In the Shadow of Christ

In the Shadow of Christ

A THEOLOGY OF CREATIONAL SUFFERING

Derek Wiertel

Foreword by
Ephraim Radner

🙢PICKWICK *Publications* • Eugene, Oregon

IN THE SHADOW OF CHRIST
A Theology of Creational Suffering

Copyright © 2025 Derek Wiertel. All rights reserved. Except for brief quotations in critical publications or reviews, no part of this book may be reproduced in any manner without prior written permission from the publisher. Write: Permissions, Wipf and Stock Publishers, 199 W. 8th Ave., Suite 3, Eugene, OR 97401

Pickwick Publications
An Imprint of Wipf and Stock Publishers
199 W. 8th Ave., Suite 3
Eugene, OR 97401

www.wipfandstock.com

PAPERBACK ISBN: 979-8-3852-3487-5
HARDCOVER ISBN: 979-8-3852-3488-2
EBOOK ISBN: 979-8-3852-3489-9

Cataloguing-in-Publication data:

Names: Wiertel, Derek, author. | Radner, Ephraim, 1956–, foreword.

Title: In the shadow of Christ : a theology of creational suffering / Derek Wiertel.

Description: Eugene, OR : Pickwick Publications, 2025 | Includes bibliographical references.

Identifiers: ISBN 979-8-3852-3487-5 (paperback) | ISBN 979-8-3852-3488-2 (hardcover) | ISBN 979-8-3852-3489-9 (ebook)

Subjects: LCSH: Creation. | Suffering—Religious aspects—Christianity. | Theology.

Classification: BT695 .W51 2025 (print) | BT695 .W51 (ebook)

Unless otherwise indicated, Scripture quotations are taken from The Catholic Edition of the Revised Standard Edition of the Bible, copyright © 1965, 1966 National Council of Churches of Christ in the United States of America. Used by permission. All rights reserved worldwide.

To Christina:
mulierem fortem quis inveniet? procul et de ultimis finibus pretium eius

Contents

Foreword by Ephraim Radner ix

Introduction: Discerning Creation in Nature's Agon xv

Chapter 1: Reading the World 1

Chapter 2: Nature's Violence 38

Chapter 3: The Figural Shape of Creation 77

Chapter 4: The Figural Coherence of Christ and the Suffering World 119

Conclusion: Nature's *Agon* in the Shadow of Christ 171

Bibliography 181

Foreword

by Ephraim Rader

THE LATE POET MARY Oliver was celebrated for her careful, and mostly grateful, description of the natural world. Not just the flamboyant or domestic beasts of mountains or homes, but especially small beings, crabs and mollusks. In a famous poem, "The Summer Day," she wonders about insects, one in particular. "Who made the world? / Who made the swan, and the black bear? / Who made the grasshopper?" Not any grasshopper, not "in general," but just *this* grasshopper whom she scrutinizes, tracing this and that minute action: "flinging" itself on the grass; eating sugar from Oliver's hand; the strange movement of the grasshopper's jaws, sideways and not up and down; its "enormous and complicated eyes."

Oliver seems to feel that such a vision demands "prayer" of some kind but admits that "I don't know exactly what a prayer is." Rather, she knows "how to pay attention" and amble quietly through the fields, watching and feeling "blessed." "Tell me, what else should I have done? / Doesn't everything die at last, and too soon?" All there is to do is to look and enjoy today. The poem's opening question, "Who made the world?" now returns, but with a sense of quiet regret that this is all there is: "Tell me, what is it you plan to do / with your one wild and precious life?" The grasshopper: a "wild," "precious," and but a momentary life.

Oliver, as she herself explained it elsewhere, was a thorough-going Epicurean, of the kind associated with Roman poet Lucretius: there is only the matter of the world swirling about in its movements, eddies, and moments, that collection of adamantine atoms born of an impersonal, impervious (yet beguilingly and deceptively personified) "mother" earth. The question, "Who made the world?" or who made the grasshopper in particular, is answered clearly in her own mind: no one. The world and its wild and precious lives "just is" and then "is not." Hence, there is no

God to who one might pray; there is only enjoyment for now. There is a tug of disappointment throughout Oliver's work, that death is simply the enveloping register of "what just is." But, as much as any writer has ever done, Oliver provides a witness to the fact that Epicurus' original vision of a life that can properly accept the nothingness of everything can, in fact, display its own measure of peaceable joy.

The Lucretian vision, as we know, had a tremendous influence on early modern thinking in the West, as the poet's manuscripts were rediscovered and began to circulate in intellectual circles. In part, the materialist presuppositions of the Lucretian worldview encouraged the development of modern empirical science. So, too, did the Lucretian philosophy's moral calling to dispassionate prudence resonate in a time of intra-religious violence and political upheaval. There was a social ethic here, and when it came to the larger natural world, one of tempered gentleness and controlled use—"sustainable" environments of modest human development. Lucretius had his own contractarian view of human society, including, arguably, animals as well, such that mutual benevolence, as it were, was meant to form the basis for a just existence among all living beings. The moral exigency of avoiding harm and mistreatment, of course, was founded on a kind of prudent utilitarianism: keep life as settled as possible so that one can enjoy one's brief existence in as quiet a way as possible.

This practical philosophy, however attractive, simply could not stand up to the realities of the truly unsettled character of human life. Except for the lucky individual here and there, few people could and can frame their daily existence in a way that avoids often horrendous loss and suffering. Wars engulf and swallow up our homes and cities; disease sweeps through the cracks of our homes' walls; the surface of the earth totters, withers, and shifts, taking with it our families and livelihoods. And, for all of Epicurus' sober advice, mental anguish is hard to banish, whatever our disciplines. "Who made the world?" and "What is it your plan to do?" have turned out to be questions impossible to let drift into the silence of the atomic whirl, despite the fetching hopes of writers like Oliver.

Whatever the pull of Epicurean materialism in the sixteenth and seventeenth centuries, and whatever the still influential consequences of this materialism in today's cultural presuppositions, the Christian alternative—"who?" is "God," and "what plan?" is "Scripture"—has refused to disappear. Yet the Christian response to Oliver, as it were, has nonetheless been confused and often even reticent in the last centuries. The Lucretian temptation was, in part, a protest against the Christian complicity in increasing the catastrophic unsettlings of European life, with its wars and social persecutions. And whatever the justice of the accusation, the seeming Western Christian missionary partnership with commercial imperialism—and its often devastating effects on what we now call the larger "biosphere"—seem to link the Christian "God" and his "words" with the increase of suffering, not its mitigation. Christan apologists have scrambled, over the past century and in the wake of chronicling the full extent of these grand unsettlings, to offer a defense of their anti-materialist option. Ironically, they have done so mostly by acceding to the very materialist presuppositions of their interlocutors: the Creator God is discerned on the basis of social history (and thus Christians have focused on the political benefits of religious worldviews), and his words are judged on the basis of the atomism of literary history. "Theodicy," or the justifying of the ways of God to man, marked this early modern Christian response. Still, the response was always built with materialist ingredients—utilitarian tools, historical trajectories, and quantifiable metrics. In the process, Christian apologists have somehow managed to ignore the implacably troubling condition of living creatures, the very condition Epicurus' proposals sought directly to address. It is, if you will, the grasshopper who still insists we give an answer. Not because the world is nothing but a grasshopper; but because just *this* grasshopper, this wild and precious life, is so precarious, here, now, everywhere, and always. This grasshopper; this human being.

Derek Wiertel's *In the Shadow of Christ* is, in this embroiled context, a breath of fresh air, bracing, invigorating, and also startling. The materialist impasse of meaning—we live, we die, we do not know why, and we try to hold it together somehow in the midst of such an emptiness with a modicum of emotional stability—foisted on the world the question of "why?" in a way that, it has turned out, could not be resolved with the tools on offer. Wiertel simply—but boldly, carefully, with critical self-awareness and explanation—goes back to the tools Christians made use of before the advent of the materialist hegemony: the Word and Spirit. That is, the articulation of the world (creation itself) by God and the divine power and being by which the world exists at all. These two realities come to us as Scripture and Scripture's divine utterer and embodiment, Jesus of Nazareth, the Messiah of Israel (Christ) through whom the world is made. To see and experience the world and our lives exhaustively within the framework of the Christ of Scripture is to give the grasshopper her meaning and purpose.

It is important to stress how Wiertel's project is a self-consciously direct and radically contrastive retort to the materialist theodicies that even Christians have entertained so broadly for so long. His volume's subtitle—*A Theology of Creational Suffering*—locates his discussion smack in the middle of these contemporary theodicies, recognizing the centrality of the natural world's distress in its entanglement with human culpability—the *agon* of creation that Wiertel identifies as an essentially true depiction of the world, not just a modern distortion of perspective. Yet, after outlining these more recent logical genealogies and ultimate incapacities, he offers as a more satisfying path their traditional antecedents. The displacement of these antecedents by early modern approaches has been so decisive and now so long-standing that we have simply forgotten their existence as viable paradigms of understanding. Wiertel's retrieval of their compelling shape—the medieval theologian Hugh of St. Victor's in particular—can seem like a welcome uncovering of a winsome artifact, even a useful implement. Yet Wiertel's work is not so much an effort in historical *ressourcement*, as it is a challenge to take up traditional Christian theological and intellectual resources for understanding the peculiarly pressing character of *modern* worries, the worries that made Lucretian materialism inescapable, if finally deeply unsatisfactory, for many. Hence, Wiertel's volume turns to an expansive engagement with contemporary philosophy, ethics, and even biology that renders his commendation of earlier modes of understanding something critically chastened and also effectively strengthened.

Simply to summarize Wiertel's main moves here—his immersion in and deployment of a Christocentric figural interpretation of both Scripture and the created world—would do them injustice, and prove reductive of the nuanced and intricate arguments he makes. Likewise, to give a thumbnail description of his "answer" to questioners like Oliver— a mysterious Creator of self-giving, whose openness to creation makes room for creation's corruption at the deepest levels of its spiritual existence (angels) and to the furthest extent of its form (worms), even as that self-offering finds divine embodiment in the sacrificial traversal and redemption of the world by Christ—would be to devalue its power and reference through abbreviation. The reader must enter into Wiertel's discussion, and be led along its paths by his patent guidance, to apprehend the existential force of the great "narrative" he presents. Yet, that force is considerable. Anyone who goes with him through this journey of theological questioning will emerge, I am certain, with a transformed sense of who they are, of what the world is, and of the fundamental grace and beauty of the God who creates and orders this world of difficult wonders. That is, *In the Shadow of Christ* is a volume of tremendous hope.

The grasshopper—to use my example, and not Wiertel's—turns out to be an actor in a great drama of both freedom and sacrifice, perversion and transfiguration, that witnesses to the being and person of God, in a mysterious yet also tangibly wondrous fashion. To see this, however, one must listen to the grasshopper of the Scriptures, not only of a momentary gazing in the field: astounding in its form; voracious in its destructive force; nourishing in its ingestion by men; paltry in its transitory weakness; carried about in swarms by the winds, alighting in power through the hand of God . . . It turns out the grasshopper struts the stage of history with all the variety, vigor, and vulnerability as Adam himself. These observations, furthermore, were made, in commentary and instruction, by both Jews and Christians in their investigation of the Bible and of the world around them. Yet, as Adam, the "plan" of their purpose is given in the great Adam of God's own self-giving, hidden within a divine heart before all worlds, striding through all worlds in both their beauty and wreckage, and taking all worlds to himself in an act "of full-ey'd love! / When thou shalt look us out of pain, / And one aspect of thine spend in delight / More then a thousand sunnes dispurse in light, / In heav'n above" (George Herbert, "The Glance").

If Jews and Christians knew this once, there is no reason such knowledge should be withheld from us today, we who pine in regret or perhaps rebel in fear before a world that often seems too hard to bear. Wiertel's witness, in this profound volume, makes good on the generous bequest of those whose wisdom he knows to be the balm of the ages.

Introduction:
Discerning Creation in Nature's *Agon*

CHRISTIAN NATURAL THEOLOGY WAS originally a type of spiritual discernment that interpreted the natural world through God's self-revelation in the person of Jesus Christ. In its late antique and medieval variants, this interpretive practice linked the vast array of entities and events of the creaturely world to the very figures given by the Holy Scriptures of Christ.[1] The ninth-century theologian John Scotus Eriugena remarks,

> Visible creation is truly the garment of the Word since, manifesting his beauty to us, it makes him known openly. But sacred Scripture has also become his garment because it too contains his mysteries . . . The first is cloaked by the sensible forms of the sensible world, the second by the outer shell of the divine letters, that is, by sacred Scripture.[2]

Under this interpretive disposition, the scriptural form of Christ's incarnate passage was perceived as unveiling the eternal divine discourse that creatively enfolded and explicated the created universe. From this remarkable vantage, with its far-reaching metaphysical and hermeneutical implications, our theological study retrieves the traditional form of Christian natural theology as a way of pursuing a sufficiently theological understanding of the disturbing wonders of nature's *agon*. The term nature's *agon* here designates the troubling character of the physical universe as an agonistic order of creaturely violence, suffering, and death. Specifically, we aim to develop theological structures that can

---

1. For a historical description of traditional natural theology in its late antique and medieval context, which envisioned Scripture and Nature as interpenetrating realities, see Mews, "World as Text," 95–112.
2. Eriugena, *Voice of the Eagle*, 198.

interpret the ontological violence of created existence in the light of God's self-revelation.³

To properly frame the scope of this inquiry, it is helpful at the start to ponder some of the concrete manifestations of the natural world's economic character. For instance, one might consider the life cycle of the liver-fluke worm (*Fasciola hepatica*) as a kind of indicative expression of nature's ontic disposition, rife as it is with aggression, dissipation, and the destruction of life as the given means for the profusion of life. This particular creature begins its life in a pond of water, where it is known for drilling itself into the lung of a water-snail. There it feeds upon the snail's internal organs, living off the less essential parts to preserve the snail's life until the worm can reproduce. Eventually, the worm's offspring drill their way out of the dying creature and settle at the water's edge in encysted form. From there, they are often swallowed by grazing sheep or oxen, where, in their stomachs, the cyst is dissolved, releasing the liver-flukes into the animal's body. The flukes feed upon the animal, causing the disease known as "sheep-rot." After three months, the worms produce new eggs, which subsequently pass out of the dying animal into the pasture, and from there, they eventually return to another water-source, where the cycle begins again.⁴

In view of such a disturbing phenomenon, questions emerge about how to understand the economy of life in terms of traditional Christian claims concerning God's divine nature. Charles Darwin himself cited the predatorial behavior of creatures like the ichneumon wasp (*Orgichneumon calcatorius*) and the domestic housecat as the source for his incomprehension regarding nature's divine provenance. In his correspondence with the famed Christian botanist Asa Gray, he writes,

---

3. I use the phrases "ontology of violence" and "ontic violence" interchangeably in this essay to describe the brutal appearance of the natural world. The terminology derives from John Milbank's study *Theology and Social Theory*. Milbank judges that behind the social and political structures of the modern age lies a metaphysical vision wherein nature (reality) is characterized by an unending flux of conflict, discord, and death. Although it appears that Milbank is correct to contrast this "war against all" ontology with the Christian theological vision of an original ontological peace, the reality that natural sciences reflect a creation that is a violence-dominated process seemingly supports the modern metaphysic Milbank chooses to reject. If Milbank's construal of the metaphysic behind modern thought is correct, then it appears that such a modern metaphysic *a la* Thomas Hobbes' *bella omnium contra omnia* captures something of the way the world actually is in terms of its concrete ontic manifestation. See Milbank, *Theology and Social Theory*, 259–76.

4. Sherrington, *Man on His Nature*, 366–67.

> With respect to the theological view of the question; this is always painful to me—I am bewildered—I had no intention to write atheistically. But I own that I cannot see, as plainly as others do, and as I should wish to do, evidence of design and beneficence on all sides of us. There seems to me too much misery in the world. I cannot persuade myself that a beneficent and omnipotent God would have designedly created the *Ichneumonidæ* with the express intention of their feeding within the living bodies of caterpillars, or that a cat should play with mice.[5]

In a rather plaintive tone, Charles Darwin recognized the theological significance of such phenomena. Here, the perception of nature's *agon* as an enveloping description of *divine creation* represents a substantial intensification of the primary form of theodicy. Namely, if the classical Christian understanding of God obtains, apprehended as omnipotent creative love, then whence come the all-embracing violence and agony of God's creatures?

Although intellectual reflection about the problem of evil and suffering, in general, abounds throughout the Christian tradition, inasmuch as the problem is bound up with the specific metaphysical implications of Christian belief concerning the nature of God and the doctrine of creation, the scope of the problem, grasped in terms of creational suffering—that is, of nonhuman animals—has been subjected to less scrutiny. It is only since the early modern period, with its specific social, political, and theological upheavals, that the problem of nature's *agon* emerged with such impressive force. Along with greater recognition of natural suffering as a theological problem for Christian belief, discernible patterns of interpretation also emerged that attempted to negotiate the world's ontological violence in view of God's traditional attributes. These interpretive patterns, categorized as eliminativist, instrumentalist, and contingent-fallenness theodicies,[6] represent the absolute reach of human rationality regarding nature's ontic strife and, as such, are eminently valuable for theological reflection. However, these interpretive strategies suffer from a certain degree of theoretical ambiguity or underdetermination, which relates to their limited engagement of the central form of the Christian faith. Specifically, the revelation of the divine-humanity of Jesus Christ—the mysterious divine utterance of infinite and finite

5. Darwin, "Letter No. 2814."
6. Both the definitional aspects of these theodical approaches and the emergent conditions for the problem of animal suffering will be examined in depth in chapter 2.

existence—exerts only a modest influence on the development and evaluation of such interpretative schemes.

Given these limitations, this theological essay aims to present a meaningful narrative of existence centrally configured by the revealed form of the incarnate Christ. The objective is not so much to seek an exhaustive explanation of the "why" of nature's *agon*. Instead, the goal is to furnish a more suitable or appropriate (*conveniens*) understanding of the grammar of existence as determined by God's trinitarian self-disclosure. The central axiom for this type of theology is that somehow all the things that constitute the world converge and find meaning in the disclosive light of the crucified and exalted one. This stress upon God's self-interpretation in Jesus Christ offers a type of regulative principle or hypothesis upon which we shall structure and evaluate our theodical reflections. In pursuit of this "fitting" interpretation, we will retrieve the traditional mode of natural theology, which displays a profound Christocentric orientation in terms of its metaphysical structure, encompassing both the biblical text and the created world. This manner of reasoning perceives scriptural figures and the world's creatures as interpretively bound together as the living discourse of the Trinity.[7] In its traditional form, this was denoted as the two books of divine revelation, *liber naturae* and *liber scripturae*, where the revelatory presence of Christ in the Spirit was also inscribed in the very phenomena of the universe. This scripturally informed character of natural theology assumed an expansive figuralism whereby the textual signs of Scripture were seen as possessing a divine reference that comprehended the entire span of creaturely existence.

This interpretive intersection of Scripture and creation under the Christological form provides the methodological disposition for my search for a fitting theological narrative of nature's *agon*. As a work of constructive theology, this essay retrieves and extends certain elements of premodern theological reasoning. Accordingly, my aim is to discern and develop interpretive structures grounded in Scripture that touch upon the metaphysical principles of the world, which in turn shape how we

---

7. Figures are defined as textually mediated persons, images, patterns and themes that constitute the Bible's semantic landscape. Figuralism broadly designates both the interpretive disposition and concrete practice of perceiving the all-encompassing mystery of Christ (the divine Word who creates and redeems the universe) in Scripture and creation. This implicitly recognizes Scripture as not merely a humanly constructed literary document, but as a mysterious reality that is connected with and derivable from the eternal Word of God. For a metaphysically robust definition of figural reading that has influenced my own view, see Radner, *Time and the Word*, 6–7.

understand both the possibility and actuality of nature's ontic violence. In essence, we seek a theological vision of creation's empirical character defined by the scripturally articulated mystery of Christ.

This traditional manner of thinking about the world and Scripture was largely submerged in the modern period by the rise of historical criticism, which remains the prevailing approach to biblical interpretation in both the academy and the church. Even with the recent wave of interest in premodern interpretive traditions among theologians, mainly through postmodern theory, the practice of figuration as the interpretive foundation for constructive theological discourse remains somewhat foreign and obscure.[8] Thus, in spite of the general recognition of the relative limitations of historicism as a mode of biblical interpretation, the current theological environment remains captive to the implicit ideological and metaphysical constraints imposed by historicism, which have hindered the renewal of such an interpretively rich approach to Scripture and the natural world. Therefore, to facilitate our engagement of Scripture's disclosive potential vis-à-vis created existence, it is necessary to substantially reorient our thinking about Scripture's metaphysical status in terms of the fundamental commitments of Christian belief.[9]

Our essay takes up the figuralism of Hugh of St. Victor for the task of reorienting our theological perceptions. This twelfth-century theologian's profound Christocentric theology exemplifies the tradition of the two books of divine revelation. For instance, in his treatise *De tribus diebus*, Hugh underscores the interpretive connection between Scripture and creation by applying the scriptural image of God writing the Decalogue

---

8. The work of the philosopher Hans-Georg Gadamer went a long way towards exposing the limitations and the inherent problems of historicist interpretation. Gadamer argued that the aim of understanding any text involved the placing of oneself in "the process of transmission, in which past and present are constantly mediated" (Gadamer, *Truth and Method*, 291). For Gadamer to understand a text like the Bible cannot be divorced from the Bible's effects upon history.

9. This study functions as work of creative retrieval inasmuch as it attempts to recover a traditional manner of thinking in order to facilitate a theologically rich interpretation of a problem that weighs heavily upon contemporary thought. The theologian John Webster aptly describes such a method's theoretical intentions as follows: "For such theologies, immersion in the texts and habits of thought of earlier (especially premodern) theology opens up a wide view of the object of Christian theological reflection, setting before its contemporary practitioners descriptions of the faith unharassed by current anxieties, and enabling a certain liberty in relation to the present. With this in mind, we begin by considering the study of history as a diagnostic to identify what are taken to be misdirections in modern theology, and then the deployment of history as a resource to overcome them" (Webster, "Theologies of Retrieval," 584–85).

(Exod 3:18) to the manifestation of the natural world under the creative providence of divine Wisdom. "For this whole sensible world is a kind of book written by the finger of God . . . and each creature is a kind of figure . . . to manifest and in some way signify the invisible Wisdom of God."[10] In terms of our theological engagement, Hugh's figuralist thought is to be retrieved and creatively extended according to two interrelated dimensions. First, we will explore Hugh's Christocentric creational metaphysics as a type of immersive therapy to reorder our thinking about Scripture's disclosive reference in terms of created being. This includes examining the foundational ontology of figuration in comparison to the ideological configurations of modern historicism. Second, from the perspective of a far-reaching Christological ontology, Hugh's figuralism will also secure the determinate point of departure for exploring the figurated landscape of Scripture in search of creation's revealed presence. Specifically, the Hugonian interpretation of Noah's ark, in the context of its scripturally networked cognates, will unveil a remarkable Christological-creational reference that will determine and guide our theological reflections. Accordingly, this network of figural cognates, uncovered by Hugh's comprehensive vision of the ark, will furnish the revelatory foundation for developing theoretical structures that reflect the mysterious space "between" God's infinite action and the manifold reality of the created world.

Regarding our constructive task, the theoretical structures discerned by our figural exploration of the Scriptures will thus form the conceptual infrastructure for a theological narrative that explicates the world's agonistic character in view of the Christological axis of divine revelation. In other words, the figuralist approach to the Scriptures will serve to anchor our reflections according to God's revealed life, where all patterns of finite being converge. Nevertheless, although this constructive engagement is grounded in the figurated dimensionality of the Scriptures, the deployment of these interpretive patterns as theoretical structures will be pursued and developed in conversation with the broader conceptual resources of the Christian theodical tradition.

In terms of this essay's trajectory, chapter 1 will examine Hugh of St. Victor's profound Christocentric figuralism, with its theologically saturated vision of nature, to uncover and develop the theoretical conditions that make such a mode of interpretation possible. We will observe that Hugh's figuralism offers a way of interpreting the natural world, including

---

10. Hugh of St. Victor, *De tribus diebus* 4.3.

its theodical elements, under the auspices of scriptural forms. In addition to considering Hugh's way of grasping natural phenomena, including the violent and dissipative economy, we will also consider the necessary conditions for retrieving this kind of figuralist thinking in the contemporary context. By considering the theological metaphysics of figuralism in light of the ontological commitments of modern historicism, we will substantiate the possibility of a renewed figuralist natural theology.

After grounding our figuralist orientation, we will turn in chapter 2 to the objective problem of natural suffering in terms of its emergence as a pressing issue for modern theology. This will involve two interconnected aspects: first, we will delineate the premodern Christian understanding of nature's *agon* and explore how animal suffering was increasingly recognized as morally significant according to the social and cultural shifts of the early modern period. Second, we will summarize the primary theodical categories adduced by contemporary theology in response to this emergence. This survey of categories will include the evaluation of their limitations in terms of traditional philosophical objections and in terms of their scriptural coherence. It is in light of these limitations that we will proceed with our creative retrieval of figuralist thinking in order to develop a theological interpretation of creational suffering.

In chapter 3, we begin our constructive task, using Hugh of St. Victor's figuralist interpretation of Noah's ark as the point of entry into the world of the Bible. By engaging the ark's extended referents in connection with its scriptural cognates, we discern interpretive patterns that will structure our theological exploration. In particular, the patterns of "traversal" and "sacrifice" in their Christic-creational overlap will press into the mysterious ontological space "between" the divine and creaturely world.

The task of elaborating these patterns in terms of their theological-metaphysical significance is taken up in chapter 4. Here, we will expand on the scriptural patterns in terms of their infinite and finite reference in order to develop theoretical structures that pertain to the mysterious relation between God's creative agency and the freedom of the creaturely world. These structures are developed in dialogue with some of the theodical categories (both philosophical and theological) outlined in chapter 2. The resultant structures will then establish the conceptual lineaments of a narrative that expresses our figurated understanding of nature's *agon* under the form of Christ's sacrificial traversal. This scripturally described form of Jesus casts light upon natural history, simultaneously revealing it as a divinely gifted reality, a fallen reality, and a reality open to an incomprehensible transfiguration.

Ultimately, the chief aim of this essay is the formation of a theological interpretation of nature's disturbing wonders, shaped by the central revelation of Christian belief: the mystery of God in the crucified and exalted Jesus. For this purpose, the creative retrieval of the traditional disposition of Christian natural theology with its rich figuralism will establish the means for understanding the world's being in all its challenging aspects. While the use of scriptural figuration as a form of natural theology is firmly grounded within Christian intellectual tradition, the challenge remains for us to pursue this task in a way that productively informs contemporary theological discussion. The ultimate justification for this approach will be adjoined with the study's provision of a fitting theological narrative that illumines the mystery of creation's *agon* in the light of God's revealed love.

1

Reading the World

ACCORDING TO THE CHRISTIAN figural tradition that flourished until the early modern period, the created world, like the semantic contours of Holy Scripture, radiated an infinite depth of meaning that was referentially founded upon and tethered to the form and content of the eternal Word of God. Under such a theological disposition, traditionally denoted as the "two books" of divine revelation—*liber naturae* and *liber scripturae*—the Christian interpreter was summoned to observe that the natural world, teeming with its creatures, was somehow enfolded by the inexhaustible meaning of Scripture, which was mysteriously identified with the paschal mystery of Christ. This metaphor of the "two books" prevailed throughout the medieval period and established the theoretical foundation for *premodern* natural theology, which interpreted the world's character through the scriptural grammar of divine revelation.[1]

We encounter this type of theological reasoning in the thought of the twelfth-century theologian Hugh of St. Victor (1096–1141), who perceived the forms and content of the natural world through the revelation of God's Wisdom in Jesus Christ, who is the "idea or pattern of all things."[2] In his treatise *De tribus diebus*, Hugh describes the "entire sensible world" as a "book written by the finger of God" to "signify the

---

1. By premodern natural theology, we refer to the practice of reading the shape of created existence according to the Christian economy of revelation. This traditional practice assumed the linkage of nature's form in terms of God's self-revealing character and was ruptured and replaced by modern natural theology that envisioned the practice of natural theology as an apologetic enterprise that inferred truths about God apart from revelatory forms. See Radner, *Chasing the Shadow*, 1–38.

2. Hugh of St. Victor, *Didascalicon* 1.6.

invisible Wisdom of God."[3] According to the Hugonian perspective, everything in the universe is comprehended as the living discourse of God's Word, and yet, the proper knowledge of this discourse is only available in its fullness through the disclosive language of Scripture. As the historical theologian Boyd Taylor Coolman remarks: "[For Hugh], Scripture alone provides the healing illumination and the revelatory patterns by which visible things can be read aright."[4] From such a vantage, the task of interpreting the world's being (theologically speaking) involves seeing the world as a densely layered "book" of signs—a living language—capable of being deciphered through the figures of the Bible. These figures are the forms, stories, patterns, and images given by Scripture, which are referentially coextensive with all things inasmuch as they are bound to the creative and redemptive action of the eternal Father in Jesus Christ and the Holy Spirit.

The traditional practice of reading the world through the revelatory images of Scripture establishes the conceptual orientation of this project's theodical agenda, which is the theological interpretation of nature's agonistic character. By nature's *agon* we mean not only the reality of ecological predation, mass extinctions, and the suffering of animals, but also the striking fact that the underlying principles of *God's* world appear defined by ontological strife. For example, creatures like the liver-fluke worm or the ichneumon wasp, whose created forms seem structured towards producing an excess of suffering in other creatures, manifest the disturbing character of creaturely existence that drives this project.

With these wonders of the natural world in mind, the scope of our essay intends to take up the church's traditional figuralist stance as a way of engaging *theologically* the endemic violence and suffering of the world. Specifically, we aim to bring the struggles of sentient animal life, which appear as an intrinsic feature of the world's evolutionary development, under the disclosive fullness of Christ.

For this theodical agenda, the figural disposition of Hugh of St. Victor's natural theology provides the orienting basis upon which we will pursue a renewed theological vision of the natural world, that is, a vision ordered by the revelatory form of the crucified and exalted Jesus. The term *figuralist* here denotes an interpretive orientation (in terms of theoretical ontology and practice) that views the Bible as *maximally* comprehensive

---

3. Hugh of St. Victor, *De tribus diebus* 4.3.
4. Coolman, "Pulchrum Esse," 181.

in its objective meaning and reference. As the Word of God, the Bible, by means of its figurated layered landscape, refers to *all things* that comprise the span of created existence, including all entities, events, and persons in their spatial, temporal, and spiritual aspects.[5] According to this view, Scripture posits an objective order that reveals the very things constituted by God's eternally creative speech. This key claim concerning the interpretive relation between the textual semantics of Scripture and the natural world logically includes the problem of theodicy insofar as both the practice of figuration and the mystery of the world's evil and suffering derive conceptually from the same Christian metaphysics of *creatio ex nihilo*,[6] which posits all things—including the destructive behavior of the liver-fluke worm, the ichneumon wasp and other creatures—as the divinely shaped work of God.

One of the central implications of scriptural figuralism as a theological stance is its challenge to the implicit positivist assumptions of contemporary biblical interpretation in both ecclesial and academic settings. Although recognition of the epistemic constraints of historicism is well established in contemporary theological circles, many modern theologies nonetheless remain largely inoculated against the conceptual purchase of Scripture's figural texture (and, by extension, its comprehensive creational scope).[7] This is due to the habituated separation of biblical interpretation from the metaphysical determinations of Christian belief. As I will argue, the practice of historical criticism conceals ontological structures

---

5. My use of the term "figural" instead of "allegorical" is conditioned by the latter's association with literary tropes (functioning as an extended metaphor). Allegory is often associated with a meaning detachable from the figure itself, which, it is alleged by some (e.g., Daniel Boyarin), dissolves its concrete historical meaning. For a critical discussion of Boyarin's dismissal of allegory, see Dawson, *Christian Figural Reading*, 19–64. By figural I refer to the broad interpretive disposition perceiving the all-encompassing mystery of Christ in Scripture. See also Radner, *Time and the Word*, 6–7.

6. The problem of evil is a scripturally given mystery for Christian theology insofar as it is tethered to the Bible's claims concerning the nature of God and the world's divine origin. Both the metaphysical status of the world and the problem of evil are conceptual structures generated, encompassed, and determined by the content of the Bible. While the perplexing nature of evil and suffering and the search for explanations have almost universally preoccupied human reflection, whether described in mythic or philosophical terms, the problem reached its most radical definition when ensconced by the Jewish and Christian understanding of creation. Indeed, the specific theological claims that flow from Scripture concerning God's nature and the doctrine of creation render the problem of evil logically opaque. For a phenomenological account of evil, see Ricoeur, *Symbolism of Evil*, 232–78.

7. For the problematic aspects of historicism for theology, see Louth, *Discerning the Mystery*, 96–131.

that are, in part, inimical to the theoretical metaphysics of traditional Christian faith. While the doctrine of creation is almost universally affirmed by Christian theologians, full acceptance of its implicative force for scriptural interpretation—*its encompassing scope*—is less prevalent.

By contrast, our agenda for exploring the meaning of nature's suffering via scriptural interpretation necessitates full admittance of a Christocentric creational ontology by which we may become more attuned to the theological depths of both the biblical text and the created world. Ultimately, the veracity of this type of interpretive stance cannot be proved by theoretical justification; rather, such a "method" will be proved by the extent to which it yields an intellectually viable natural theology of the world's suffering. Convincing readers of the propriety of figuration for theodical reflection cannot be sustained apart from actual performance. Nevertheless, before pursuing a figural-theological rendering of creation's *agon*, we must situate the conceptual parameters of figuralism for contemporary thought.

This chapter will outline the theoretical commitments that ground the figuralist orientation in contradistinction to modern historicism. To begin, we will examine how figuration shaped premodern natural theology by considering the work of Hugh of St. Victor. Hugh's theology embodies the traditional interpretive intersection of text and world under a figuralist perception, which forms the prevailing structure of premodern Christian hermeneutics. However, despite its exemplary use of figuration to grasp the meaning of the world, Hugh's interpretation of nature's character is of limited use in its material conclusions, which are shaped by premodern perspectives concerning the moral status of animals. Animal suffering did not emerge as a *major* theological problem for Christian belief until the early modern period. Nevertheless, the formal disposition of Hugh's thought displays the necessary orientation to animate our study of the world's being in relation to Scripture's content. Our engagement of Hugh's theology is based on his profound Christological figuralism, wherein Scripture "saturates" his perception of the natural world. This saturated perception provides a way of reading the form of the world, including the existence of liver-fluke worms or ichneumon wasps, as filled with divine meaning tethered to the mystery of Christ.

Ultimately, this engagement with Hugh's figural practice is intended to shape our thinking about the world, with its strife and suffering, to accommodate a broader theological-metaphysical perception. In pursuit of this expansive theological vision, our project will begin by stressing the traditional role of figuralism in relation to nature *via* Hugh's thought. The chapter will then explore the *conditions of possibility* for retrieving this natural theological practice of reading text and world together figurally for contemporary theodical reflection. This will involve plunging into the theoretical foundations of figural theology in relation to questions concerning theological metaphysics, hermeneutics, and historical criticism.

CREATION AND FIGURATION: PREMODERN NATURAL THEOLOGY AND HUGH OF ST. VICTOR

Both the conceptual architecture of figural reading and the problem of theodicy are essentially structured by the metaphysical implications of the Christian doctrine of creation. The concept of *creatio ex nihilo* refers to the ontological narrative wherein the triune God posits *all things* into existence from absolute nothingness.[8] This act implies that the world itself possesses no intrinsic logical or metaphysical necessity but is a reality born mysteriously out of the incomprehensible freedom and power of God's creative love. Notably, its metaphysical grammar is not a conceptual deduction of theoretical reason developed to explain the appearance of the world; rather, the doctrine is a revealed scriptural claim impressed upon the mind of the church.[9] One might say that the Bible's narrative of salvation provoked the development of this unique theoretical structure, capturing the metaphysical distinction between God and the world[10] and

---

8. The metaphysical shape of *creatio ex nihilo* refers to the Absolute's positing of the contingent dimension of Being as a whole. This positing does not presuppose the "existence" of "nothingness" as if it were a shadowy form of Being; on the contrary, absolute nothingness is an impossibility (a pseudo-concept) that serves to clarify the Truth that God's absolute origination of all things is not constrained by any other reality than God's unrestricted Being. For an important discussion of these metaphysical issues, see the philosopher Lorenz B. Puntel's insightful and challenging *Being and God*, 236–52.

9. For a brief discussion of the biblical basis of the Christian doctrine of creation, see McMullin, "Creation Ex Nihilo," 11–23; Anderson, "Creatio Ex Nihilo," 15–26; Bockmuehl, "Creatio Ex Nihilo," 253–70. While I maintain that the Christian doctrine of creation is a scriptural reality (in its substantial content), this does not mean that the apprehension of the meaning of *creatio ex nihilo* was given in "ready-made" form; rather, the doctrine was epistemically derived from a process that engaged the substance of Scripture in light of the prevailing concerns of the sub-apostolic period.

10. For the importance of the unique ontological distinction between God and the world for Christian theological developments, see Sokolowski, *God of Faith and Reason*, 1–51.

setting the conceptual context for the church's figural hermeneutics and the development of its dogmatic claims.

Based upon this theoretical ontology, the church perceived that both the universe and the revealed text of Scripture were divinely given mediations of the eternal Logos of God.[11] For instance, the third-century theologian Origen describes this revelatory intersection as follows: "For once one admits the Scriptures are from the Creator of the world, one must also be convinced that whatever they discover, who search for the meaning of creation, must also be true of the meaning of Scripture."[12] This vision culminated in the medieval articulation of the two divine books of revelation, as previously noted, which serves as the conceptual basis for Hugh of St. Victor's interpretation of the natural world. According to this interpretive tradition, the divine Word of God is articulated or expressed in varying degrees of similitude through the biblical text and the creatures of the world.[13] On this point, the perception of the *divine origin and status* of both the *world of creation* and the *world of the Scriptures* grounded the interpretive junction of creatures and figures as they were both shaped in accordance with the mystery of the divine Word. This mutual involvement of text and world established a way of narrating creaturely reality—including the death and violence of the nonhuman creation—on scripturally given terms, i.e., according to the figures and themes given by the biblical text. Historian Peter Harrison describes this mutually involved character as follows:

> The interpretation of the two books, moreover, took place as part of an integrated hermeneutical practice, premised on the

---

11. Along with church's interpretive stance, it should be noted that traditional Jewish interpretations of the natural world in the divine economy was framed by the same creational metaphysics with its concomitant figuralist orientation. In this sense, the Torah as the Word of God is the foundational divine speech that frames all of reality "Just so did God look into the Torah and create the world" (Genesis Rabba 1:1, cited in Kugel, *Traditions of the Bible*, 69). As an example of Jewish figuralism, the Rabbinic Aggadah places animals within the enveloping framework of God's creative purpose, wherein they possess an extensive symbolization. Animals not only carry out God's purpose in their divinely assigned natures, but they also address the particularities of human existence and encompass questions concerning the wider theological meaning of history as displayed by Scripture. For a discussion of the role of Bestiaries in the Aggadah, see Neusner, *Praxis and Parable*.

12. Excerpt of Origen's Commentary on Psalms 1, 3, in Origen, *Spirit and Fire*, 90. The theoretical notion of the two books is also made by Augustine in his commentary on Psalm 45:7. See Augustine, *Exposition of the Psalms 33–50*, 315.

13. For a description of the role of figuration in relation with the "books of Nature and Scripture," see Harrison, *Bible, Protestantism*, 1–63; Pedersen, *Book of Nature*.

principle that the meaning of the words of scripture could not be fully known until the meanings of the objects to which the words referred were also known. Linking the words of scripture with the objects of nature was the universal medieval practice of allegorical interpretation. Allegory was not, as we sometimes tend to think, a strategy for reading multiple meanings into the words of texts, but was rather a process through which the reader was drawn away from naked words to the infinitely more eloquent things of nature to which those words referred.[14]

As a result of this interpretive disposition—a disposition that formally influenced Christian exegetical practice until the eighteenth century—many theologians embraced a *scripturally saturated* natural theology: a vision of the world's creatures structured by the figural economy of the Bible. Significantly, reading the world according to the Bible was not born from an idle curiosity regarding creatures; it was grounded upon concerns essentially *theodical* in nature. For instance, the figuralist perspective helped elucidate the sheer existence of so many harmful and noxious creatures that ostensibly lacked an easily discernible purpose. Again, Harrison writes:

> During the first sixteen hundred years of the common era, those thinkers who directed their attention to the natural world had tended to be preoccupied neither with questions of how animals came into being nor with the direct causes of their various operations but rather with the question of why they existed at all.[15]

A figural comprehension of nature was thus one of the essential ways of making sense of the universe and its profusion of creatures in relation to God's creative purpose. Such natural theologies perceived the material phenomena of the world (including the appearance of ontic strife and suffering) as symbolizing theological and moral truths while also reflecting the expansive Wisdom of the divine Word of God, who had bestowed a providential order and divine meaning upon the things of the world. This brings us to the life and work of Hugh of St. Victor, whose theology embodies this interpretive practice.

---

14. Harrison, *Bible, Protestantism*, 26.
15. Harrison, "Virtues of Animals," 463–65.

Hugh of St. Victor's Life and Work

Regarded in his lifetime as an *alter Augustinus* (a "second Augustine"), Hugh of St. Victor was one of the most influential theologians of the early twelfth century. While the precise location of his birth is unknown, he came to the Abbey of St. Victor just outside Paris around 1115–1118.[16] Hugh served as the head of the monastery after the departure of its founder, William of Champeaux. Hugh's literary output elevated the status of the Victorine abbey, which became an important center of learning amidst the intellectual ferment of the twelfth-century renaissance.[17] Offering an education to novices and outsiders, the abbey of St. Victor established an integrated form of intellectual and religious life that united the liberal arts within the expansive framework of scriptural interpretation.

For Hugh, the whole intellectual edifice of philosophical learning was ordered towards the *re-formatio* of the human intellect and will according to the archetypal Wisdom of God, who comprehended and unfolded both the created world and the history of salvation in Scripture. Boyd Taylor Coolman describes Hugh's thought as a program of reform that integrated theological, exegetical, and spiritual practices as a means of perceiving the truth about God and the world and, thus, of restoring the human soul to its original beauty. He writes, "Hugh conceives of Christian existence in this life as aiming at the construction of a dwelling place, an *aedificatio* for the presence of God within human persons, through their reformation in the image of God, accomplished through ordered practices."[18]

In pursuit of this theological program, Hugh composed a series of works ordered towards re-formatio, including the first summa of the faith, *De sacramentis Christianae fidei*, and an important pedagogical work on scriptural interpretation, *Didascalicon de Studio Legendi*. He also wrote a range of texts that exemplify the figural rendition of creation that typified the dominant stance of premodern Christian thought. Namely, Hugh's ark-treatises (*De arca Noe morali* and *De arca Noe mystica*) and his treatise *De tribus diebus* display a remarkable sacramental figuralism, wherein the world's being is brought under the disclosive shape of the scriptural narrative. *De tribus diebus* interprets the phenomena of the

---

16. For a brief description of the debate concerning Hugh's origin, see Harkins, *Reading and the Work of Restoration*, 1–3.

17. See the collection of essays in Chenu, *Nature, Man, and Society*.

18. Coolman, *Theology of Hugh of St. Victor*, 3–4.

natural world as a landscape of signs that refer to its trinitarian foundation. The ark treatises represent the same figuralist disposition turned towards a multi-level apprehension of creation as a totality. In particular, the ark-treatises engage the image of Noah's ark with its scriptural cognates as a sweeping synthetic figure that apprehends the mysterious relation that obtains between God and *all* created things, including the universe, nature, history, and the individual human soul. The figure of the ark as a "synthesis of reality"[19] comprehends the content of God's works of creation (*opus creationis*) and restoration (*opus restaurationis*), which are to be contemplated for the re-structuring of one's soul.

> Now therefore, enter your own inmost heart, and make a dwelling-place for God. Make Him a temple, make Him a house, make him a pavilion. Make Him an ark of the covenant, make Him an ark of the flood; no matter what you call it, it is all one house of God.[20]

These figuralist works represent the symbolist mentality of Christian antiquity that beheld the biblical text and the creaturely world as mutually referential realities in regard to their divinely given character. Following the interpretive precedents set by Augustine of Hippo (among many others), Hugh recognized that biblical signs (*signa*) referred to objects (*res*) that bore a multiplicity of meaning due to their provenance in God's creative positing of the whole cosmos. Scripture's objective reference possessed "as many different meanings as there are forms, figures, properties, and natures."[21] For Hugh, the figural character of the Bible, as given in its literal-narrative form, referred to all things, including the divine nature and the particularities of creation's history. Theologian M. D. Chenu remarks,

> Consideration of sacred history involved a biblical interpretation which took literal history (*littera*) as the basis for continuous reference to supra-historical realities figured in terrestrial events. Upon such reference the entire doctrine of the four senses of scripture was postulated. In Christian terms this doctrine was no mere literary technique; the very nature of the

---

19. Coolman, *Theology of Hugh of St. Victor*, 18.
20. Hugh of St. Victor, *De arca Noe morali* 1.3.
21. Hugh of St. Victor, *De scripturis et scriptoribus* 17.

Judaeo-Christian revelation posits an ongoing interrelationship among things that underlay this hermeneutic approach.[22]

Under such a perspective, it was only fitting that Hugh perceived a scriptural figure like the ark as a structuring form that captured the extensive theological character of the world's being. To reiterate, the interpretive coherence of world and text was founded upon the archetypal role of the divine Word of God in the works of creation and restoration. For Hugh, the mystery of Christ is the formative "idea or pattern"[23] of the created world and the primary content of scriptural revelation.

With respect to Scripture's Christological form, Hugh remarks: "For the whole Divine Scripture is one Book, and that one Book is Christ, for the whole divine Scripture speaks of Christ and is fulfilled in Christ."[24] Concerning nature's Christological form, he writes, "this whole sensible world is a kind of book written by the finger of God, that is created by divine power, and each creature is a kind of figure, not invented by human determination, but established by the divine will to manifest and in some way signify the invisible wisdom of God."[25] Notably, the "invisible wisdom of God" is ontologically identical with the incarnate form of the crucified and exalted Jesus. Thus, the various elements that make up the creaturely world and Scripture enfigurate the same Jesus who created them.

Hugh of St. Victor's Natural Theology

Hugh's figuralist disposition—ordered by a Christocentric metaphysics—facilitates a theological interpretation of the created universe. We should note, however, that Hugh's figural perception is not directly applied to creation's violent economy, especially given the fact that the problem of animal suffering was largely overlooked in premodern theological discourse. Nevertheless, the formal aspect of his figural interpretation of creation is instructive in its attempt to coherently integrate the phenomenal world (including its bizarre and destructive appearances) within the encompassing scope of the scriptural economy. In this regard, Hugh

---

22. Chenu, *Nature, Man, and Society*, 110–11.
23. Hugh of St. Victor, *Didascalicon* 1.6.
24. Hugh of St. Victor, *De arca Noe morali* 2.11.
25. Hugh of St. Victor, *De tribus diebus* 4.3.

"reads" the natural world as an allegorical expression of the truths of the Christian faith, which function as soteriological and pedagogical signs.

As a figuralist rendering of creaturely being, the Hugonian interpretation of nature assumes two primary functions: first, nature's objective order serves as a compendium of moral and spiritual truths that guides the faithful into salvific action; second, this objective order also manifests the invisible nature of the triune God—that is, in the concrete reality of the finite world the "invisible wisdom of God shines forth."[26] Hugh summarizes these interrelated pedagogical functions: "By contemplating what God has made we realize what we ourselves ought to do. Every nature tells of God; every nature teaches man;[27] every nature reproduces its essential form, and nothing in the universe is infecund."[28] In regard to the first function, Hugh derives tropological[29] significance from nature's creatures, including those that appear harmful and dangerous. For instance, he writes in *De tribus diebus* that creatures "both good and bad . . . speak to humanity in such a way that its members [must] attend to what great zeal they should show in fleeing eternal evils and seeking eternal goods."[30] The specific disposition of creatures, whether benign or malignant, bears an instructive message that cohered with the moral and spiritual content of the Bible. Under this figural perception, nonhuman animals were interpreted as exemplifying the interior dispositions that characterize the human traversal of time.[31] Although such an account

26. Hugh of St. Victor, *De tribus diebus* 4.5.

27. Please note that the use of the term "man" for humanity is only used when quoting other authors and translators.

28. Hugh of St. Victor, *Didascalicon* 6.5.

29. Tropology is an aspect of the wider category of allegory (or figure) that pertains to moral instruction—that is what one must do in terms of the shape of Christian living. Hugh of St. Victor writes, "Tropology is when in that action that we hear was done [in Scripture] we recognize what we must do. Whence it rightly receives the name 'tropology,' that is, converted language or replicated speech, because we certainly turn the language of a foreign narrative toward our own instruction when, by reading the deeds of others, we conform ourselves to their example of living" (Hugh of St. Victor's Prologue to *Chronicon*, in Harkins, *Reading and the Work of Restoration*, 38–39).

30. Hugh of St. Victor, *De tribus diebus* 10.

31. While this type of theological interpretation of the natural world is ubiquitous in Patristic and medieval interpretation, its most influential articulation is found in the *Physiologus*, an anonymous second-century text that offered a scripturally infused commentary on animals, plants, and other creaturely elements. This text profoundly shaped all subsequent Christian interpretation of the natural world until the early modern period. For example, in the *Physiologus*, lion cubs are perceived as figures of the risen Christ when they, after being born dead (as it was traditionally believed), come to

is not an explicit explanation that makes sense of creational suffering, it does function as a kind of indirect theodicy insofar as it meaningfully interprets the world's ambiguous elements, albeit in an anthropocentric fashion.

Although moral interpretations abound with respect to nature's phenomena, this did not exhaust Hugh's figural appraisal of creation. Indeed, with respect to its second function, Hugh's figuration affirmed that the entire creaturely universe was imbued with a fertility of meaning that was revealed in light of the mystery of the divine Word. Namely, all things in their distinction and variety represented (or signified) some aspect of the triune God. In this respect, Hugh's thought adhered to the scriptural claim that "the Word made what can be seen and is seen through what He made."[32] In this sense, the creaturely world's being is bound to the revealed form of Jesus, as is the Bible's overall scope and meaning. Boyd Taylor Coolman writes that Hugh envisioned "a variegated universe of creatures in one degree or another participating in, and thus reflecting through their beauty, the Wisdom that is the second Person of the Trinity."[33] The primary content of Hugh's theological elaborations concerning creation's Christological form is also expressed in his *De tribus diebus*, where he examined and elaborated how the variegated creatures of the material cosmos manifest divine "power, wisdom, and kindness," which correspond to the properties appropriated to the distinct persons of the triune God. Each one of these characteristics is displayed in creatures, which Hugh then further subdivides into a wide range of creaturely properties.[34] This figural cast of mind is extended to the "monstrous" and "ridiculous" elements of the natural world.[35] He interpreted these elements as declaring

---

life after three days. This type of tropological or spiritual application—which integrated all created things, including the perplexing and bizarre elements of nature, into a theological landscape—formed the primary way of grasping the creaturely world's meaning in Patristic and Medieval thought. As Peter Harrison writes, "For the church Fathers and their medieval successors, the natural world was a book, a repository of rich and varied symbols which bore important meanings. So it was that whatever properties a creature had—physical characteristics, behaviors, life histories, passions, all potentially taught some moral lesson or signified some eternal verity" (Harrison, "Virtues of Animals," 465–66). For a historical description of this remarkable text, see Michael J. Curley's "Introduction" to his accessible translation of *Physiologus*.

32. Hugh of St. Victor, *De tribus diebus* 1.1.

33. Coolman, *Theology of Hugh of St. Victor*, 88.

34. For analysis of the figural dimensions of Hugh's *De tribus diebus*, see Cizewski, "Reading the Word as Scripture," 65–88.

35. Hugh of St. Victor, *De tribus diebus* 11.2.

the profound depths of God's providential wisdom. In describing nature's strange creatures, he writes,

> The more their shape is alien to human reason, the more readily it can compel the human mind to amazement. Why does the crocodile not move its lower jaw when it is eating? And how does the salamander stay unharmed in the fire? . . . And the ant that knows winter is approaching and so fills her granary with grains? The spider, too, fashioning its webs from its own innards to capture prey? They are witnesses to the wisdom of God.[36]

In line with the figural rendition of the world as a reflection of God's being, Hugh maintains that the mortality and violence of the nonhuman creation are creatively encompassed within God's overarching purpose for the world, which is ultimately centered upon humanity. For instance, in his *Adnotationes*, a collection of notes on Genesis, Hugh writes that everything that God made (plants, animals, elements, etc.) was for the sake of humanity, and all nonhuman creatures were intrinsically endowed with "change, and mortality."[37] In this respect, Hugh's thought echoes both scriptural passages (e.g., Ps 104; Job 38–41) and the prevailing Christian theological tradition that envisioned death and animal predation as a manifestation of God's providential wisdom.[38] For Hugh, animal death in the prelapsarian world reflects the Christian Neoplatonic notion that natural limits are divine gifts bequeathed to creatures for the sake of the universe's overarching beauty. In describing Hugh's cosmological perspective, Coolman writes, "The original creation was a highly differentiated world, wherein all things were arranged in hierarchical gradations of power, subtlety, wisdom, freedom, such that each had its proper 'measure, mode, and end.'"[39] The existence of what we have described as nature's ontic strife is ordered toward the display of an ever-greater beauty as it is graciously given to the world by God's creative love. Hugh writes,

---

36. Hugh of St. Victor, *De tribus diebus* 11.2.

37. Hugh of St. Victor, *Adnotationes*, 66.

38. As representative of wide streams of Patristic thought, both Basil and Augustine express a view in which animals are created as intrinsically ordered to violence (see Basil, *Homily* 9.5). Basil perceives that animals exist for the sake of humanity, both for consumption and as an example of virtue; e.g., the struggle of animals to survive teaches human beings courage (Basil, *Hexaemeron* 9.5). For Augustine's position, see *Literal Meaning of Genesis* 3.25. The premodern approach to animal suffering in Christian theological tradition will be examined in the next chapter.

39. Coolman, *Theology of Hugh of St. Victor*, 86.

> First of all, if you gaze at the structure of this universe, you will find that the composition of all things is perfect because of wonderful thought and wisdom. How apt, fitting, seemly, how complete in all its parts! In it not only do similar things protect concord, but also diverse and incompatible things, which come into existence by the Creator's power at the command of wisdom, come together in some way in one friendship and federation.[40]

According to Hugh and the prevailing tradition, the problematic aspects of nature's conflictive character—the wastefulness and struggle of life in time—are sublimated to an overarching harmony and fecundity that is a manifestation of God's dynamic and creative Word.

By evincing the prevailing Christian approach to the nonhuman creation in premodern Christian thought, Hugh of St. Victor's interpretative disposition embodies a figural theology that explicates the meaning of the world within the scope of the scriptural economy. This effectively connects the phenomenal world of nature (as it appears to premodern thought) with the interior dimensions of the Bible's theological architecture. As a consequence, this interpretive disposition yields a type of indirect theodicy whereby the perplexing features of creaturely existence are meaningfully located within theological discourse. This figural disposition provides a formal interpretive structure that enables one to grasp the problem of nature's *agon* in a theological manner. This engagement of the problem of animal suffering from the perspective of figuration is advantageous, given that it operates within the grammar of Christian creational thought. Nevertheless, while figural reasoning is logically consistent with respect to Christianity's ontological commitments, two major problems emerge: first, the employment of figural reading challenges prevailing interpretive assumptions concerning the Bible *and* nature in contemporary thought; second, the concrete interpretive outcomes rendered by such an engagement are not entirely acceptable to modern perceptions concerning nature and ethics. Therefore, while much of the *material* content may prove insufficient for addressing the contemporary problem of creational theodicy, Hugh's theology provides a figural orientation grounded upon the mystery of Christ that will prove interpretively fruitful. This retrieval of Hugh's figuration in view of contemporary theodical concerns will be the subject of the latter half of this study. Before we commence with this

---

40. Hugh of St. Victor, *De tribus diebus* 4.7.

retrieval it is necessary to examine the primary objections associated with such an approach.

Our adoption of Hugh's figuralist perception as a formal theological principle remains controversial in an intellectual context profoundly shaped by the theoretical assumptions of modern historicism. If the proposal for a renewed figuralist natural theology is to hold any conceptual purchase for contemporary theodical reflection, it is necessary to consider and develop the conceptual assumptions of scriptural figuration in light of higher criticism. This task will occupy the rest of this chapter. A second problem concerns Hugh's assumptions regarding the nature of the physical world (its scientific description) and the nature of animal suffering (its moral ontology), both of which have been dramatically reconfigured by the epochal changes of the modern period. This shift and its implication for theodical reflection will be examined in the next chapter.

FOUNDATIONS FOR THE RENEWAL OF FIGURATION

The Living Words of God: Creation and Scripture

The theoretical ontology of creation expresses the Christian revelation that all things are made and providentially shaped *from nothingness* by the eternal act of the Trinity. This forms the *sine qua non* of figuralist thinking. Significantly, this indispensable ontological structure both animates the figural interpretation of Scripture and is itself a truthful disclosure about God and the world established by Scripture's encompassing significance in the revelatory economy. Consequently, the theoretical structure of creation depends epistemically upon a more comprehensive claim regarding the nature of Scripture as inspired discourse, grasped as the words of the Word of God. This brings us to a series of conceptual distinctions we must consider regarding the *nature* of Scripture and its *status* vis-à-vis the divine personhood of the Word of God.

A sufficient theological account of the Bible cannot ignore the fact that for most of the church's history it was viewed as a divinely revealed text read to discern the mind and will of God. As we observed with Hugh of St. Victor's figuralism, the act of reading the Bible as Scripture was governed by a mysterious and elusive ontology that recognized the text as simultaneously identical to and distinct from the eternal Word of God. It is precisely this mysterious identity of Scripture that established the interpretive practices that consequently shaped and governed the church's theological discourse.[41] This expansive vision of the Bible's metaphysical status is the spring that nourished the church's interpretive tradition, giving form and life to the church's way of being in the world. To state the traditional ontology boldly, the words of Scripture are the *divine* discourse that unveiled the mind of God concerning the meaning of the world, both human and cosmic. Thus, when Hugh of St. Victor describes the Bible as "divine utterance" he is only exemplifying the principal disposition that animates the broad sweep of Jewish and Christian assumptions concerning Scripture's mysterious character. For instance, the profoundly influential Augustine describes this vision of the Bible as divine discourse in the fourth century, writing from the divine perspective in his *Confessions*:

> Listen, human creature: what my scripture says, I myself say, but whereas scripture says it in terms of time, my Word is untouched by time, because he subsists with me eternally, equal to myself. What you see through my Spirit, I see, just as what you say through my Spirit, I say. You see these things in terms of time, but I do not see in time, nor when you say these things in temporal fashion do I speak in a way conditioned by time.[42]

The affirmation that Scripture is the living discourse of God in time presses the issue further concerning the relationship between Scripture's textual referents and the hypostatic Word. For his part, Hugh's theological reasoning displays the ambiguity of this question while coming close to affirming a direct identity between the Bible and Christ. He writes, "For the whole Divine Scripture is one Book, and that one Book is Christ."[43] Here, the church's traditional perception of the ontological status of scriptural speech straddles the uncreated-created distinction without a

---

41. The apprehension of the biblical text according to the Christian creational metaphysic led to interpretive practices that recognized a temporally complex relationship amongst the Bible's referents. This perception yielded the four-fold method of scriptural interpretation called the *quadriga*. As the theologian Charles Scalise put it: "The history of 'precritical' Christian biblical interpretation is characterized by methods such as typology and allegory, which uses levels of time and eternity to ground various levels of meaning. This pattern may be discovered in the classical fourfold levels, which move from the 'historical or literal level' (the past) to the 'allegorical level' (connecting past and present) to the 'moral or tropological level' (what shall be done in the present and immediate future) to the 'mystical or anagogical level' (the future of eternity)" (Scalise, *Hermeneutics as Theological Prolegomena*, 1).

42. Augustine, *Confessions* 13.29.

43. Hugh of St. Victor, *De arca Noe morali* 2.11.

clear categorization. As divine discourse, the Bible is bound up with both God's eternal being and the created content of the universe. The mysterious character of Scripture thus appears to find a conceptual correspondence (or analogy) with the function of the divine ideas in traditional Christian metaphysics.[44]

The doctrine of divine ideas provided a way for Christian thinkers to negotiate the unique relation between God and the world by means of a theologically transposed Platonism. Whereas Platonists ostensibly viewed the intelligible forms of the world as eternally subsistent realities, Christian thinkers adopted and reconfigured this concept by placing it within the eternity of the Word of God, who fully shares the divine nature.[45] The Word of God (who is Christ) thus *enfolds* all the ideas of creatures within himself, and He is, by extension, *unfolded* or *explicated* in all the elements of the world, in the very creatures and events of time. A problem emerged, however, concerning the ontological status of these forms in view of God's uncreated and unchanging nature. The question arises: How are the ideas or forms of created existence related to the eternal nature without violating the principle of divine simplicity? Without going into its historical evolution, it is enough to say that the divine ideas were emptied of their status as *real* being (*esse reale*) and were reconceived as a form of *intentional* being (*esse intentionale*) "contained" within the Word's eternal act of filiation. In the Father's eternal utterance of the Son, God exhaustively knows (timelessly by way of transcendence) all the ways in which the divine essence can be participated

---

44. I am using the term "divine ideas" in a wide sense to cover the various ways theologians have conceived of the pre-existence of creation within the eternity of the divine Word: from Augustine's *rationes seminales* to Maximus' *logoi spermatikoi*, John Scotus Eriugena's *praedestinationes*, to Bonaventure's and Aquinas' *divinae ideae*. These fascinating metaphysical concepts attempt to delineate the relationship between God and creation in a manner that preserves the contingency of creation while affirming the doctrine of divine simplicity and immutability. For a discussion of the role of divine ideas in Christian theology, see McIntosh, "Maker's Divine Meaning," 365–84.

45. Even though Middle-Platonists and Neoplatonists placed the archetypes and forms of the world within the *Nous* (or *Logos*), this was distinct from the Christian reformulation of the platonic account. Notably, the Platonists were able to avoid the problem of the multiplicity of real ideas within the *Nous* by means of an emanationist ontology. Since the *nous* or *logos* were not "God of God," but derived subordinate hypostases, the truly divine One was unaffected by the multiplicity of creation. By contrast, the Christian identification of the *Logos* with the divine nature of the Father (God from God) raised the issue of how these ideas were ontologically found in the eternal unity of God's nature. For how this was worked out in Christian orthodoxy, see Clarke, "Problem of the Reality," 65–88.

in by creatures. In this respect, the intentional ideas of the world were eternally conceived *as* the atemporal content of the divine Word—the "ideas" of creaturely being were "spoken" within the very subsistence of the hypostatic Word without destroying the simplicity of the divine nature.[46] Regardless of whether one accepts the conceptual import of this tradition, the ambiguous character of the divine ideas in relation to God's Word underscores its analogical correspondence with the strange and indefinable nature of the Bible's ontology. The words of Scripture, in their semantic reach, appear in both Western and Eastern theological traditions to hover around the same metaphysically opaque terrain. Scripture belongs to the disclosive creativity of God; it is tethered to and contained by the inexhaustible depths of the triune nature, while its being remains intrinsically mysterious and elusive.

This parallel between the divine ideas and Scripture's ontology accentuates the unique interpretive relation obtained between textual figures and creatures, a relation grounded upon the mysterious connection of both with the Divine Word's creative comprehension. Such a theological metaphysics enabled someone like Hugh of St. Victor to discern the truth of God's Wisdom in the "monstrous" and "ridiculous" appearances of creatures, including things predatory and destructive like "the spider . . . fashioning its webs from its own innards to capture prey."[47] Under such an interpretive lens, it is theoretically possible to "read" the shape of the world and its creatures, including its ontic violence, as an index of divine truth. Here, the reality of nature's agonistic economy—including things like the liver-fluke worm consuming a sheep's internal organs or hyenas chasing down and tearing the flesh of wildebeest—speaks of *some* revelatory truth about the world. What that truth might be will be pursued in later chapters.

Grounded upon this Christocentric ontology, scriptural signs and the physical world are referentially implicated as disclosive mediations of God's trinitarian life. This pronounced vision of the Bible and nature, according to Ephraim Radner, "renders the world as an ordered whole, if grasped from a spiritual perspective, where everything must (and does)

---

46. In traditional scholastic terms there is no *real* distinction between the ideas and God's essence but a *logical* distinction. For an historical account of the reception of "divine ideas" among Christian thinkers, see Clarke, "Problem of the Reality," 65–88; Doolan, *Aquinas on Divine Ideas.*

47. Hugh of St. Victor, *De tribus diebus* 11.2.

in fact refer to everything else."[48] This metaphysically "thick" perception establishes allegorical figuration, which is defined by a vision of the Bible as the communicative *enscripturation* of the divine Logos, whose eternal filiation from the Father encompasses all things. Again, Radner writes, "The 'figural' import of the text is simply built into the structure of reality as created. The redemptive aspect of the scriptural 'revelation' is tied, conversely, to the fact that this creation and its articulation is given in the Word who is Christ Jesus."[49] Radner perceives the expansive interpretive practice of premodern Christianity as intrinsically tethered to this ontology, i.e., a *Christocentric* perception of reality, which grounds Scripture's semantic polyvalence. In its concrete manifestation, this type of figural exegesis is noteworthy for its rich (and at times extravagant) deployment of biblical figures as a resource for theological discernment.[50] Historically speaking, the Bible was engaged in a manner that related the variegated textual figures to its unifying theological referent (Christ) and, by extension, with the creaturely realities established in and through Christ.[51]

---

48. Radner, *Time and the Word*, 63.

49. Radner, *Time and the Word*, 56.

50. By reading the Scriptures figurally, premodern Christians were not simply inventing and projecting a framework in order to give the Scriptures narrative coherency. The canonical texts themselves presuppose (and authorize) such a figural extension of meaning. For example, in 1 Corinthians 10:4, Paul deploys a figural reading of the Exodus narrative wherein he identifies the physical rock from which Israel drank in the wilderness as the person of Christ. Furthermore, the Gospels, especially in the passion narratives, invoked the Old Testament Prophets and Psalms, which re-colored and reframed how those preceding texts were received and interpreted by the church. For the authors of the New Testament (and the church Fathers), the use of Old Testament texts in reference to Christ was not an abandonment of the immediate referents of the texts (e.g., the Davidic laments of Pss 22, 31, 109), but instead a "thickening of meaning" conditioned by the figurative order of the biblical text itself. The Bible displays an extension of meaning vis-à-vis its various figures, which ultimately enveloped the form of Christ (cf. Luke 24:27). As such, for the early Christians the Bible's figures were canonically expanded beyond the immediate historical concern of the various texts and ultimately found their ontological clarity in Christ himself. Peter Leithart offers some helpful treatments of the figural texture of Paul's usage of the Old Testament in *Deep Exegesis*, 36–52. It should be noted that scriptural figuration is not exhausted by predictive or typological relations within Scripture's discourse. Instead, such elements belong to and presuppose the broader creational ontology articulated here, based upon the divine arrangement of the cosmos (both time and being) as a divinely shaped totality.

51. Daley, "In Many and Various Ways," 609.

The Decline of Figuration: Scripture in an Uncreated World

The figuralist orientation remained the primary mode of interpretation for Christian ecclesial bodies (Catholic, Protestant, and Orthodox) well into the eighteenth century before being displaced by modern historiography.[52] The fundamental claim behind what would later be denoted the "historical-critical method" asserted that Scripture, as a humanly authored document, ought to be studied in conformity with the applicative criteria of other forms of ancient literature. According to its proponents, this method was intended to secure the factual meaning of biblical texts by constraining "fanciful" elaborations of figuration, which had become highly suspect in light of the new ontology of time and being that emerged gradually in the late Renaissance and Early Modern periods. This new ontology of history perceived temporal events as discrete sequential "happenings" that accorded with a materialist account of event causation. As a result, Scripture's objective reference was narrowed to one that was initially linked to evidenced temporal events (the "brute facts" of history) and subsequently to authorial intention. This new interpretive practice also manifested a dramatic reduction (or bracketing) of the Bible's traditional status, whereby it became merely another literary artifact amongst many others. In his seminal 1860 essay *On the Interpretation of Scripture*, the great proponent of biblical historicism Benjamin Jowett writes,

> Although the interpretation of Scripture requires "a vision and faculty divine," or at least a moral and religious interest which is not needed in the study of a Greek poet or philosopher, yet in what may be termed the externals of interpretation, that is to say, the meaning of words, the connexion of sentences, the settlement of the text, the evidence of facts, the same rules apply to the Old and New Testaments as to other books. And the figure is no exaggeration of the erring fancy of men in the use of Scripture, or of the tenacity with which they cling to the interpretations of other times, or of the arguments by which they maintain them.[53]

For Jowett and subsequent generations of historical critics, the authentic meaning of the Bible was exhaustively determined by what could

---

52. The prevalence of figural readings among various ecclesial bodies (with varying forms of creational frameworks) until the eighteenth century is demonstrated by Radner, *Time and the Word*, 111–62; cf. Frei, *Eclipse of Biblical Narrative*.

53. Jowett, "On the Interpretation of Scripture," 337.

be discerned through historical interrogation. This method included a special emphasis on historical facticity, the "real" event behind the text as opposed to its narrative presentation, and the constriction of literary signs (words) to a meaning that cohered with the surrounding historical and cultural milieu of the original author.

Contraction of the semantic depth of Scripture also applied to the wider figuralist perceptions concerning the natural world. The reading of creation as endowed with divine meaning reflective of scriptural discourse was largely abandoned or revised into a new mode of natural theological reasoning. This modern method of natural theology abandoned the theological investigation of creatures in terms of scriptural content and shifted towards a discourse that emphasized the remarkable discoveries of the emerging scientific method, especially in terms of the mathematical precision of nature's laws. It is not so much the case that God disappeared from this new mode of natural theology but that the scripturally revealed character of God's nature was largely displaced by an abstract portrait governed by an emerging vision of creation as discerned by scientific discovery rather than Scripture's theological texture.[54]

This fundamental contraction in the interpretive posture of the church with respect to the theological meaning of Scripture and the natural world was principally conditioned by the extensive social, political, and metaphysical upheavals of the early modern period, which included the ecclesial fragmentation of Western Christianity, the emergence of secular modern nation-states as the primary political reality, and the technological mastery displayed by the scientific revolution.[55] Within this cluster of changes, the historical-critical analysis of the Bible and the scientific interrogation of nature emerged as the primary ways of getting

---

54. For this movement from figuralist natural theology towards its modern form that seeks to infer knowledge about God from created realities, see Radner, *Chasing the Shadow*, 1–38.

55. Notably, part of the generating conditions for modern biblical historiography were the ecclesial divisions, which led to the "Wars of Religion" in the early modern period. To mitigate the violence that was in part tethered to biblical interpretation, the movement towards a modern historicist perspective was animated by the belief that historical analysis could operate in a manner similar to that of the natural sciences. Under the discerning eye of the historian the authentic meaning of the Bible, which had been entirely subjugated to ecclesial polemics and theological projections of traditionalist interpreters, could be set free from the occluding character of theological exegesis. It was believed that only a neutral scientific analysis of the historical shaping of the text would yield the determinate meaning that lies behind the text in the mind of the original author. For an account of the political dimensions of historical criticism see Legaspi, *Death of Scripture*.

at the "real" meaning of things without succumbing to the "distorting" ideological projections of religious interpretation.[56] These methods presupposed that strict scientific analysis of the text and the world, divorced from distorting theological claims, would yield a stable determinate meaning that avoided the interpretive conflicts and diversity that had prevailed since the time of the Reformation.[57]

Behind the social and political ferment of the modern period and the drive to subdue the disruptive nature of scriptural interpretation evinced in Catholic-Protestant debates, there lies a gradual reconstitution of metaphysical assumptions that ultimately reconfigured the church's figuralist perception of reality. The Christocentric creational metaphysics that once framed *all things* was at first displaced by an abstract theistic ontology. This thinned-out theism slowly transformed (culturally and socially) into the implicit metaphysical materialism that frames contemporary cultural perceptions concerning nature and history.[58] Accordingly, the implicit

---

56. Modern historiography presented itself as an epistemically neutral discipline that imitated the emerging natural scientific exposition of the natural world. Historical theologian Andrew Louth summarizes the purportedly objective character of this practice: "It has what appears to be the great merit of objectivity: both in the sense that the object of study seems clear—it is what the author of a text had in mind when he wrote it—and in the sense that the truth discovered is independent of the one who discovers it" (Louth, *Discerning the Mystery*, 99).

57. The intractable social and political dimensions of the shift away from a classical premodern hermeneutic is described by George Lindbeck, who writes, "The basic causes of its [the church's classical hermeneutic] demise, as I have already suggested, antedate the rise of historical criticism. Confessional rivalries culminating in wars of religion, on the one hand, and the mentality associated with the development of modern science, on the other, each played a part. The two phenomena are interconnected. Communal certainties were undermined by Christian fratricide (much more unsettling than ever before in the West because it was between established churches), and many turned for firm foundations to individual reason and experience" (Lindbeck, "Scripture, Consensus, and Community," 84). Under such conditions, the science of "dispassionate historical analysis" promised to yield certain knowledge about its object of study (the Biblical texts and the ancient past), and thereby obviate the divisive currents of ecclesial interpretation while subordinating unverifiable theological convictions to the emerging secularism of the modern European state.

58. The origin of the displacement of creational metaphysics is not entirely straightforward. Some figures (notably Louis Dupré in *Passage to Modernity*) have maintained that the nominalist impulse of the late-medieval period conditioned the gradual externalization of divine action, which led ineluctably to a materialist ontology. Yet, such an account is insufficient. The metaphysical conditions of early modernity cannot be divorced from the concrete social and political conditions that shaped the period. While the loss of a participationist framework may be significant for the emergence of a non-creational ontology (this is debatable), I believe the socially disruptive aspects of intra-ecclesial battles seems to form the primary conditions for a gradual purge of

materialist ontology of modernity, aided by the technological success of the natural sciences, reframed the universe as an objective, mathematical, and mechanistic reality. As a result, both nature's creatures and Scripture's content were perceived as discrete objects subject exclusively to the limited "neutral" methodologies that *bracketed* (or replaced) the fundamental metaphysical claims of Christian belief. Created being and time were sealed off epistemically from the disclosive form of the Scriptures. The gradual loss of this sense of *Creation* led to the contraction of figuralist thinking.[59] Previously, both Scripture and the universe were seen as the mediative expressions of God's creative love, which conditioned their manifold significance. The new science of nature and history, under the pretense of metaphysical neutrality, operated in a culturally *posited* world that was conceptually sealed off from Christian claims.

A consequence of this metaphysical shift was shown by the way early modern thinkers reconsidered the issue of nature's violent and destructive forms. As we saw with Hugh of St. Victor, premodern thought was able to include the "monstrous" aspects of nature in light of scriptural patterns, which effectively provided a type of narrative explication that made such realities an index of divinely revealed truth about the world. With the decline of the figuralist perception, the implicit theodical problem of nature was exposed. Peter Harrison writes:

> A clear indication of the new, non-symbolic status of living creatures is provided by the re-emergence of the problem of useless or hostile animals and plants. Indeed, in the seventeenth century the more general problem of evil reasserts itself in an acute way, signaling the disintegration of those epistemic structures which had given meaning to nature. No longer could it be confidently asserted with the Fathers that apparently purposeless features of the created world actually represented higher things of considerable import. If the natural world was again to make sense,

---

theology and creational metaphysics from the collective mind of Europe's intellectual elite.

59. Peter Harrison argues in *The Bible, Protestantism, and the Rise of Natural Science* that the displacement of figural (or allegorical) exegesis by Protestantism was one of the primary conditions that factored into the emergence of the natural sciences in the early modern period. While Harrison is right to link the figural perspective of nature with its scriptural interpretation, it seems that Harrison overstates the case for Protestantism as the primary source of the contraction of figuration. As Ephraim Radner has demonstrated, various types of figuration were practiced across denominational lines well into the eighteenth century, many associated with natural philosophers. See Radner, *Time and the Word*, 111–62.

some new account of innumerable creatures which served no obvious purpose had to be found.⁶⁰

The emergence of creational theodicy as a substantial problem for modern Christianity thus appears bound up with the declension of the Christocentric creational metaphysics and its resultant delimitation of the Bible's objective reference. The tools of analytic history had pried the Bible apart into a diverse array of sources with disparate ideologies and varying degrees of historical facticity.⁶¹ That which was traditionally thought to have been a coherent unity that made sense of the world was exposed as a multi-layered, historically conditioned, all-too-human document whose meaning was tethered to an inert past. Because of this strict delimitation, Scripture could no longer speak of any reality beyond that which was discernible to the historical critic. Biblical interpretation was held captive by a materialist ontology that effectively silenced its ability to speak meaningfully about the world and its creatures.

Under such a contracted vision, the problem of nature's suffering was gradually pursued according to the type of abstract reasoning that characterized early modern natural theology. For instance, the eighteenth-century philosopher G. W. Leibniz represents a trajectory of thought that perceived nature's ontic strife as a necessary feature of created existence. According to Leibniz, "one must believe that even sufferings and monstrosities," like the liver-fluke worm or ichneumon wasp, are part of an

---

60. Harrison, *Bible, Protestantism*, 162.

61. The general approval of the historical-critical method as the proper mode of interpretation invites the conclusion that the church failed to properly discern the real meaning of its sacred texts for most of its history because it was submerged in distorting confessional frameworks at odds with the "objective" science of modern intellectual culture. Thus, not only were Christian theologians wrong to apply scriptural categories to nature, but scriptural categories themselves were historically suspect and inapplicable to the problems at hand. According to Stephen Fowl, the wholesale adoption of historical-critical exegesis by theologians "force[d] Christians to view the overwhelming majority of the history of Christian biblical interpretation as a series of errors, of failed attempts to display the meaning of the text" (Fowl, *Engaging Scripture*, 36). Similarly, Andrew Louth writes, "How can one accept their results if one does not accept their methods? It might be possible to argue that if they had had the benefit of the historical-critical method they would still have ended up at Chalcedon. But on the one hand such a claim seems a bit far-fetched, and on the other it is so unhistorical a notion as to be scarcely coherent" (Louth, *Discerning the Mystery*, 100). Oddly enough, those theologians and biblical scholars who affirm both traditional dogma and the interpretive insufficiency of figuration are thrown into a rather strange juxtaposition as they accept traditional theological ontological claims concerning God and Jesus Christ but dismiss the epistemic processes that yielded such formulations.

order that contributes to the "best plan of things."[62] On the one hand, Leibniz's perspective recapitulates the broadly Neoplatonic perspective that nature's ontic violence and dissipative form are direct expressions of God's creative Wisdom; on the other hand, his explication of this divine Wisdom, while not untethered from its Christic orientation, is less apprehended by scriptural forms than it is grasped by a calculative logic.[63] This contraction in figuralist thinking manifests the *growing* detachment of the world's meaning from the scriptural narrative and the centrality of the crucified and exalted Jesus. In this way, the theological depth of nature, including its predatory and destructive character, becomes more opaque as it is shifted further apart from the figural texture of Scripture.

By stressing the necessity of recovering the figuralist perception in theological interpretation, I am not claiming that the tools of historical criticism (and of modern science in general) have not yielded authentic insights that enrich our understanding of their targeted domains. The historical-critical approach has rightly emphasized the importance of historicity with respect to the biblical text, which is inherent to the church's confession.[64] Moreover, the method's exposition of various layers of the biblical text has also provided a more textured, theologically rich account of its literary dimensions, which adverts to fruitful avenues of interpretation. However, despite this, historical criticism's pretense to a totalizing description of "the real" masks an assortment of claims that are fundamentally inimical to the church's foundational commitments concerning

---

62. Leibniz, *Theodicy*, 276, 280.

63. See the Christic orientation in Leibniz, *Causa Dei*, 114–45. In terms of his broader theodicy, Leibniz envisions this universe as "the best possible world" inasmuch as it is the one in which God becomes human in the person of Jesus Christ. This emphasis upon the Christic element challenges many popular accounts of Leibniz as a rationalistic metaphysical optimist. Nevertheless, even with his theological orientation, his natural theology expresses the trajectory of thought that perceived divine Wisdom in terms of the mathematical precision of the physical properties of the universe.

64. To what extent is historical "happened-ness" a necessary feature of Christian discourse? On one level, a set of core claims are necessarily tethered to a notion of historical actuality (e.g., the birth, death, and resurrection of Christ); however, on another level, there are a great range of figures where it is not clear how they are to be construed in "historical" terms (e.g., Noah's flood). Historically speaking, the notion of "happened-ness" is not as straight-forward in the Christian tradition as it is assumed to be by our modern mono-causal sense of historicity. For example, Origen readily admits that some of the described events of the biblical narrative escape a literal historical referent while serving a signifying function with respect to the immaterial properties of the creaturely world. Perhaps, in light of God's providential ordering of text and reality, our notion of "happened-ness" must be construed differently and expanded. See Origen, *On First Principles* 4.3.

God, creation, and the nature of Scripture. The use of historical criticism as the *primary* approach to scriptural meaning can only undermine the interpretive richness of the scriptural text, as it assumes a rival ontology that is theoretically underdetermined and conceptual incongruent with Christian revelation. Moreover, this contracted vision subverts and limits our ability to think theologically—defined in terms of the primacy of scriptural revelation—about the world's being in general and animal suffering in particular. Hence the renewal of figuralist thought that I support requires a profound re-apprehension of Christianity's creational ontology in view of scriptural hermeneutics and natural theology.

Figuralist Thinking and Historicism

The re-integration of scriptural interpretation within the wider tradition's Christocentric creational ontology is an indispensable condition for a renewal of the figuralist perception. Yet, the manner of this re-integration must attend to the conceptual purchase historicism has claimed upon the mind of the church and the academy. There has been a growing openness among theologians towards the re-appropriation of theological exegesis, largely in terms of postmodern hermeneutical theory. However, the practical deployment of *figuration as a theological orientation* has remained largely untapped due to prevailing non-creational metaphysical assumptions concerning temporal events, historical causality, and the nature of written texts. The retrieval of figuralist thinking, which foregrounds a traditional creational metaphysics, also helpfully dovetails with the postmodern critique leveled at historicism's foundationalist epistemology. For the rest of this chapter, I intend to expose some of the suppositions that underlie the historicist tradition to allow us to stretch the theological imagination beyond the interpretive limitations imposed by intellectual convention. We will examine the metaphysical assumptions of historicism along with its postmodern critique. It is my hope that challenging some of the conventions of modern historicism will contribute towards a livelier retrieval of the figural perception of reality, which can aid us in dealing with the challenge presented by creation's suffering character.

The underlying theoretical ontology driving the historical-critical project construes the events of history as "brute" entities that are defined as such by an implicit materialist ontology hidden under a pretense of epistemic neutrality. This pretension masks a host of theoretical structures (or presuppositions) concerning the objects in question and their ontological status (their *being*), which in turn mediates what can be said of them.[65] According to the theologian Matthew Levering, historical criticism implies a "linear temporal continuum" in which all things are assumed to be discrete atomistic entities sealed off from God's creative shaping of time and being.[66] All creatures and "happenings" of time are accounted for by their placement within an extrinsic unidirectional causal sequence, which is abstracted from the chaotic flux of temporal existence.

If this account of being and time is used in a limited fashion as a heuristic device to construct minimalist narratives of the past without becoming a totalizing ontology, it is amenable to theological discourse. However, when the heuristic is inflated to a metaphysical vision in which the extrinsic determinations of events exhaust their meaningfulness, such an account is contrary to the church's theological ontology and is profoundly underdetermined in its own right. The biblical scholar Francis Martin describes the implicit ontology of historicism, writing, "For modern history, time is succession, a dubious and uneven march toward an indeterminate future. The study of history, now capable of genuine

65. The assumption that the natural sciences are in and of themselves value neutral is untenable. For example, the philosophical work of Thomas Kuhn and Michael Polanyi have called into question the assumption that the sciences are methodologically objective by asserting that all scientific investigations proceed from within an elaborate conceptual framework that determines the perception and interpretation of data. Accordingly, no scientist is able to operate outside such frameworks because the scientific mode of inquiry depends upon implicit beliefs that shape analysis. Polanyi writes, "I hold that the propositions embodied in natural science are not derived by any definite rule from the data of experience, and that they can neither be verified nor falsified by experience according to any definite rule. . . . These maxims and the art of interpreting them may be said to constitute the premises of science but I prefer to call them our scientific beliefs. These premises or beliefs are embodied in a tradition, the tradition of science" (Polanyi, "Stability of Beliefs," 218–19). Polanyi's identification of the epistemological structure of scientific knowing illuminates the reality that all forms of knowledge are grounded within tradition-based communities. Consequently, the epistemological assumptions that informed the pretensions of modernity, and subsequently, modern historiography, have also been shown to be the product of a particular social and cultural context. In other words, claims to know reality objectively whether scientifically ("what is the case") or historically ("what really happened") is built upon a range of background assumptions that condition emerging narratives of meaning. Thus, the historical enterprise, as conceived according to the dictates of modern historicism, is not a metaphysically neutral enterprise. Claims to have bracketed theological or metaphysical structures is itself built upon assumptions regarding the ultimate nature of reality that condition how textual meaning is grasped.

66. Levering, *Participatory Exegesis*, 3–7.

reconstruction and insight, records this march. As we have seen, it resolutely eschews any consideration of transcendence, any search for causality that exceeds the forces and resources of what is fundamentally a closed system."[67] According to Martin, the inflation of the historicist accounting of time into an all-embracing ontology is fundamentally inimical to the Christian perception of *created* time as "succession with the dimension of presence."[68] In sum, a sufficiently theological account of time and being must be set within the bounds of the creative eternity of the Father, Son, and Holy Spirit, who absolutely posits and shapes all contingent things in their coming-to-be. As Levering puts it:

> The modern (metaphysical) understanding of history as a solely linear continuum, insofar as this understanding has taken hold in biblical scholarship, is incapable of accounting for the theological and metaphysical reality of human history. *History cannot be confined to what can be known by linear historical modes, important as those modes are; the historical includes participation in realities known by faith.*[69]

The inflation of historicism's heuristic into a far-reaching ontology inevitably displaces the creational metaphysics requisite for theological reasoning and ultimately deforms the apprehension and interpretation of all contingent beings, both creatures and temporal events.

Under the ontological implications of an inflated historicism, one's perception of the world is sealed away from the structuring insights that flow from Scripture's revelatory discourse. In this respect, the distinct figurations of created realities found in the Scriptures possess little conceptual purchase upon one's discernment of the world. This occurs in two ways: first, the perception of the world and its creatures is deformed in its theological significance insofar as both world and creatures are construed, historically and theoretically, as brute realities subjected to the deforming projections of materialism. Second, under such a vision of being, one's apprehension of the meaning of Scripture is reduced to the reconstructed intentions determined to lie behind the formation of the text. Such historical interpretations are interpretively inert with respect to the wider meaning of created existence. As a result, the referential reach of Scripture's figures cannot speak of the theological shape of nature.

---

67. Martin, "Revelation as Disclosure," 243.
68. Martin, "Revelation as Disclosure," 244.
69. Levering, *Participatory Exegesis*, 6.

This is not to say that historical criticism—as a set of theoretical procedures—does not afford some insights into the nature of the biblical texts as humanly composed documents. The methods of critical analysis, when conducted with the expressed aim of understanding the writings as historically conditioned forms of human writing, are entirely appropriate. The problem lies with the totalizing impulse that inflates historical analysis to a form of exhaustive discourse that severely contracts textual meaning. Concerning this impulse, the biblical scholar Luke Timothy Johnson remarks:

> The historical-critical paradigm is peculiarly hegemonic. It has claimed exclusive right to designate itself as "critical" and scientific, relegating other approaches to the Scripture—at least by implication—to the realm of the uncritical or "imaginative." ... In subtle ways, the literal sense of Scripture has come to be more or less identified with the historical sense, and the historical sense has taken on normative authority. It is not simply that all interpretations must respect the literal sense, a proposition to which all gladly and rightly agree. It is also that the original meaning of the text, a meaning determined only by historical exegesis, functions as a limiting control to all other interpretations.[70]

In line with Johnson's assessment, the historical-critical method's orientation towards an inflated ontology belies the faulty assumption that authorial intent exhausts meaning.

For instance, in the case of the scriptural depiction of the natural world's ontology, the Bible encompasses a diversity of texts that divergently describe nature's economy. In Job 38–41 and Psalm 104, the violence of the natural economy is presupposed as God's providential will for creatures.

> Is it by your wisdom that the hawk soars, and spreads his wings toward the south? Is it at your command that the eagle mounts up and makes his nest on high? On the rock he dwells and makes his home in the fastness of the rocky crag. Thence he spies out the prey; his eyes behold it afar off. His young ones suck up blood; and where the slain are, there is he. (Job 39:26–30)

> The young lions roar for their prey, seeking their food from God. (Ps 104:21)

---

70. Johnson and Kurz, *Future of Catholic Biblical Scholarship*, 15.

Other scriptural texts, such as Isaiah 11:6–9 or perhaps Genesis 1:30, depict nature's economy as divinely ordered toward ontological peace.[71]

> The wolf shall dwell with the lamb, and the leopard shall lie down with the kid, and the calf and the lion and the fatling together, and a little child shall lead them. The cow and the bear shall feed; their young shall lie down together; and the lion shall eat straw like the ox. . . . They shall not hurt or destroy in all my holy mountain; for the earth shall be full of the knowledge of the LORD as the waters cover the sea. (Isa 11:6–9)

> "And to every beast of the earth, and to every bird of the air, and to everything that creeps on the earth, everything that has the breath of life, I have given every green plant for food." And it was so. (Gen 1:30)

For the historical critic, this divergence in descriptive ontology is merely a reflection of the discrete cultural/ideological intentions of the respective authors and/or communities. As such, these contrary perspectives in Scripture are not subjected to some interpretive theological comprehension but instead are perceived as contingent historical expressions only extrinsically related by some artifactual convention (e.g., literary canon). The meanings of these texts are thereby submerged into an ossified reconstructed past insofar as they only depict the limited, perhaps naïve, perspectives of ancient peoples.

The key problem with such an assumption regarding authorial intent and textual meaning is that it is notoriously underdetermined. The theologian Stephen E. Fowl remarks,

> One can see that in periods when there is a large degree of interpretive agreement, agreement both in terms of methods for attaining meaning and in terms of interpretive results, there is an illusory plausibility to the notion that interpretation is determinate. Problems, however, arise when someone questions the very definition of meaning, thus, throwing the object of any textual mining expedition into question. As the history of literary criticism over the past fifty years has shown, someone has only to ask, for example, "Why should something like the author's intention count as the meaning of a text?" to make both

---

71. Consideration of these distinct creational ontologies in Scripture will be pursued in the next chapter.

the contingency and the fragility of those interpretive agreements clear.[72]

For Fowl, the claim that meaning resides solely with authorial intent is ultimately grounded upon circular reasoning in which textual meaning is axiomatically predetermined to align with the author's intent. The elevation of authorial intention as the exclusive determinant of meaning simply begs the question.[73] The practice also commits a type of genetic fallacy by equating the purported originating conditions of a text with its interpretive extension. Furthermore, in terms of its implicit ontology, such a contracted sense of scriptural reference runs against the wider theological claim that the biblical text possesses *divine* authorship that supervenes through the humanly mediated configuration.[74] At once, the claim of divine authorship plunges the interpreter into a thicket of theological metaphysics and the problem of negotiating fundamental background assumptions regarding the nature of being, time, and the biblical text.

My adverting to the problematic nature of the claim that authorial intent *exclusively* determines textual meaning should not be construed as a denial that communicative intentions are discernible within texts; rather, it is intended to disclose how background commitments antecedently condition judgments concerning meaning.[75] I must stress that I do not

---

72. Fowl, *Engaging Scripture*, 35.

73. In conjunction with this general philosophical objection, it appears that identification of textual meaning exclusively with authorial intent also suffers from a practical problem. Because most "scriptural texts cannot be treated as the product of one human author or one human intention," the notion that there is a single determinate meaning to be recovered is implausible (Ayres and Fowl, "[Mis]Reading the Face of God," 520). In effect, the critical judgment that diverse layers of redaction constitute the Bible (a claim demonstrated by historical criticism) precludes the restriction of meaning of the text to a single intention. Further, the anonymity of the Bible's authorial and redactive provenance further obscures the task of identifying and reconstructing the determinate motivations and intentions behind the texts.

74. One theologically sensitive approach to the issue of authorial complexity is presented by the canonical approach developed by Brevard Childs. For Childs, the various tradents that constitute the biblical texts are subsumed within the deliberate form of the final redacted text, which displays its own comprehensive intentionality. This intentionality "supervenes" upon the text by taking up the authorial and redactorial intentions. While Childs offers an intriguing approach as to how one may perceive the objectivity of a text's canonical form amidst the flux of its diachronic formation, I believe Childs' account necessitates a more robust theological metaphysics that justifies both the process and final form of the text. See Childs, *Biblical Theology*.

75. Along with the inherent complexity associated with basing textual meaning

believe that the communicative intentions of any given author/redactor are entirely submerged by the textual deposit, as is maintained by some radical theorists[76] (e.g., Derrida, Fish, et al.); on the contrary, I believe that such intentions are theoretically discernible to varying degrees of apprehension.[77] For instance, the communicative intentions of texts like Isaiah 11:6–9 or Psalm 104 display a real divergence in terms of their depiction of creation's ontology. However, the grasping of this divergence is not objective, value-free, or an entirely straightforward process.[78] Nor

---

upon authorial intention, the wider historiographical claims regarding the "re-constructability" of the historical past also rest upon questionable epistemological conventions that ultimately fail to deliver what is promised. Luke Timothy Johnson observes that historical exegesis "has not in fact led to an agreed-upon historical reconstruction of ancient Israel, of the human mission of Jesus, or of the development of early Christianity. In fact, the opposite is true: the more scholars have pursued these questions, the more elusive such agreement appears" (Johnson and Kurz, *Future of Catholic Biblical Scholarship*, 14). In line with the multi-valence of historical reconstruction, Arthur C. Danto remarks that the historiographical enterprise in general depends "upon non-historical significance," which is a "matter of the local attitudes and interests of the historian" (Danto, *Narration and Knowledge*, 33). The subjective plays an essential role in accounting for the diversity of interpretation within historical exegesis. Though I do not share Danto's general skepticism regarding knowledge about the past *per se*, I believe that his analysis profitably exposes the interpretive fissures in the nature of the historical enterprise that effectively undermine any pretension to deliver the "real" behind narrativized accounts. Indeed, the perspectival nature of historical knowledge is most on display when it comes to epistemic verification. Danto insists that despite claims to the contrary, the historian's method is not a detached set of operations that enable an authentic *discovery* of the past; rather, historical accounts are positive *constructions* shaped by social, political, and cultural factors that motivate and determine the explanatory scope of any narrative account of the past. The truth-value of these narrative-based reconstructions of historical data (e.g., documents and other sources) is always underdetermined to a significant degree—i.e., most historical constructions, especially of the distant past, have no substantial way of being evaluated apart from a previously accepted framework which is itself a result of the same constructive enterprise. This is not to deny the value of historical inquiry. Rather, I want to expose the reality that historical constructions involve conceptual leaps that depend upon assumed conventions regarding what is already true about the past and what is *metaphysically* possible. Thus, the meaning of the scriptural text is strictly delimited by the theoretical ontological commitments brought to bear upon it by the reader. For a robust articulation of the impossibility of historical knowledge, a claim that I do not share, see Meiland, *Scepticism and Historical Knowledge*.

76. See Fish, *Is There a Text in This Class?*

77. For a defense of the necessity and possibility of discerning authorial intention, see Vanhoozer, *Is There a Meaning in This Text?*, 197–280.

78. As Hans-Georg Gadamer puts it: "In the process of understanding, a real fusing of horizons occurs—which means that as the historical horizon is projected, it is simultaneously superseded. To bring about this fusion in a regulated way is the task of what we called historically effected consciousness" (Gadamer, *Truth and Method*, 306). This

do I admit that the recovery of these intentions (pace historical criticism) is solely determinative of these texts' meaning; rather, the discernment of communicative intentions is simply one aspect of grasping what the philosopher Paul Ricoeur calls "the direction of thought opened up by the text."[79] In this regard, I affirm Ricoeur's emphasis upon the "distanciated text," whereby the reader encounters not the author's intentional consciousness but the "world propositions" that constitute the subject matter of the text. Accordingly, Ricoeur's emphasis on the power of a text to project an entire world of meaning places the focus of interpretation within the instantiated text as it is constituted in its written form, not in the inferred reconstructed mentality of the author. He writes, "Understanding has less than ever to do with the author and his situation. It seeks to grasp the world propositions opened up by the reference of the text. To understand a text is to follow its movements from sense to referents: from what it says to what it talks about."[80]

By highlighting certain features of postmodern hermeneutics, we can discern certain advantages with reference to natural theology, figuralism, and theological metaphysics. First, by locating meaning within the world proposed by the text, such a position can sidestep the historiographical problem of the Bible's authorial complexity, i.e., the reality that the Bible was shaped by a multiplicity of authors and redactors, most of whom are hardly recoverable by historical-critical exegesis. Second, the Ricoeurian recognition that the proposed world of the text is endowed with an expansive meaning fits well with the metaphysically dense perception of Scripture as infinitely fertile with respect to its interpretation. This focusing upon the text as a world unto itself seemingly comports with the traditional perception of the Bible as substantially multivalent with respect to its generative meaning.

Yet, even with the recognition of the expansive "objectivity" of distanciated texts that indicates an inherent interpretive multiplicity regarding human literary artifacts, the question arises: Is the Bible to be regarded any differently than other texts in terms of its interpretive value (e.g., Chaucer's *Canterbury Tales*)? While figuralist or symbolist readings

---

emphasis upon the mediative dimension of textual interpretation under Gadamer's image of the "fusion of horizons" does not eliminate the so-called objective meaning of texts (its ontological aspect) but it certainly complexifies the degree to which that meaning is absolutely determinate and stable.

79. Ricoeur, *Interpretation Theory*, 92.
80. Ricoeur, *Interpretation Theory*, 87–88.

may be applied to other texts, the specific nature of the Bible as Scripture—the reason we regard it differently than other texts—is irreducibly tethered to its ontological constitution as the mysterious revelatory discourse of God. Consider the conceptual idiom of Augustine who claims that the Scriptures give in "terms of time" that which *eternally* "stands together" with the very being of the divine Word of God.[81] Once again, the hermeneutical question concerning the Bible cannot escape metaphysics. The church's practice of reading Scripture thrusts us into the realm of ultimate commitments regarding the nature and source of the being of the world. Thus, when comprehended within a Christocentric creational ontology, the expansive nature of textual meaning, as posited by poststructuralist hermeneutics, opens out upon the very shape of the universe. This includes the problem of creation's suffering. Under such a metaphysical comprehension, ostensibly divergent scriptural perspectives concerning nature's ontology become disclosive of the actual world inasmuch as they are bound up with the triune God's creative presence.

In summation, I want to reiterate that the theoretical practice of historical criticism seals the world off from the Bible's referential depth and is not a theologically or metaphysically neutral perception,[82] but the result of specific socio-cultural assumptions that shape and limit interpretive possibilities. This recognition that antecedent metaphysical (and ideological) structures determine hermeneutical judgments establishes an important condition for retrieving the figural perception of the Bible and the world. Indeed, the act of reading the Bible within the horizon of creation, and not within the modern historicist's thinned-out ontology of time and being, sets the appropriate context for the recovery of figuralist thinking and traditional natural theology. This practice opens up interpretive possibilities for understanding the theological significance of nature's ontic strife by bringing it within the shaping pressures of Scripture and its all-encompassing Christological depth.

---

81. Augustine, *Confessions* 13.29.

82. One of the theoretical assertions associated with modern non-creational metaphysics is the pretension to epistemic neutrality as its foundation—as if a non-creational account of reality is self-evident. Such a claim to epistemic neutrality is simply unsustainable. All metaphysical systems, whether creational, non-creational, non-materialist, or materialist, all operate out of theoretical pre-commitments that are not self-evident (see Thiel, *Nonfoundationalism*).

CONCLUSION

The foundation for figuralist thinking as a means to explore creational strife depends upon certain theological-metaphysical commitments that underwrite the possibility of reading the Bible and the world as saturated with divinely given significance. Indeed, the central claim of figural theology is that the Bible is the disclosive Word of God that preeminently communicates the divine will for creation. According to this account, the triune God is the absolute author of both the world of creation and the world of the biblical text through his creative and providential ordering of secondary causes, conditions, and circumstances. In line with this claim, all of history is "suffused" with God's creative presence, which shapes and orders all things according to the divine will. As Matthew Levering puts it,

> While temporal reality is a "linear" unfolding of moments, it is so precisely as participating in the triune God. Moment follows moment in succession, and yet these moments are not atomistic, but rather constitute an organic web of interrelation. . . . This metaphysical and Christological-pneumatological participation in God joins past, present, and future realities in a unified whole, so that through God's presence each moment is related intrinsically, not merely extrinsically, to every other moment.[83]

For Levering, a Christian view of time is necessarily conditioned by a creational theology in which the triune God configures all finite being in its variegated dimensions (spatial, temporal, and spiritual). Accordingly, there exists an intrinsic relation between all creaturely entities (persons, creatures, and events) and God; all things possess a potentially infinite depth of meaning due to their connection to their divine source and the infinite set of relations with other creaturely realities that this source makes possible. In the words of Hugh of St. Victor: "The meaning of things is determined by the will of the Creator. . . . The meaning of

---

83. Levering, *Participatory Exegesis*, 1. Although the creational theological metaphysic is the *sine qua non* of theological exegesis, it is not clear that Levering's assertion is correct and that a participationist ontology is absolutely necessary for figural interpretive practice. Ephraim Radner has effectively argued that the figural perception of the Scriptures was maintained even with the growing dominance of nominalism with its ontological and epistemological claims. This suggests that the collapse of traditional reading practices in the church resulted from more than a reconfigured ontology. That being said, I am sympathetic to Christian platonic metaphysical accounts and find them more amenable to the creational metaphysics of figural hermeneutics than other metaphysical stances.

things is much more manifold than the meaning of words . . . a thing can mean as many other things as it has visible or invisible properties in common with other things."[84] This radical ontological claim concerning the intrinsic relation of all things to God provides the context for the figural apprehension of the Bible and the creaturely world, granting them an interpretively "thick" meaning rooted in God's creative being.

Within this theological horizon, the dynamic elements of creaturely history, including the diachronic elements of the Bible's historical constitution, are given ultimate coherence. Whereas modern historical criticism mounts a view of time conditioned by materialistic patterns of meaning, the figural perception unveils a depth to historical experience that is only discernible to the scripturally saturated mind. Thus, the modern dynamic account of history may be synthetically integrated within a wider creational ontology wherein the unfolding tensions of historical becoming are reconceived in relation to God's providential order. All things are configured according to the incarnate life of the eternal Son, the form and exemplar of Scripture and creation.[85] Within this comprehensive creational account, the written Word of God is disclosed as the truthful expression of God's loving will for the world. While the divine Word of God contains all the dynamic ideas and sequences of creation's historical form, the *enscripturated* Word of God displays a world of figures that constitute God's truthful discourse about creatures. This disclosive co-inherence of text and world is fittingly expressed by the thirteenth-century theologian Bonaventure. Influenced by Hugh of St. Victor, he writes: "Scripture, then, deals with the whole universe, the high and the low, the first and the last, and all things in between. It is, in a sense, an intelligible cross in which the whole organism of the universe is described and made to be seen in the light of the mind."[86] Behind Bonaventure's interpretive claim resides the mutual disclosure of text and world in the mystery of Christ, which opens a perceptual vista shaped by the figures of Scripture. When discerned under the ontology of divine creation, the scriptural text is charged with a referential density that obviates the sort of discrete atomistic understanding of history evinced by the historical-critical method. Hence, the Christocentric creational ontology that lies

---

84. Hugh of St. Victor, *De scripturis et scriptoribus* 17.

85. The Christological exemplarist account of creation is found in varying forms throughout both Eastern and Western theological traditions. See Blowers, *Drama of the Divine Economy*, 139–87.

86. Bonaventure, *Breviloquium* Prologue 6.4.

behind figural thinking cracks open the imposed limits of the historical sense and reveals a hermeneutically fertile vision of the scriptural text and the created world. To read the Bible under the metaphysical auspices of the church's theological convictions is to be summoned to a figural or allegorical form of thinking.

The preceding analysis thus leaves us with a set of prospective claims that will animate the development and scope of this project. First, the objection that figural reading cannot be deployed as a mode of theological reasoning because of historical criticism's interpretive priority has been shown to rest upon questionable epistemological and ontological assumptions. Second, our emphasis on the importance of metaphysics with respect to scriptural hermeneutics provides the impetus for recovering figural thinking as an intrinsic aspect of the Christian vision of creation. Third, the priority of creational metaphysics for theological discourse implies an intrinsic conceptual relation between figuration and the problem of theodicy. Thus, engaging creational thinking by means of scriptural figuration appears logically (and metaphysically) consistent with the conditions that gave rise to the issue at hand. Regarding the development of a figural theology of creation's *agon* (the scope of this project), our constructive approach proposes to *retrieve* and *extend* Hugh of St. Victor's theological engagement of the Scriptures as a means to this end. As demonstrated in the first part of this chapter, Hugh narrated creation (as it appeared to premodern thought) by means of a figuralist reading of Scripture. In the words of Boyd Taylor Coolman, he perceived in the Scriptures "the revelatory patterns by which visible things can be read aright."[87]

Before we commence with this interpretive retrieval and extension, it is necessary to grasp more adequately the state of the problem of creation's ontological strife. The appearance of the creaturely world for Hugh of St. Victor differs significantly from how it appears to us. Thus, his figural rendition of creation is conditioned by antiquated assumptions concerning the nature of the world (its scientific description) and the nature of creational suffering (its moral ontology), which consequently reshape how we will deploy his figuration in view of such realities. Therefore, in order to retrieve the figuralist perception so as to shape a theology of creational suffering, it is necessary that we first grasp the problem of creational suffering as it presents itself to contemporary thought. To this task we now turn.

---

87. Coolman, "Pulchrum Esse," 181.

2

Nature's Violence

IN THE PREVIOUS CHAPTER, we saw that Hugh of St. Victor's practice of reading the creaturely world by means of scriptural figures sufficed as a sort of implicit theodicy that explained the appearance of the world given the moral, scientific, and ontological acceptances of his day. However, this way of narrating creation as bound to God's self-revealing form has since been undermined in two significant ways. First, as previously discussed, the widespread collapse of figuralist thinking as the primary mode of theological interpretation was part of a metaphysical shift that severed the world's appearance from its ontological source in God's creative Wisdom. This provided the context for a "secularized" rendition of natural being that was ignorant of its spiritual grammar. Second, the collapse of the figuralist perception was also accompanied by profound cultural changes that re-constituted how creatures were perceived by human beings in Western societies. How these shifts impacted theodical reflection will be the subject matter of the present chapter. We will explore how the moral recognition of animal suffering undermined the traditional view that interpreted animals within an enveloping theological horizon centered upon human beings. With the collapse of scriptural figuration and the gradual shift in moral perception, the problem of animal suffering emerged in the modern period with a previously unknown clarity and sharpness.

This chapter will examine the modern perceptions that have challenged traditional theological approaches to nature's *agon*. This will involve two interrelated components: the first part will delineate the historical emergence of animal suffering as a live problem for Christian thought; the second will present the primary theodical forms adduced by contemporary theology as a response to this emergence. Accordingly, the first part will outline the traditional Christian perception of animals and attend to the cultural changes that reframed animal suffering as an intellectual and moral conundrum. The second part will attend to the present state of the theodical question for Christian thought by means of a description and critique of the primary theodical forms applied by modern theologians and philosophers. As will be seen, the basic structure of these contemporary theodicies will correspond with their premodern antecedents, albeit denuded of their scientific and cultural assumptions. It will also be concluded that these contemporary theodicies display a certain degree of theological indeterminacy that is tied up with the modern obscuration of Scripture's figural character. This recognition of the limited nature of modern creational theodicies thus establishes the context for our subsequent retrieval of scriptural figuration as the means for developing a theology of creational suffering that is ordered by Scripture's Christological form.

THEOLOGICAL PERCEPTIONS OF ANIMAL SUFFERING AND CREATIONAL VIOLENCE

Premodern Theology: The Major Tradition

Hugh of St. Victor represents the prevailing character of natural theology in premodern Christian thought: according to its premodern form, natural theology interpreted the meaning of natural phenomena within the encompassing reference of Scripture. This approach, which I am designating the *major interpretative tradition*, narrated (or explained) the concrete forms of creation in two primary ways: first, natural phenomena, like the liver-fluke worm or the ichneumon wasp, were perceived as divinely enacted signs that accorded with scriptural images that disclosed the spiritual condition of human creatures;[1] second, the created world

---

1. Although this approach conceded that creational violence was a divinely determined reality, the character of nature received important qualifications. Namely, the violent and destructive aspects of the nonhuman creation (e.g., poisonous plants and dangerous animals) were only perceived as evil in relation to how they engaged the human world. The world was created ontically violent; however, it was only when human beings fell into sin that nature's violence turned against human beings and thus became an evil. On the relationship of nature to human beings in view of the fall, see Harrison, *Fall of Man*. In describing the Patristic perspective, Harrison writes, "For a number of the Fathers, the Fall had wrought a dramatic inversion of the natural hierarchical

was viewed as a theophany of divine Wisdom's infinite fullness. Under such a vision, something like the ghastly behavior of the liver-fluke worm, which eats away at animals from the inside, could be interpreted as a sign of sin's interior wounding of the soul *and* as a manifestation of creation's ordered beauty. Thus, the major interpretation depicts the natural world as entirely determined by God's creative action in all its aspects. The diversity and profusion of creatures, including their violent interactions and dissipative ends, are expressive of God's nature as revealed in Christ. This theological reading of nature had important conceptual advantages. First, this type of narrative was able to admit the world in its phenomenal appearance without postulating additional theological categories to explain its current state. It is precisely this world, with all its disturbing aspects, which God has made in Christ. Second, this vision corresponded with scriptural locutions describing God's unrestricted shaping of the world. For example, Psalm 104, Job 38–41, and Isaiah 45:7 depict God's creative mastery over all natural phenomena and the events of history.

> Can you hunt the prey for the lion, or satisfy the appetite of the young lions, when they crouch in their dens, or lie in wait in their covert? Who provides for the raven its prey, when its young ones cry to God, and wander about for lack of food? (Job 38:39–41)

> The young lions roar for their prey, seeking their food from God. ... O Lord, how manifold are thy works! In wisdom hast thou made them all; the earth is full of thy creatures. (Ps 104:21, 24)

> I form light and create darkness, I make weal and create woe, I am the Lord, who do all these things. (Isa 45:7)

According to such a scriptural vision, the entities and patterns that made up the world's form—including the predatory economy of nature—were simply identified with God's creative Wisdom.

This identification of God's will with the world *as it is* did not mean that the major tradition failed to engage questions concerning the perplexing character of natural violence and death. For instance, in his *Literal Meaning of Genesis*, Augustine directly addressed the question,

---

relationships. At a cosmic level Adam had rebelled against God. This insurrection was mirrored in the newly created world where animals became wild and no longer acknowledged Adam's authority. Even the earth itself became barren and no longer provided abundant food" (Harrison, *Fall of Man*, 26). See also Augustine, *Literal Meaning of Genesis* 3.27.

"Why do beasts injure one another, though they neither have any sins, so that this kind of thing could be called punishment?" His answer: "For the simple reason of course, that some are the proper diet of others. . . . All things, you see, as long as they continue to be, have their own proper measures, numbers and destinies."[2] For Augustine and Hugh of St. Victor, and the majority of premodern interpreters, ontic violence and death were contingent derivatives of creation's divine order that unveiled God's sublime Wisdom. Augustine writes:

> Since, then, in those situations where such things are appropriate, some perish to make way for others that are born in their room, and the less succumb to the greater, and the things that are overcome are transformed into the quality of those that have the mastery, this is the appointed order of things transitory. Of this order the beauty does not strike us, because by our mortal frailty we are so involved in a part of it, that we cannot perceive the whole, in which these fragments that offend us are harmonized with the most accurate fitness and beauty. And therefore, where we are not so well able to perceive the wisdom of the Creator, we are very properly enjoined to believe it, lest in the vanity of human rashness we presume to find any fault with the work of so great an Artificer. At the same time, if we attentively consider even these faults of earthly things, which are neither voluntary nor penal, they seem to illustrate the excellence of the natures themselves, which are all originated and created by God.[3]

The scriptural depiction of God's creative determination of the nonhuman world through wisdom found a certain degree of conceptual coherence with Neoplatonic tradition, albeit shaped in view of Christian claims concerning God's trinitarian life and the metaphysical implications of creation *ex nihilo*.[4] Accordingly, this ontological narrative depicted the interactive patterns of nature—the economic relations of material creatures that displayed violence, decomposition, and death—as

---

2. Augustine, *Literal Meaning of Genesis* 3.25.
3. Augustine, *City of God* 12.4.
4. For the biblical tradition of God's creating through Wisdom see Prov 3:19; 8:22–31; Jer 10:12; 51:15; Ps 104:24; Sir 1:1–10; 16:26–30; cf. John 1:3; Wis 7:22; Col 1:16. The combustive engagement between biblical wisdom and Hellenistic philosophy was already well established in both Jewish and Christian traditions well before Augustine, especially attested in the so-called deuterocanonical material (e.g., Wisdom and Sirach), the works of Philo of Alexandria, and a range of pre-Nicene Christian thinkers like Justin and Origen among others.

providentially manifesting an overarching beauty, harmony, and purpose.⁵ Thus, the world's phenomenal form with its ontological shadows was simply the outworking of God's divine Wisdom in a created idiom. Hugh of St. Victor writes,

> He conceived in eternity in his wisdom, which is coeternal with him, the forms of all creatures. These forms are coeternal with that wisdom and are called the "reasons" (*rationes*) of things in the divine mind, or "ideas," or "notions." And these primordial forms of all things are what can be described as primordial causes, reasons of things established from eternity in the divine mind.⁶

And,

> If in creatures the lack of some good is fitting, through this the universe appears more beautiful because in some part of some good a defect appears. Just as superior goods are judged more beautiful compared to inferior ones, so the least goods are set off more favorably when compared with evil. Just as the good of the whole is more beautiful because the good of part is less, so it should be more beautiful because some part suffers a defect of the good.⁷

It is significant that the major tradition posited no ontological interval or hiatus that would remove God from being directly accountable for the destructive and dissipative form of the world's creatures. In this respect, the agonistic order of nature did not register as a moral or theological problem. How was this so?

Direct identification of the world's form with God's creative volition adverts to the question: how does *created* natural violence comport with traditional claims regarding God's nature?⁸ While seemingly counterintuitive, Christian Neoplatonism was able to navigate the tension between

---

5. This metaphysical vision is given greater explication in the thought of Thomas Aquinas, who writes, "As, therefore, the perfection of the universe requires that there should be not only beings incorruptible, but also corruptible beings; so the perfection of the universe requires that there should be some which can fail in goodness, and thence it follows that sometimes they do fail. Now it is in this that evil consists, namely, in the fact that a thing fails in goodness" (Aquinas, *Summa Theologica* 1, q.48, a.2; cf. Augustine, *City of God* 12.4–5).

6. Hugh of St. Victor, *Sententiae de divinitate* 2.

7. Hugh of St. Victor, *Sententiae de divinitate* 2.

8. For a recent description and defense of classical Christian theism, see Hart, *Experience of God*.

the agonistic existence of material being and the notion that God is the infinite fullness of love by means of two specific claims that accompany this participationist ontology. The first claim maintains that defects and evils suffered by creatures are simply an expression of divine goodness, which is perceived within the comprehensive order of the universe. For example, God's creation of both the timber wolf (*canis lupus*) and white-tailed deer (*odocoileus virginianus*) displays the wonder of divine beauty in distinct ways, even while defects are entailed in their encounter.[9] The encounter itself, with its violence and death, when framed in cosmic (or ecological) terms, is viewed as manifesting a beauty that would otherwise be lacking without it.[10]

In conjunction with this claim, the major tradition also embraced an ontic hierarchy of souls that constrained the meaning and value of animal suffering. The Stoic and Aristotelian conception of a rigid demarcation of souls as vegetal, sensitive, and rational exercised a profound influence on Christian thought.[11] Under the Stoic-Aristotelian categorization, it was

9. In its development within the Thomistic tradition, which is informed by the participationist Neoplatonic ontology, the dissolution of a creature was not considered an evil *per se* because, ontologically speaking, evil was a privative absence parasitic upon a good *owed* to the essential form of a creature. Accordingly, God only *directly* wills the formal good of a creature (that which is due to their essence) and only *indirectly* wills the privative consequences that result from the complex interactions of the created economy. For example, such an account claims that God wills the essential forms of both the timber wolf (*canis lupus*) and white-tailed deer (*odocoileus virginianus*), including all the positive properties specific to each creature, without directly willing the defects that come about through their encounter. This account claims to have sidestepped the implication that God directly wills evil, on account of the metaphysical axioms that evil is not a substantial reality and that God can only will the substantial perfections of being as such. For a helpful explanation of this ontology as it specifically relates to Aquinas, see Davies, *Thomas Aquinas on God and Evil*, 67–70. Also see Keltz' essay, *Thomism and the Problem of Animal Suffering*.

10. This type of vision of the comprehensive beauty that supervenes throughout nature's diverse interactions might be related analogously to the notion of "trophic cascade," which denotes the extended positive net effects of reintroducing predators into an ecological sphere. See Weiss et al., "Societal and Ecosystem Benefits."

11. The Christian adoption of the Stoic-Aristotelian account of animal souls marks the endpoint of the debate between Platonists and Stoics concerning animal welfare. The church largely accepted the Stoic-Aristotelian position with its impressive disjunction between human beings and animals, which eventually became the dominant theological position in Christendom. Whereas Christianity found a substantial degree of philosophical correspondence with Platonism with its dualistic conceptualization of divine and creaturely realms and its ontology of participation the church tacitly sided with the explicit anthropology and zoology of Stoicism. It may appear odd that the Platonist position did not exert more influence upon Christianity's perception of animals, especially given the fact that certain Old Testament texts expressed at least a modicum

only the rational soul that was subject to moral obligations. By contrast, the vegetal and sensitive soul lacked the requisite properties—a reflective consciousness and intellect—reckoned essential for moral consideration.[12] Consequently, the widespread adoption of an ontic hierarchy with such sharp discontinuities shaped the Christian moral landscape and submerged the problem of animal suffering from antiquity until the early modern period. While there are some exceptions,[13] the wider Christian tradition largely followed the intellectual sentiments of Augustine, who re-enforced the ontic and moral distinction between animals and human beings. Augustine writes,

> When we say, "Thou shall not kill," we do not understand this of the plants, since they have no sensation, nor of the irrational animals that fly, swim, walk, or creep, since they are dissociated from us by their want of reason, and are therefore by the just appointment of the Creator subjected to us to kill or keep alive for our own uses . . . the commandment is, Thou shall not kill man.[14]

Strikingly, this diminished moral vision of nonhuman creatures did not include an outright denial of the experiential authenticity of animal suffering. On the contrary, Augustine affirmed the reality of animal pain; however, the moral criteria implicit within the ontic division of souls designated such suffering as a morally neutral feature of the world's overarching goodness.[15] Thus, the influence of the Stoic-Aristotelian conception of animal souls led interpreters to conclude that animals could not be moral subjects, and thus, the nonhuman experience of violence, decomposition, and death had no *theodical* bearing upon God's creative power or benevolence.

---

of moral consideration for nonhuman animals. However, the Stoic's exceptionally high view of the human person, above the rest of the created order, seemingly formed a conceptual parallel with those passages in the Bible, particularly in Genesis, that describe human beings as made in the image and likeness of God, and gave dominion of the creaturely world to this image-bearer. See Sorabji, *Animal Minds and Human Morals*.

12. For this classical Western perspective see Steiner, *Anthropocentrism and its Discontents*, 126–31.

13. Although the perspective that denied the moral significance of animals was dominant in antiquity among both Christians and pagans, there were some notable exceptions. See Arnobius, *Against the Heathen* 7.9. See also the discussion of Macarius of Alexandria in Vivian, "Peaceable Kingdom," 487–88.

14. Augustine, *City of God* 1.20.

15. See Augustine, *On the Morals of the Manichaeans* 17.59.

Premodern Theology: The Minor Tradition

Along with the major tradition, there existed a secondary *minor* tradition that viewed predatory violence and suffering as fundamentally inimical to God's foundational will for creation. This position, displayed in the thought of Theophilus of Antioch (183–185), Irenaeus of Lyon (130–202), and Ephrem the Syrian (306–373), concluded that the present shape of the creaturely world—the manifestation of animal predation and death—was directly tethered to the Fallenness of the world that occurred at the dawn of history.[16] Reflecting on the change wrought by the entrance of sin into the material creation, Theophilus writes,

> And the animals are named wild beasts [θηρία], from their being hunted [θηρεύεσθαι], not as if they had been made evil or venomous from the first—for nothing was made evil by God, but all things good, yea, very good,—but the sin in which man was concerned brought evil upon them. For when man transgressed, they also transgressed with him. For as, if the master of the house himself acts rightly, the domestics also of necessity conduct themselves well; but if the master sins, the servants also sin with him; so in like manner it came to pass, that in the case of man's sin, he being master, all that was subject to him sinned with him. When, therefore, man again shall have made his way back to his natural condition, and no longer does evil, those also shall be restored to their original gentleness.[17]

---

16. It is important to note that there existed other variations of how the Fall shaped the world in gnostic literature of early Christianity. Indeed, among the Valentinians and other groups elaborate speculations were made concerning the cosmic fall of divine aeons that brought about the material cosmos. The problem with this type of literature (among other things) was that they ran against the comprehensive witness of Scripture as grasped by the early church. Notably, the sub-apostolic theologian Irenaeus displays a remarkable and vigorous engagement and refutation of gnostic speculations. Pre-Irenaean Christianity (e.g., Shepherd of Hermas and Athenagoras) revealed a more substantial role for non-divine spiritual powers in shaping/governing the world. Significantly, after Irenaeus' challenge to gnostic renditions of the world, the populated vision of spiritual powers in the creation undergoes a remarkable (albeit not complete) decline. See Gavrilyuk, "Creation in Early Christian Polemical Literature," 22–32.

17. Theophilus of Antioch, *To Autolycus* 2.17. This perspective is also found in Irenaeus. He writes, "But although this is [true] now with regard to some men coming from various nations to the harmony of the faith, nevertheless in the resurrection of the just [the words shall also apply] to those animals mentioned. For God is rich in all things. And it is right that when the creation is restored, all the animals should obey and be in subjection to man, and revert to the food originally given by God . . . that is, the productions of the earth" (Irenaeus, *Against Heresies* 5.33.4). See also Ephrem the Syrian, *Commentary on Genesis* 2.9.3.

According to this interpretation, the original peace of the first creation was causally transposed into the vulturine world of conflict, violence, and suffering by humanity's rebellion. The entrance of *sin* into history marred the beauty of the first world and plunged nature into an economic cycle of predation and creaturely agony. Such an account depended upon a contested interpretation of the hexaemeron that seemingly depicted natural violence as a deviation from God's foundational purpose. "And to every beast of the earth, and to every bird of the air, and to everything that has the breath of life, I have given every green plant for food" (Gen 1:30a; cf. Isa 11:1–9).[18] Furthermore, such an account also conformed to the Pauline notion that creation was subjected to "futility" and "bondage to decay" (Rom 8:19–21), which invited the conclusion that the present world was enthralled to its suffering condition in anticipation of God's redemptive purpose in Christ. The minor tradition thus reflected a figural disposition insofar as the bondage of creation *mirrored* the corrupted spiritual life of humanity. Nature's unruliness was a concrete figuration or manifestation of the wickedness of rational creatures. Although such a figural macrocosm-microcosm relation was obtained in both major and minor traditions, each pressed the relation in different ways. The major tradition defined the scope of sin in view of humanity's relationship with nature and not with the created world itself. By contrast, the minor tradition viewed sin's influence in the very interstices of nature's arrangement and function. Under this vision, things like the liver-fluke worm, the ichneumon wasp, and the wider predatorial form of the ecosphere represent the cascading effects of the mystery of iniquity in the nonhuman creation.

The conceptual advantage of the minor tradition resides in its metaphysical transparency vis-à-vis God's beneficent character in view of creation's *agon*. This scriptural interpretation, which placed an ontological hiatus between the present empirical world and God's antecedent will, seemingly avoids some of the conceptual difficulties associated with the doctrine of creation.[19] Unlike the major tradition's laborious use of meta-

---

18. As to whether the original stipulation of Gen 1:30 is indicative of vegetarianism is subject to an ongoing debate by historical critics. For a view that ascribes to Genesis an original ontological peace, see Fretheim, *God and the World*, 51. For a contrary perspective concerning the protological vegetarianism of Genesis, see Wenham, *Genesis 1–15*, 33–34. Even if we concede that Genesis presumes an original ontology of peace among creatures, the biblical text indicates that this foundational vegetarianism is subsequently re-ordered after the deluge (Gen 9:1–7).

19. While the minor tradition comports well with classical theism, the attribution

physical distinctions to free God from direct culpability for the world's suffering form, the minor tradition outlines a narrative framework that refuses the direct linkage of nature's *agon* to God's being in any primary way. Accordingly, the world's strife was not indicative of God's desire; rather, nature's form was shaped by a spiritual "fallenness" that diverged from God's creative purpose.

To summarize, Christian antiquity displays two interpretive traditions that construed the origin and meaning of ontological violence in the material creation. The minor tradition (exemplified by Theophilus, Irenaeus, and Ephrem) held that it was the manifest consequence of sin in the rational creation. It claimed that the world's protological form was defined by a relational peace amongst all creatures, whereas subsequent disruptions of natural violence and death were causally determined by human sin. With respect to the role of figuration in this account, the manifestation of creatures as predatory, violent, and death-conditioned reflected the disruptive character of sin as it grew both within the collective heart of humankind and in the interstices of the creaturely world. While this position effectively moralized natural violence by attributing it to a rational agential cause, this account never maintained a significant hold on the collective vision of the church's theologians. Apart from a brief renewal of interest in creation's fallenness during the Renaissance and Reformation, this minor tradition was largely eclipsed during the premodern period.

The major tradition, by contrast, viewed creaturely dissipation as a foundational property of the world's original form, indicating that creation itself was constituted by violence that was primordial and divinely willed. This striking theological claim, which calls into question God's goodness, was mollified in two ways. The first used certain ontological structures that enfolded creaturely agony within the positive order of nature's beauty and goodness. The second involved an ontic hierarchy wherein animal suffering was not morally freighted in a way that was theologically problematic. These ameliorating factors proved sufficient as long as the major tradition prevailed, as it did throughout the premodern period.

---

of nature's ontological violence to a temporal fall creates other theoretical problems. Indeed, the fragility problem looms largest. Why would God create the world so inherently fragile that non-rational creatures would suffer in the wake of human disobedience? By all accounts, the fall narrative merely pushes the problem into the mystery of God's creative will.

The major tradition's cultural dominance was eventually called into question by vast changes in the modern period. Specifically, changes in the moral perception of suffering entailed the emergence of theodicy with a forcefulness that was previously unknown. This new historical epoch displayed a moral sensitivity to the suffering of creatures that profoundly altered the basic terms of the problem and undermined the overall suasiveness of the major tradition. We will now turn to examine the historical emergence of the modern problem of animal suffering.

Creational Violence in The Modern Epoch

As narrated in the discussion of scriptural figuration, the modern epoch was shaped by a gradual decline of the conceptual purchase of traditional creational theology upon European intellectual culture. Whereas premodern Christians perceived the phenomenal world as *creation*, a manifestation of eternal Wisdom in its variegated wholes and parts, the modern epoch was increasingly characterized by an ontology that relegated the meaning of nature exclusively to the determinate results of scientific inquiry. This declension of the theological perception of creation was inversely related to a vision of the natural world as a brute reality (*bruta facta*) exclusively accessible by means of empirical investigation and mathematical abstraction. The gradual advancement of a world known primarily through scientific interrogation, which was ostensibly confirmed by technological application, was also accompanied by an expanded moral consciousness characterized by an increased sensitivity towards sentient animal life. In particular, the modern period displayed a change with respect to how animals were perceived in moral terms, exhibited by the founding of humane societies and a growing body of literature that pertained to animals.[20] While this growing social concern for nonhuman life was influenced by a scientifically reordered cosmos, which eventually leveled some of the sharper ontic distinctions between human beings and animals, this cannot account entirely for the moral revaluation of animals. In fact, the cultural recognition of their moral significance preceded the materialist leveling of nature's hierarchy. Thus, the rise of public concern with animal suffering appears part of a wider moral shift concerning the magnitudes of human suffering in the early modern period. This shift in moral perception was marked by an increased

20. Kalof, *Looking at Animals*, 97–136.

sensitivity towards members of society who were previously despised, including criminals and the mentally disturbed. This shift towards the experiential dimension of suffering as a basis for ethical reflection is also extended to nonhuman animals. Though it was not universally acknowledged, social concern for animals and their ethical treatment came to the fore in the early modern period in a way previously unheard of in Western societies. As a result, the interpretive traditions that had previously been used to make sense of nature's *agon* theologically seemed inadequate and had to be recast into new conceptual forms that could account for this re-ordered vision of nature's moral landscape. To understand the character of modern theodicy, we will analyze the way this problem was reshaped and advanced by both a new scientific narrative of the universe and the shifting moral landscape of modernity.

Modern Science and Animal Suffering

To what extent did modern science shape the problem of nature's *agon*? Its influence largely pertains to the scope and context of the theodical problem and not to its originating conditions. While the modern scientific picture of the world paints a dramatic image of nature's ontic violence (far beyond that envisioned in premodern thought), it does not on its own establish animal suffering as a problem in isolation from the socio-cultural context through which animals were perceived and used. Changes in the socio-cultural engagement of animals *and* human beings provided the practical conditions that gave rise to animal suffering as a theodical problem in the first place. Nevertheless, scientific knowledge certainly plays a formative role in structuring our contemporary understanding of the magnitude of the problem. This conceptual enlargement was initially correlated with the gradual recognition of geological deep time (cf. James Hutton) and evolutionary biology (cf. Charles Darwin) in the nineteenth century. These developments signaled the death knell for Christianity's minor tradition since they decisively undermined the notion that creaturely death and predation were bound to humankind's originating sin. The fossil record indicated that long before the emergence of *homo sapien sapiens* (between 400,000 and 150,000 years ago), the natural world was already shaped by competition, violence, mass extinctions, and a prodigious amount of suffering and waste.[21] This picture

21. See Benton, *History of Life*.

of nature's death-shaped history has since become radicalized in view of contemporary physics. The second law of thermodynamics describes the universe as *intrinsically* shaped by a unidirectional degradation of matter and energy into a disorganized and unusable form. This property, which appears as a universal constant, assures that all things (inanimate and animate) decompose into simpler elements over time. However, this principle of increasing entropy simultaneously conditions the emergent order and developmental richness of creaturely existence. The theologian Robert John Russell describes the importance of entropy in a particularly poignant way:

> In this world time has an arrow and a claw, and the talons of time lacerate lived experience with a breaking of symmetry, a fracturing of structure, a loss of an irretrievable past, and a staining of the present with the marks of its birth through successive passage and epiphanies.[22]

What this means is that organismic development and dissipation—the positive and negative poles of nature's historical form—are bound to each other due to the world's entropic character. Death as an ontic reality appears woven into the very heart of creation.[23] Hence, the presence of such

---

22. Russell, "Entropy and Evil," 451.

23. Although death appears as a necessary aspect in the concrete development of the biosphere, the degree to which it is *intrinsically* necessary to evolutionary development is more questionable. Under the gene-centric view of the modern neo-Darwinian synthesis, natural selection and random mutations constitute the most significant factors in the evolutionary story of life's coming-to-be. In contradistinction, the fields of developmental biology and molecular biology have called into question the gene-centric view with its heavy emphasis on natural selection and random mutation as the process that yields morphogenetic development. According to developmental and molecular biology, the evolutionary story of life is characterized by a whole host of alternative factors, including epigenesis, symbiogenesis, organismic self-organization, and developmental systems theory, which altogether reframe the story of life. Such revised accounts of evolution from the molecular level underscore the fact that the evolutionary process is highly structured and constrained and characterized by a profound range of cooperative factors. Within the revised accounts of molecular biology, natural selection plays a subtractive rather than a generative role. The role of organismic competition and death (standard features of the modern synthesis) do not appear as intrinsically necessary for the development of elaborate forms of life; on the contrary, it is theorized that evolutionary transformations would have occurred regardless of the historical contingencies of creaturely competition and death. Nevertheless, even if we grant this account of the evolutionary process, which de-centers competition and natural selection, we are still left with a phenomenal world characterized by a great deal of violence, suffering, and death.

For a highly gene-centric view of these issues see Dawkins, *Selfish Gene*. For revised accounts, see Margulis, *Symbiotic Planet*; Kauffman, *At Home in the Universe*;

troubling creatures like the liver-fluke worm, whose operative properties serve to prolong the agonies of other creatures, is founded upon and conditioned by the ontic principles of the universe, which fundamentally shape this world in terms of its beauty and its sorrows.

While the scientific perception of nature as inherently entropic establishes the context for modern creational theodicy, I want to again stress that science itself does not account for how animal suffering was (and is) a problem for Christian thought. Indeed, the contemporary scientific narrative of evolutionary development is amenable to the major tradition of premodern theology. On this subject, the major tradition's depiction of a providentially ordered cosmos that sublimated creaturely violence as a theophanic expression of divine Wisdom comports with the wide contours of the world's evolutionary and entropic form. In point of fact, it is worth noting that the major tradition (broadly construed) has continued to function as a widely posited theistic response to evolutionary theodicy in the contemporary setting.[24] This raises the important question: if modern scientific accounts of evolutionary development conform to premodern theological depictions of the world's form (again broadly construed), how is it the case that animal suffering provokes a significant theological problem? To answer this question, it is necessary to revisit the social location of animals in premodern Christian thought and explore the cultural reasons for the shift in their moral evaluation.

The Moral Status of Animal Suffering

How did premodern Christians view the moral significance of animals? According to tradition, animals and other nonhuman creatures possessed significance to the extent that they *figurally* reflected the scriptural world. In this respect, nonhuman animals were morally relevant in view of how they symbolized the scriptural economy of creation and redemption (e.g., the hostile world of predatory animals potentially symbolized the disordered soul and its ruptured relationship with God). Although there are some notable exceptions,[25] the theological perception of animals did not

---

Goodwin, "Evolution and Generative Order"; Morris, *Life's Solution*. For excellent theological interpretations of these issues, see Cunningham, *Darwin's Pious Idea*; Hanby, *No God, No Science*.

24. For a salient example of this type of approach, see Farrer, *God Is Not Dead*.

25. While animals were formally regarded as non-participants in the human moral community and thus not subject to moral concern due to their lack of a rational nature,

invite any significant degree of moral scrutiny in the premodern period. The reason for this, as previously discussed, is the hierarchical categorization of creaturely souls, which ineluctably determined animal suffering as morally neutral.[26] However, over the last 150 years, this ontic hierarchy of souls has been destabilized by an evolutionary account of biological development. This has led some to regard the purported evolutionary kinship between human beings and animals as the primary reason for

---

in concrete practice premodern societies displayed a more complex set of attitudes. Strikingly, this complexity was exemplified by the so-called animal trials. These trials, which occurred in both secular and ecclesiastical courts, subjected animals to dictates and parameters of human justice, including the provision of legal representation. Although the animals in question were formally regarded as non-rational, they were subjected to provisions of natural justice that would normally be granted to rational agents. It could be argued that this blurring of categories was simply a case of anthropocentric projection, but it also appears that this sense of justice in relation to animals flow from a theological concern that animals are entitled to their divinely given mandates. In this regard, the concern for justice—defined as a rightly ordered world—afforded animals some limited degree of moral concern. See Cohen, *Crossroads of Justice*, 100–133.

26. This premodern Christian approach to animals provided the decisive *terminus* for the philosophical problem of animal valuation in antiquity. At the time of the church's birth, there existed within the Roman world a lively debate concerning animal souls and to what extent animals ought to be subjected (or not) to moral and ethical consideration. Richard Sorabji's study *Animal Minds and Human Morals* provides an effective narrative outlining the ways various proponents of animal welfare constructed their arguments in the ancient cultural milieu. Sorabji claims that the two primary positions in this debate were held by two pervasive philosophical systems in antiquity: Platonism was largely more amenable to the ethical consideration of animals, and Stoicism followed Aristotle in maintaining a rigid disjunction between human beings and animals. The debate itself was largely fought over to what extent animal souls participated in reason. Both Stoics like Chrsippys and Middle Platonists like Plutarch held that moral consideration was grounded in the concept of a community of "likeness" or "relatedness" denoted by the term *oikeiosis*. For Plutarch, animal souls existed in a gradual continuum with human beings. As such, they displayed behaviors that are only explicable in terms of rationality. Furthermore, Plutarch's middle-Platonism perceived the universe under the auspices of a participationist ontology, wherein all beings reflected some aspect of *nous*. Indeed, it was this participationist ontology that would form a nuptial fit with the theological convictions of the early church. As a consequence, most notable antique theologians were Platonists, including Origen, Gregory of Nyssa, and Augustine. In contradistinction to this perspective, the Stoics argued that animals are fundamentally irrational and that all their "reason-like" behaviors were explicable according to the sensitive capacities of the soul. Gary Steiner maintains that the Stoics represented a radicalization of the position of Aristotle, who also denied animal rationality. The Stoics affirmed that animals were fundamentally irrational and created simply for the instrumental use by those who possessed reason. This debate continued well into the third and fourth centuries of the Common Era with Porphyry and Celsus criticizing Christianity for its treatment of animals. See Sorabji, *Animal Minds and Human Morals*; Steiner, *Anthropocentrism and its Discontents*.

the ethical revision of animal suffering. Summarizing this position, the moral philosopher Robert Wennberg writes,

> Many, including critics of animal consciousness, judge that the most powerful consideration on behalf of animal consciousness is the argument from evolutionary theory. If we grant that both humans and existing animals developed by a process of gradual change from previously existing forms, and consequently, if we reject a special creation of each individual species as an immutable life-form, then we have reason to believe that there is no radical discontinuity between human beings and all other animals.[27]

According to this argument, all living organisms (human beings, animals, and plants) share a common ancestry evinced by morphological and genetic continuities. The perception of a shared lineage that encompasses all biotic creatures challenges the vestigial ontic hierarchy that prevailed in premodern thought. This type of argument from biological evolution has been amplified and enhanced by a growing body of literature that describes the neurophysiological similarities between human beings and animals.[28] Furthermore, in addition to the evolutionary frame of reference, contemporary ethological research has also proffered accounts of animal mindfulness as evidence of a rich cognitive life in many nonhuman creatures. For example, the ethologist Donald Griffin has compiled extensive (albeit circumstantial) evidence of animal consciousness and cognition. He provides fascinating accounts of animal "communicative actions" and "behavioral versatility" to novel situations, both of which are (at least) suggestive of first-order perceptual consciousness in nonhuman animals.[29] Thus, given such evolutionary and ethological considerations, it would appear reasonable to affirm that there is much more going on with respect to animal minds than has been traditionally recognized.

While such descriptive claims concerning the similarities between human beings and animals have contributed to the cultural revaluation of animals, the historical reasons for the heightened moral concern withstand any simple correlation with the blurring of the human-animal ontic

---

27. Wennberg, *God, Humans, and Animals*, 97.

28. For exposition of some of the neurophysiological similarities, see Rollin, *Unheeded Cry*. See also Marino, "Cetacean Cognition," 227–39; Elwood and Appel, "Pain Experience in Hermit Crabs?," 1243–46.

29. Griffin, *Animal Thinking*. See also Ristau and Marler, *Cognitive Ethology*.

distinction.³⁰ On the contrary, there had already been a significant moral transformation vis-à-vis animal suffering that antedated evolutionary accounts. This points to the conclusion that the socio-cultural recognition of animal suffering was conditioned by other factors. That is to say, from the late seventeenth century to the mid-nineteenth century (the pre-Darwinian period), there was already a substantial increase in public concern for animals with respect to both moral practice and intellectual reflection.³¹ Indeed, the fact that influential thinkers like G. W. Leibniz felt compelled to address animal suffering as a moral problem was indicative of a tremendous shift in the moral perceptions of Western culture.³² Although influenced by changing scientific accounts of the world, the expansion of moral concern to animals appears to be conditioned by more fundamental social and cultural factors that were stirred up by the modern epoch.

According to this account, multiple pressures emerged within the foundational matrix of modernity that socially transformed animals

---

30. It is notable that despite evolutionary theory and ethological research into the issue of animal consciousness, many psychologists, biologists, and philosophers have been hesitant to ascribe consciousness to animals. Robert Wennberg notes that this unease with respect to animal consciousness is bound up with social-cultural factors as well as with the prevailing philosophical conundrum of mind/body relations. See Wennberg, *God, Humans, and Animals*, 84–90.

31. Without this transformation or expansion of moral concern, it is hard to see why animal suffering would be problematic for the major tradition. Contemporary theories that suggest a high degree of animal cognition and consciousness (including the experiential phenomena of suffering) fit with the over-arching moral ontology of the major tradition. That is to say, the major tradition recognized a certain degree of experiential awareness in animals (including pain) while rejecting the moral implications of that experience. Thus, the theodical problem of creaturely suffering required a revaluation of animal suffering—not simply the recognition of an ontological proximity between animals and human beings. Strikingly, the major tradition possesses a remarkable durability with respect to modern scientific accounts.

32. As mentioned in chapter 1, Leibniz perceives animal suffering to be the inevitable result of creaturely finitude while also being ordered towards the comprehensive perfection of the universe. Leibniz recognizes that animals are sensitive creatures that feel pain and are not mere biological machines. However, he stresses that animals do not suffer to the same extent as human persons due to the absence of rational reflection (apperception). He states: "One cannot reasonably doubt the existence of pain among animals; but it seems as if their pleasures and their pains are not so keen as they are in man: for animals, since they do not reflect, are susceptible neither to grief that accompanies pain, nor to the joy that accompanies pleasure" (Leibniz, *Theodicy*, 281). In many respects, Leibniz's understanding of animal life corresponds with the major interpretive tradition: animals do possess a sensitive soul, and are subjected to feelings; however, they cannot be subjected to moral duties because they are not rational.

into moral creatures, at least in certain contexts. The sociologist Linda Kalof has argued that the growing intellectual consideration of animals in Western societies occurred by means of "three rapidly spreading trends: the popularity of vivisection in the new experimental science, increasing urbanization and commodification of animals for food and labour, and the widespread availability of print media."[33] She maintains that these factors reconfigured the social perception of animals and contributed to the emergence of a new philosophical debate over the moral placement of animals within human societies. While these factors played an important role, the historian Keith Thomas has suggested that the change was also tethered to a more fundamental moral shift occurring with respect to human beings and human suffering. Thomas notes that growth in the moralization of animals in eighteenth-century Britain was correlated with a substantial growth in the public recognition of human suffering in all its forms. He writes:

> The concern for animal welfare was part of a much wider movement which involved the spread of humane feelings towards previously despised human beings, like the criminal, the insane or the enslaved. It thus became associated with a more general demand for reform, whether the abolition of slavery, flogging and public executions or the reform of schools, prisons and the poor law.[34]

Following Thomas, I believe that the increased recognition of animal suffering, manifested by the development of humane societies and legislation prohibiting animal cruelty, was part of a powerful cultural drift toward greater recognition of human misery, which gradually transformed the way animals appeared to human beings. Moreover, the inclusion of animals in the expanded moral universe of modernity is also likely related to the changing perceptions of death in Western culture. Namely, changes in socio-cultural practice, as the result of the expansion of the human lifespan as facilitated by modern medicine and the outsourcing of food production, have created a new interpretive horizon by which human beings engage and understand other living creatures. The condition of modern life where death in all its forms (both human and animal) is largely masked in relative social invisibility has subsequently contributed

---

33. Kalof, *Looking at Animals in Human History*, 97.
34. Thomas, *Man and the Natural World*, 184.

towards a fragmented ethical evaluation of animals in modern culture.[35] Paradoxically, contemporary perceptions of animals involve greater moral recognition for some (e.g., pets, endangered species, etc.) and simultaneously an ever-increasing disregard and systematic exploitation of others (e.g., factory farm animals).[36] In light of these reasons, the present form of the theodical problem of animal suffering appears inextricably tied to concrete changes in the human social order that have precipitated the phenomenological recasting of certain animals as potential moral subjects.

The modern revision of the moral universe and the scientific reconfiguration of nature's history have compounded the problem of nature's *agon* for contemporary Christian discourse. Once it is recognized that animals deserve some degree of moral consideration, the major tradition can no longer sufficiently narrate the meaning of animal suffering. Additionally, the loss of theology's figural character (as discussed in chapter 1) magnified the theodical problem as it robbed the church of an interpretive disposition that engaged the obscurities of nature in a way that was meaningfully ordered by Christian revelation. Instead, the moral and scientific transformations coupled with the loss of figuration led ineluctably to the rendering of nature's sufferings as a theological problem to be

---

35. The importance of the drastic expansion of human lifespans in the late nineteenth and early twentieth centuries cannot be understated. This complex reconfiguration of human life, little studied in its cultural significance, is tethered to an accumulation of factors (nutrition, sanitation, medical, and educational) all of which have reframed the practical apprehension of mortality and violence in human societies. It seems likely that this remarkable change in human existence, with its ostensible banishment of death, has configured the moral shape of creatures. On the one hand, the gradual evacuation from social visibility of animal death for human consumption has played into the "banishment" trend, as the blood and cries of the creatures we consume are largely hidden from view. On the other hand, this banishment has also granted creaturely violence, with its inherent ferocity an irruptive effect upon the social framework when it reasserts itself in its natural force. The particular social configurations of death and violence thus heighten the apprehension of natural violence when manifested. For an excellent discussion of the social, ideological, and theological impact of the expansion of human lifespans, see Radner, *Time to Keep*, 21–35.

36. With the increased moralization of animal life, evinced by the creation of anti-cruelty laws and organizations, there has also been a paradoxical expansion in the usage of animals for human consumption. This expansion corresponds to an increase of mechanized factory farming that performs the killing and transformation of animal flesh into meat. This fragmented approach to animal life that at once extols the moral worth of animals while subjecting animals to deplorable conditions characterizes contemporary Western societies. For a descriptive history of animal moral reflection, see Wennberg, *God, Humans, and Animals*, 1–28.

solved. Because such phenomena stood outside of, or even contradicted, a literal construal of the scriptural narrative (e.g., the presence of violence and death in nature prior to human existence), the question arose whether Christian theology could adequately narrate the existence of animal suffering in light of its traditional claims concerning God's nature and the doctrine of creation.

MODERN THEODICIES OF CREATIONAL SUFFERING

In the wake of the modern shift in metaphysics and culture, the traditional scope of theodicy was extended to nonhuman creatures in a fragmentary fashion, which ineluctably compounded the phenomenal perception of suffering within the world. This modern awakening to the scope of nature's *agon* has generated a range of responses that have attempted to render the world intelligible in view of traditional theistic claims concerning God's divine aseity. Significantly, these modern theodicies share important conceptual continuities with their premodern antecedents, albeit revised in view of the contemporary intellectual environment and denuded of the tradition's figuralism. With the absence of figuration, the present theological engagement of Scripture is largely reserved to a rather ad hoc use of thematic correlations that relate some scriptural element (e.g., eschatology) to a stated problem. Modern theodical forms are thus only peripherally related to the Bible as scriptural content is marshaled in a secondary way to lend support to theodicies whose foundation resides elsewhere, primarily in philosophical traditions.[37] Amidst the diversity of contemporary approaches, three primary categories of interpretation

---

37. I am not dismissing the important role of philosophy for theodical reflection; instead, I want to advert to the fact that most modern creational theodicies approach their task assuming a rather thin relationship with the central theological dimensions of scriptural revelation. This is understandable considering the state of scriptural interpretation, determined by the dictates of historical criticism, cannot adjudicate the various theodicies in any theologically significant way. With respect to many modern creational theodicies, it appears that philosophical accounts provide the foundational content whereupon scripture is subsequently supplemented, if at all. To my mind this is backwards. Theodical reflection like all forms of theological reflection ought to be grounded upon a metaphysically thick (figural) engagement of the Bible, which can then subsequently establish the conceptual parameters for engaging and evaluating philosophical resources. Furthermore, the "method" I am prescribing presses the question of adjudication. I mean by this that if we grant the metaphysically freighted role of the Bible according to the figural disposition, then such an account yields a theological basis for articulating a theodicy grounded in God's self-revelation.

have been applied to nonhuman suffering. These interpretations include (1) *Eliminativist* (or *Neo-Cartesian*) *theodicies* whereby nonhuman creatures are denied the mental requisites necessary for morally significant suffering; (2) *Instrumentalist theodicies* that sublimate nature's ontic violence within an overarching creative process; and (3) *Contingent-Fallenness theodicies* that posit some type of divergence within the universe's temporal development.[38] I want to stress that this schematic serves as a conceptual map and not as an exhaustive treatment. As an abstraction, this schematic loses some of the permutations and conceptual overlap that characterize individual theodicies. Nonetheless, the various explanations of *creational suffering* presented in modern literature (both philosophical and theological) are discernible within this typology. The rest of this chapter will examine the main contours of each type of theodicy, consider some salient examples, and evaluate the benefits and problems associated with each type in light of Christian claims. This descriptive and evaluative exercise will demonstrate the "open character" of the problem of creational suffering whereby any one of these approaches may be adopted as a possible explanatory narrative. I conclude that without some theologically determinative criteria or goal, the problem remains endlessly deferred. The retrieval of figuralist thinking with its Christocentric metaphysic will ultimately provide a guiding theological framework for navigating the interpretive possibilities afforded by these speculations.

Eliminativist Theodicies

The most controversial interpretation of animal suffering in contemporary discourse is based upon the assertion that animal consciousness is of a drastically different quality than that of human beings. Consequently, it is asserted that animals do *not* experience authentic suffering in a way that is morally compelling. The most famous articulation of this perspective is attributed to René Descartes (1595–1650), whose ontological vision of a mechanistic universe constituted by two distinct substances, mind (*res cogitans*) and material extension (*res extensa*), effectively evacuated

---

38. My typology of animal suffering theodicies approximately correspond with that presented in Lloyd, "Are Animals Fallen?," 147–60. Lloyd designates the range of theodicies concerning creation's endemic cycle of violence: (1) "It is not bad"; (2) "It is bad but necessary and worthwhile"; or (3) "It is bad, and not the work or will of God." As abstract categories, these broad theodical perspectives can encompass the possible rational responses to the problem of nature's ontological violence.

consciousness from animal subjectivity. According to Descartes' ontology, the *immaterial* properties of mind, which included reason and perception, could only be grounded in the existence of a transphysical rational soul, whereas material substances could be sufficiently (and exhaustively) explained in terms of mechanistic causal principles. The behavioral patterns of nonhuman animals could be entirely explicated without recourse to categories of mentation and consciousness. In view of this ontic disjunction between rational mind and irrational matter, animals were described as temporal configurations of matter devoid of mental properties that would be indicative of a reflective consciousness. In his *Discourse* 5, Descartes writes, "There is nothing which leads feeble minds more readily astray from the straight path of virtue than to imagine that the soul of animals is of the same nature as our own."[39] It appears that Descartes' position is simply a modern variation of the traditional Stoic-Aristotelian division of souls that characterized the major interpretation of premodern theology. One important aspect of the major interpretation was that the absence of animal rationality consigned animal suffering to moral insignificance.[40] Although Descartes himself did not directly apply his ontic division of reality to the issue of animal theodicy, many of his followers embraced it to explain why nature, in view of God's character, was so violent.[41]

Descartes' universe of two distinct substances was eventually overtaken by a dynamic evolutionary account, but the Cartesian perspective of animal consciousness has continued to exercise significant influence upon both secular and theological perspectives of animal cognition. For instance, in his article "Theodicy and Animal Suffering," the philosopher Peter Harrison adopts what could be considered a neo-Cartesian perspective of animal consciousness based upon an evolutionary account of pain. In his theodicy, Harrison argues that animal responses to noxious stimuli need not entail the existence of a conscious mental state. For Harrison, the adaptive value of pain resides solely in its survival value for

---

39. Descartes, *Discourse on Method and the Meditations*, 76.

40. It is possible that Descartes did not deny all feelings (*passions*) to animals, but only those feelings (*sentire*) that required a reflective consciousness. Harrison, "Descartes on Animals," 219–27; Cottingham, "Brute to the Brutes?," 551–59; Leiber, "Descartes," 365–75. For a critique of this revision of Descartes, see Steiner, *Anthropocentrism and its Discontents*, 132–52.

41. The most notable Cartesian who explicated the theological implications of Descartes' understanding of animal pain was Malebranche in his *De la recherché de la verita* 7.2.7.

organisms. By contrast, the mental awareness that accompanies human pain is potentially debilitating in its effects. This indicates that mental states of severe pain are maladaptive because they might incapacitate an organism and hinder its survival. Harrison writes,

> The canons of evolutionary dogma do not enable us to entertain the view that animals might be love-sick or grief-stricken, because such behaviours would not confer any obvious selective advantage, but rather the contrary. The same is true of debilitating physical pain. Any pain or mental state which impinges upon an animal's normal routines—the things it needs to do to survive and reproduce—are counter-productive and serve no obvious function in the economy of natural selection.[42]

For Harrison, the human experience of mental anguish is linked to humankind's highly developed cognitive capacities that extend beyond that which is necessary for creaturely survival. Since excruciating mental states of pain allegedly offer no survival value, Harrison makes the assertion that it is unlikely that animals possess this experiential dimension. Similar to Harrison's account, in *Nature: Red in Tooth and Claw*, the philosopher Michael J. Murray explores recent research into human and animal neuroanatomy and posits that most animals, except perhaps some of the higher mammals, lack the requisite neurological structures such as the prefrontal cortex and right neo-cortex that appear necessary for second-order mental states, which is another way of describing the unified experience of consciousness—that is, a conscious awareness of self.[43] Murray's position is similar to Descartes' in that it neither denies the phenomenal reality of animal pain and its associated behavioral response nor first-order consciousness in animals. Rather, it posits that animals lack the neurological basis for a second-level cognitive function that enables the *conscious* awareness of pain.[44]

Although the *eliminativist* (neo-Cartesian) position presents a solution to animal suffering, the postulate is severely weakened by its underdetermined character, both in terms of its scriptural foundation and in its conceptual implications. The assertion that nonhuman creatures do not

---

42. Harrison, "Theodicy and Animal Pain," 82.

43. Murray, *Nature*, 41–72.

44. Murray holds that there are indications that most animals lack the necessary neural pathways for nociception. One pathway appears to detect the cognitive dimension of noxious events whereas another is required for the associated affective dimension. It is this second affective pathway that most animals lack. Murray, *Nature*, 68.

suffer might accord with the scriptural description of animals as "irrational" or "unreasoning" (Jude 1:10; 2 Pet 2:12; Ps 73:22), which could arguably be stretched into an *eliminativist* accounting of animal sentience. However, along with this description of animals as irrational creatures, Scripture, in its figural texture, also depicts creatures as engaging in actions that defy such an account. Animals "cry" to God (Job 1:20; 38:41), animals "praise" God (Ps 148; 150:6), animals "honor" God (Isa 43:20), the nonhuman creation "groans" in travail (Rom 8:38). Indeed, the life (blood) of an animal is subjected to God's accounting, which disrupts any merely *instrumentalist* account of animal value. While all this may be considered metaphorical or poetic, it nevertheless appears to invest the nonhuman creation with an implicit moral significance reflected in God's creative love and concern (Ps 36:5–6; Wis 11:24). The figural language of Scripture navigates the tension between the moral subordination of animals to human beings while also granting intrinsic value to animals insofar as they are God's creatures. This view of the nonhuman creation as both subordinate and valued does not sit easily with the claims of the *eliminativist* position, which attempts to read creational suffering as entirely devoid of moral weight. Instead, it gestures towards a more comprehensive and morally complex vision of creation wherein the divinely ordered *economia* with its violence and suffering belong to God's creative purpose.

In terms of its conceptual implications, the *eliminativist* position's depiction of animal behavior also appears substantially underdetermined. While comparative studies of human and animal neuroanatomy are significant as they bring to light possible insights with respect to animal cognition, this research cannot underwrite the conditions necessary for accepting the *eliminativist* perspective. The neurological comparisons, while suggestive, are ultimately ambiguous in relation to animal consciousness. The fact that human consciousness remains an impenetrable mystery in spite of overwrought claims to the contrary suggests that the problem of animal consciousness is no nearer to a definitive account.[45] Notably, the fundamental limitations presented by philosophy's mind-body problem effectively constrain overly optimistic

---

45. Against the materialist conception of mind, see Nagel, *Mind and Cosmos* and the collected essays in Koons and Bealer, *Waning of Materialism*. For contrary perspectives regarding the nature of the mind, see Armstrong, *Materialist Theory of Mind*; Dennett, *Consciousness Explained*.

suppositions regarding the experiential status of animal suffering.[46] At most, this research indicates that we may theorize that animal pain is not as significant or debilitating as it is for human beings, but even this assertion suffers from epistemic problems.[47] Altogether, I maintain that acceptance of an *eliminativist* theodicy ultimately depends upon whether we have justified reasons for recasting the phenomenal experience of animal suffering. Is it reasonable to designate animal behavior as automated behavioral responses that do not entail mental anguish? In my view, the inability to grasp the inner life of an animal severely constrains any definitive evaluation. Consequently, without overwhelming evidence to the contrary, we are left with the presumption that animal suffering is real: anything less would be ethically irresponsible. While the *eliminativist* perspective, if true, would unquestionably solve the problem of creation's suffering, its underdetermined character and inadequacy in comporting with the phenomenal appearance of animal behavior render it untenable.

Instrumentalist Theodicies

The *Instrumentalist theodicy* designates a conceptually extensive category that depicts the existence of creaturely suffering as instrumentally related to the acquisition of some overarching benefit with respect to God's creative purpose. Broadly construed, most *instrumentalist* theodicies depict the natural world's dynamic and agonistic character as the antecedent ground for the manifestation of some higher purpose for creaturely existence. This vision of nature's utility comprehends an extensive range of perspectives that include "soul-making" theodicies, "natural-law" theodicies, and "free-process" theodicies.[48] Each theodical variation of

---

46. For a general account of the Mind-Body problem, see Feser, *Philosophy of Mind*.

47. The perspective that animal suffering is real yet substantially diminished in comparison to human beings is presented in Hick, *Evil and the God of Love*, 314. For a perspective that challenges the notion that animal suffering is somewhat less experientially substantial than human beings, see Akhtar, "Animal Pain and Welfare," 495–518.

48. The traditional soul-making theodicy is developed by John Hick's work (see especially *Evil and the God of Love*), where animal sufferings somehow provide the "epistemic distance" necessary for the formation of authentic human persons; this type of approach has been recently adapted by the philosopher Trent Dougherty in a creative attempt to include animals as moral subjects in the soul-making purpose of the creaturely world, see Dougherty, *Problem of Animal Pain*. For "Natural law theodicies," which typically depict the creative regularities of nature as the generative instruments of creation, see Farrer, *God Is Not Dead*; Murray, *Nature*, 130–92. "Free-Process" theodicy depicts natural evil as the result of an ontically free creation that exists in a manner analogous with human freedom; see Polkinghorne, *Faith of a Physicist*.

an instrumental perspective admits that a contingent universe involves the inevitability (or even necessity) of creaturely decomposition, suffering, and death for the sake of the procurement of some outweighing good. Among the various instrumental forms, the existence of suffering in the nonhuman creation has been associated with a range of diverse goods that have included: (1) the cultivation of morally virtuous persons in an ambiguous and dangerous environment, as in the "soul-making" theodicy of the philosopher John Hick; (2) perceiving the sublime beauty of the universe as a theophany of God's mysterious being, as found in Thomistic and Neoplatonic metaphysics;[49] and (3) the good of there being a universe characterized by ontic freedom at all variegated levels of creaturely being, as in the thought of the scientist and theologian John Polkinghorne.

Irrespective of the offsetting good to be achieved, the *instrumentalist* theodicy attempts to describe and narrate suffering by depicting it as the inevitable shadow-side of some willed good. Note that contemporary *instrumentalist* theodicies bear a striking resemblance to the major tradition that prevailed in premodern theology, albeit abstracted from the broader scriptural-figural context in which it was located. Indeed, it appears that the basic structure of the major interpretation is the most prevalent option adopted by theologians in the contemporary setting. The pervasiveness of this type of theodicy may be attributed to both its historical lineage, connected as it is to traditional Christian metaphysics, and its ability to admit the broad scientific description of the phenomenal world without recourse to extra-scientific categories. *Instrumentalist* theodicy can take the world "as is" without recourse to additional theological categories (e.g., the positing of fallenness or additional spiritual beings). Furthermore, this upholding of the world's phenomena as directly willed by God finds evidentiary support in the Scriptures wherein the prevailing order of the natural world, its seasonal rhythms (Gen 8:22) and creaturely interactions (Ps 104; Job 38–41), are considered evidence of the sublime glory of God who is not only "love" (1 John 4:8), but the one who makes "weal and creates woe" (Isa 45:7).

Nonetheless, despite their rather parsimonious correspondence with modern science and their theological basis in both Scripture and tradition, *instrumentalist* theodicies have remained relatively limited in explanatory persuasion vis-à-vis nonhuman suffering. The modern shift

---

49. Levering, *Engaging the Doctrine of Creation*, 109–44.

with respect to the moral character of animals has severely dampened the explanatory potential of contemporary reformulations of the major tradition. Consequently, the major tradition cannot be affirmed without significant restructuring that accounts for the moral dimensions of creaturely violence, suffering, and death.

One of the more viable articulations of this type of *instrumentalist* theodicy—one that accounts for the moral dimension of animal suffering—is found in the work of theologian Christopher Southgate. In his study, *The Groaning of Creation: God, Evolution, and the Problem of Evil*, Southgate affirms the basic form of an *instrumentalist* theodicy in view of evolutionary suffering. In a word, he maintains that the morally troubling aspects of the creaturely world (decomposition, death, and suffering of creatures) are the inevitable and necessary result of the evolutionary process through which God exercises his creative omnipotence. While Southgate acknowledges that creaturely suffering and death are "intrinsic features of creation that evolve according to Darwinian principles," he attempts to mitigate the moral culpability of God's creating a world imbued with an inherent ontology of violence by recourse to his "only way" argument.

> Because my faith tells me that a loving God created this cosmos out of absolutely nothing, and my understanding of evolutionary biology (and of thermodynamics) tells me that, in a cosmos such as this, suffering is an inevitable concomitant of sophisticated sentience, I presume that the only way a God of love could have created a world of complex and feeling creatures . . . was by a process to which suffering was intrinsic.[50]

On this score, God elects to create an evolving cosmos with its accompaniments of violence, suffering, and death because it is the only way by which God is able to achieve a world characterized by "beauty, diversity, sentience, and the sophistication of creatures."[51] Although broadly similar to the major tradition, Southgate diverges from his premodern predecessors in that he does not deny the moral significance of animal suffering. He recognizes that the instrumental value of suffering does not reduce its absurdity with respect to claims regarding God's beneficent nature. To escape the logical implication that God *directly* wills an ontology of violence, Southgate posits that the intrinsic goods of creation

---

50. Southgate, "God's Creation," 247.
51. Southgate, *Groaning of Creation*, 16.

are *necessarily* related to the law-like regularities of the evolutionary biosphere. The authoring of values such as diversity of species, creaturely sentience, consciousness, and agency is logically bound to the violent existence of the actual world. Southgate writes,

> I acknowledge the pain, suffering, death, and extinction that are intrinsic to a creation evolving according to Darwinian principles. Moreover, I hold to the (unprovable) assumption that an evolving creation was the only way in which God could give rise to the sort of beauty, diversity, sentience, and sophistication of creatures that the biosphere now contains.[52]

Although he attempts to avoid problematic implications regarding God's creative agency by arguing that it was logically impossible for God to create in any other way, an intellectual maneuver that has the pedigree of being reminiscent of Leibniz's "best possible world," such a position cannot avoid the inference that violence and suffering are forever lodged in God's creative will. This narrative of creation's ontological form—a world shaped *intrinsically* by violence—establishes a vision of God's character that is morally impenetrable. If we accept the scriptural claim that God's being is reflected in the created world (Rom 1:20), what does this disclose about God's nature? Southgate stresses that this world of resplendent beauty and immense suffering is simply the mysterious expression of divine glory, which resists domestication to any sentimental idealization. Yet, Southgate attempts to ameliorate the moral challenge that flows from the description of nature's *agon* as an expression of God's character by marshaling scripturally based concepts to recast God's relationship with the world. Most notably, he posits an *intratrinitarian kenosis* wherein God reveals himself as a fellow sufferer with the world[53] and suggests that

---

52. Southgate, *Groaning of Creation*, 16.

53. It is noticeable that many Christian theologians who affirm an *instrumentalist* theodicy that weds the world's form directly to God's creative purposes attempt to mitigate the implication that God is the direct source of evil and death by recourse to a theology of kenosis, often in conjunction with the abandonment of the classical attributes of the divine nature. Although I find certain kenotic interpretations of divine omnipotence to be compelling (e.g., Sergius Bulgakov and Stephen R. L. Clark) their usefulness in establishing "space" between God's will and creation's *non-volitional* freedom appears problematic, insofar as they ultimately cannot avoid the implication that this creation remains the highest expression of God's will. I wonder if the invocation of God's kenotic nature without any notion of creation's fallenness is no more than window dressing for a Leibnizian "best-of-all-possible-worlds" theodicy. Use of various forms of kenotic theology to address evil may be found in Haught, *God After Darwin*; Polkinghorne, *Faith of a Physicist*; Clark, "Progress and the Argument from Evil," 181–92; Bulgakov, *Lamb of God*; Edwards, *Breath of Life*.

creation itself will somehow be redeemed through an eschatological fulfillment.[54] With these additions, Southgate completes an entire theodicy that is admirable in its capacity to admit the world's phenomena without remainder. Nevertheless, while I commend Southgate for his willingness to grasp the nettle with his comprehensive identification of the world's form with God's will, I am concerned that such an account inevitably implies that God is the metaphysical ground of all creational violence in a direct way.[55]

54. I am not certain that Southgate's positing of an eschatological redemption does not subvert his "only way" defense of God's creative act. Indeed, it appears somewhat incoherent that a God who is bound by logical necessity to create in a certain way (with intrinsic violence and suffering) is also able to transform and redeem the world (including all creatures) so that all are eschatologically fulfilled. Does this not create major disjunctions in both the notion of God's power (God is both unable and able to bring about a non-violent world) and in God's will (God both wills a violent world and a subsequent nonviolent world)? Perhaps there are ways of construing this that avoid formal contradiction, but such an account seems incongruous with the ontology of peace that Christian theological tradition has associated with God's nature.

55. This objection is shaped by my affirmation of the traditional metaphysical description of God's transcendent nature that presupposes that God's simplicity is the transcendent fullness of beauty, truth, life, and peace. By extension, the divine creative act is grounded in and expressive of God's transcendently harmonious and peaceful nature. I want to maintain the traditional scriptural notion that the creation expresses the being of God. (Metaphysically speaking, the admittance of creation's capacity to disclose the creator operates along the analogical bridge of God's creative causality.) Given my traditional metaphysical understanding, this creates tension with respect to the entropic shape of creation (at least as it has been realized in the concrete). Namely, does the violence of creation reflect God? In the traditional metaphysical picture the answer typically trades on the privative nature of evil in order to exclude the darkened hues of the world from God's will (see Davies, *Thomas Aquinas on God and Evil*); yet this seems deeply unsatisfying to me, largely because it avoids recognizing animal consciousness and the "subjective" experience of suffering among nonhuman creatures. Another option is to reorder the traditional metaphysical picture of God and creation. One might revise God's nature in two different ways. The first is process thought, which entangles the divine nature in the process of nature's becoming and recasts God's divine aseity (omniscience, omnipotence) in a way that is hard to distinguish from a finite agent. The second approach grasps the nettle and admits that nature's ontological violence is part of God's willing of the world without remainder. This appears to necessitate a profoundly apophatic conception of God that, in the face of creation's mysterious form, renounces any pretension towards solving the opacity of the world's being. Recognition of the mystery of God may prove to be the inevitable destination of all theodicies; however, I believe that because of the revelation of God in Jesus Christ, more can be said about God's nature. While not solving the mystery, this points towards certain claims that we are compelled to affirm: namely, the important theological notion that nature's cycle of violence is not the proper or necessary means of achieving the greater good but that the good of creation, which God intends to bring to pass in spite of the mysterious presence of evil, is willed by God from eternity.

The major difficulties with creational theodicies like Southgate's are twofold: first, it is unclear whether the magnitude of creaturely suffering is logically linked to the existence of certain goods and whether the acquisition of these goods sufficiently outweighs the suffering endured by the world's creatures. Under Southgate's proposal, the benefits conferred by a Darwinian account of evolution are indelibly linked to the emergence of higher orders of creaturely beings. Yet, it is uncertain whether the attained goods justify the concrete suffering experienced. The problem is fundamentally epistemic. More to the point, is it possible to attain a conceptual vantage point from which to evaluate the world's suffering in relation to the benefits generated? The *instrumentalist* theodicy is subject to endless deferrals of justification because its postulates cannot be ascertained or denied without a sufficient grasp of the whole of reality. And even if we could somehow verify that creation's violent form is sufficiently outweighed by benefits, do we not end up with a God whose omnipotent creative love is constrained by a utilitarian logic that merely sublimates violence and suffering? From this perspective, the traditional Christian claim regarding God's transcendent goodness conflicts with a narrative that perceives violence as part of God's will. The *instrumentalist* theodicy's most advantageous aspect is also its most significant liability: that is, such theodicies can admit the world as it appears without recourse to additional conceptual categories, yet this fusion of God's will with the suffering world forms a moral aporia with respect to traditional claims concerning God's beneficent nature and omnipotent agency.

When compared to the figuralist approach to creational theology, the "reductive" nature of *instrumentalist* theodicy, which reduces everything to God's direct creative will, seems at odds with other creational claims of Scripture. For instance, in terms of its scriptural basis and comprehension, *instrumentalist* theodicy trades upon a real dimension of Scripture that depicts God as the all-determining source of nature's being. This captures an important aspect of the Christian understanding of God's transcendent action in positing the universe from nothingness. However, alongside the texts that affirm a connection between the visible manifestations of nature and God's providential governance, there are other scriptural passages that appear to challenge the *instrumentalist* theodicy insofar as they depict creation as subjugated to a fallen order. Specifically, Scripture depicts the created cosmos "in bondage to decay" (Rom 8:21) and subjected to other created "powers" and "principalities" (Col 1:16; Eph 6:12). Strikingly, Scripture also seems to depict an ontologically peaceful creation *sans* ontic violence at its eschatological consummation (Isa 11:6–9; Rev 20–21). This seems to indicate that the present world is not entirely reflective of God's desire, as creation's final state diverges considerably from its present condition. However, recognition of an ontological deviation in creation's developmental history is exactly what an *instrumentalist* theodicy like Southgate's rejects. Instead of describing the present shape of nature with the language of "fallenness" (however construed), the world, in its ontic violence and agony, appears entirely determined by God's creative desire.

The narrowness of the *instrumentalist* theodicy is made apparent by its limited connection with Scripture's figured order. Scripture's imaging of the natural world expresses a mysterious tension of which the *instrumentalist* theodicy grasps only one aspect. This tension is between God's creative omni-causality that seemingly locates all things within God's antecedent will and a vision of the natural world as languishing in a state of misery and awaiting an eschatological transformation. In this regard, *instrumentalist* theodicy fails to take full comprehension of the pressures of the scriptural landscape. This leads to a limited theological portrayal of finite existence: nature and its violence appear as just the method of God's creative purpose. By contrast, a figuralist account preserves Scripture's diverse portrayal of creation in order to perceive the complex truth of God and the world within its tensive articulations. Alongside the scriptural description of creation's foundation in God's transcendent creativity lies a vision of the created world as a contingently fallen reality wherein all that happens is not always commensurate or identical with God's creative purpose.

Contingent-Fallenness Theodicies

The last category—the *Contingent-Fallenness theodicy*—relates nature's ontic violence to sin's causal influence within the creaturely world. According to this perspective, the present condition of the world is a chiaroscuro of being's divine radiance and the murky shadows of disorder. It is a world that fails to correspond with God's protological (or antecedent) intention; instead, the structure of the world is riven by moral and ontic darkness that originates from some secondary causal agency or power. In premodern Christianity, this view corresponds with the minor tradition found in the writings of Theophilus of Antioch, Irenaeus, and Ephrem the Syrian (amongst others), who regarded the death-conditioned properties of nature as a form of fallenness. While the minor tradition possessed limited influence upon premodern Christianity, this construal of nature influenced some forms of post-Reformation Protestant Christianity, which have lasted until the present day.[56] In view of modern scientific accounts, however, it is clear that such an etiology of creaturely suffering cannot comport with the chronological history of the natural world, seeing that death and predation are exhibited in the fossil record. Yet, despite the range of chronological and metaphysical problems presented by the traditional form of the *contingent-fallenness* narrative—one centered upon humankind's agency—a growing number of modern theologians have attempted to recast the concept of *contingent-fallenness* into a form that comports with the basic acceptances of contemporary science. Here, the notion of a cosmic fall or spiritual fall has become a significant resource for developing a theodicy of creational suffering.[57] Based upon scriptural passages that allude to the fallenness of creation (Rom 8:18–23) and its subjugation to evil spiritual principles (Eph 4:12; 1 John 5:19), the world appears in such theodical accounts as a conflicted reality that bears the wound of some anterior disorder.

One contemporary variation of this type of narrative invokes the notion of a *non-hypostatic* fall of creation, wherein the present world cannot be squarely identified with God's protological design or will. The most compelling form of this non-hypostatic theodicy is found in the work of Celia Deane-Drummond, who retrieves Sergius Bulgakov's language of "Shadow Sophia" to convey a sense of creation's divergence from God. Drummond argues that the world is imbued at its foundation with mysterious potentialities that are open to divergence. Accordingly, the world's divergent pathways are metaphorically construed as "the culmination of tendencies already latent in the natural world, rather than a specific work of a mythological figure of Satan."[58] According to Deane-Drummond, the possibility of creaturely evil and suffering is conditioned by the entropic

---

56. The Adamic Fall interpretation of creation is present in Calvin, *Commentary on the Epistle to the Romans*. This interpretation is quite prevalent among the various fundamentalist variations of Protestant Christianity, especially those associated with the "creationist" movement.

57. Some contemporary proponents of the angelic fall theodicy include Louis Bouyer, E. L. Mascall, Michael Lloyd, and Paul Griffiths. See Bouyer, *Cosmos*; Mascall, *Christian Theology*; Lloyd, "Are Animals Fallen?"; Griffiths, *Decreation*.

58. Deane-Drummond, *Christ and Evolution*, 187. Another variation of a nonhypostatic fall is displayed in Creegan, *Animal Suffering*; Williams, *Ideas of the Fall*.

form of the cosmos, yet the specific direction of nature's evolutionary development—the way the thermodynamic flux of energy manifests itself in history—is entirely contingent. In this way, Deane-Drummond's vision corresponds with Robert John Russell's notion of evil as a "universal contingent," whereby all forms of natural evil (waste, suffering, and death) lack metaphysical necessity but are nonetheless inevitable in any created universe.[59] Although notable for its recovery of fallenness language, this type of account suffers from definitional and conceptual ambiguity: what does it mean for *impersonal* elements to turn away from God? The notion of a non-hypostatic fall—that is, one that avoids the ontic density of personal secondary agencies—amounts to little more than a re-description of the mysterious presence of suffering in God's creation. Indeed, no matter how vigorously one affirms that contingency provides the ontic conditions for evil in the cosmos (a metaphysical truism), without the notion of personal agency and free action, one is left with a conceptual surd that cannot adequately explain how evil *inevitably* emerges from the divine establishment of non-personal elements.

In contrast to a non-hypostatic cosmic fall, the notion of a personal spiritual (one might say, *hypostatic*) fall that has somehow affected the intrinsic structures of space and time is both coherent in its definitional aspect and substantially present within the Christian tradition. In this respect, some modern theologians have attempted to retrieve the notion of personal spiritual powers as a way of rendering the natural world intelligible for Christian theodicy. This type of interpretation characteristically trades upon two interrelated notions from the Christian tradition: first, the notion of the mediative role of angels in creation's governance; second, the notion that some angels have rebelled against God's vision for the world. With respect to the notion of angelic mediation, this vision of nature's governance is evinced throughout the tradition from the sub-apostolic period (e.g., Athenagoras, Papias, and the Pastor of Hermas) all the way through to the medieval period (e.g., Thomas Aquinas) and beyond.[60] For instance, in the early second century AD, Athenagoras describes the role of angels as follows: "For this is the office of the angels—to exercise providence for God over the things created and ordered by Him."[61] In conjunction with this concept of angelic mediation is the

---

59. Russell, *Cosmology*, 244.

60. Shepherd of Hermas, *Visions* 3.4; Papias, *Fragment 7*. For Aquinas, see *Summa Theologica* 1, q.110, a.1.

61. Athenagoras, *Plea for Christians* 24.

notion of the angelic fall, a ubiquitous notion in the Christian tradition from the New Testament until the early modern period. Together, these two notions provide fixed points around which one might construct a theological narrative of creational suffering. It is apparent that within Christianity's metaphysics of creation, there resides the possibility of a more textured dualistic cosmology, which allows for some divergence of the world from God's creative desire.

Advocates for this sort of fall narrative typically point out that it is not invented out of contemporary need but is present to the tradition as a secondary residual idea. For instance, E. L. Mascall remarks:

> This suggestion is the more compelling because the doctrine of an angelic fall was certainly not originally postulated in order to account for the existence of evil in the material world before man. . . . It is therefore striking that the twin beliefs that the angels had charge of the material world and that many of them had fallen away from God before the commission of the first human sin were, so to speak, stored away in readiness for answering a problem as yet unthought—of, namely that of possible distortion and deviation in human evolution.[62]

In making this claim, Mascall asserts that Christian tradition had never used the notions of angelic mediation and the angelic fall in a way that specifically addressed the shape and conditions of the natural world. Mascall's statement ought to be qualified in two ways: first, the doctrine of the fall of the angels was used in view of traditional theodical concerns. It was posited as an explanation for the prior circumstances that anticipated and conditioned humanity's temptation and fall. In this respect, the concept of fallen spirits served a theodical role vis-à-vis human sin and its consequences. Second, Mascall's claim that the angelic fall was not applied to the natural world is not entirely accurate. While he is correct insofar as the vision of fallen immaterial agents shaping the natural world is largely a modern concern, there are notable exceptions. Extant witnesses of the sub-apostolic period indicate a much more populated and active role for fallen spirits in the governance of the world. Accordingly, in the second century, Athenagoras describes Satan as the "prince of matter" and writes,

> Some, free agents, you will observe, such as they were created by God, continued in those things for which God had made

---

62. Mascall, *Christian Theology*, 303.

and over which He had ordained them; but some outraged both the constitution of their nature and the government entrusted to them: namely, this ruler of matter and its various forms . . . and he became negligent and wicked in the management of the things entrusted to him.[63]

Although such an account depicts fallen angels as abusing their authority over nature, this condition is a reality that follows from and is shaped by the human fall. The corrupted governing function of the angels over nature was a consequence of Adam's sin and not a reality that antedated human existence.[64] On this subject, Mascall is largely correct in claiming that the angelic fall—as a separate ontological event—was not applied to the shaping and governance of the *pre-human* natural world.

If we admit the possibility that these ideas of fallenness may be retrieved and reformulated to explain nature's *agon*, in what way would such an account offer a better explanation than other theological narratives? According to the moral philosopher Robert Wennberg, such a vision has the benefit of viewing creational violence as a deviation not directly willed by God's creative act. Wennberg comments, "It remains the case that the theory of the angelic fall does at least serve to place God one step removed from the physical evil in the world. . . . Importantly, then, it may be felt, the supposition of the angelic rebellion enables us to preserve the principle that God never directly wills or creates evil."[65] Wennberg's statement addresses one of the major difficulties with attributing the existence of evil solely to the contingency of creation: it is hard to see how non-personal elements might diverge from God's will, seeing that they are protologically established and governed by God. However,

---

63. Athenagoras, *Plea for Christians* 24.

64. Within early Christianity and the wider context of Second Temple Judaism, widespread belief in fallen spiritual beings was tethered to the mysterious passage of Genesis 6:1–4, wherein the Sons of God have intercourse with the daughters of men. F. R. Tennant posits that this story was *the* first Hebraic fall narrative that explained the provenance of evil. He argued that this explained its relative prominence in the extant pseudepigraphical literature of the Second Temple Period (e.g., the Ethiopic Book of Enoch). Tennant, *Sources of the Doctrines*. However, as noted by Norman Williams, by the time of the Common Era the prominence of this "angelic fall" story in Genesis 6 was displaced and subordinated to the story of Adam's Fall in Genesis 3. Williams, *Ideas of the Fall*. Notably, for someone like Athenagoras, the angelic fall is ostensibly identified with the account in Genesis 6, which is an event *after* Adam's fall. Athenagoras, *Plea for Christians* 24–25. In other variations, the angelic fall is either prior to the Adamic fall (e.g., Augustine, *Literal Meaning of Genesis* 2.17–19; 11.17–37) or chronologically coterminous with human sin (Justin Martyr, *Dialogue with Trypho* 124).

65. Wennberg, *God, Humans, and Animals*, 331.

if we posit some form of personal agency at the root of creation's divergence, this makes more sense in accord with the basic acceptances of the Christian faith. By this, I mean that the notion of personal agencies capable of divergence from God's will is part of the basic structure of the Christian tradition. Indeed, one of the most essential aspects for narrating and explaining the human experience of evil has been the idea of sin's volitional character, which is grounded in the mysterious reality of human personhood.[66] Thus, the upshot of the hypostatic fall of the angels is that it simply expands upon conceptual realities inherent to the Christian faith. These include claims regarding personhood, creaturely freedom, and the contingency of sin.

While such an account appears to remove the present world's ontological violence from God's creative will—thereby preserving the divine peace of classical Christian theism—the position is not without significant scriptural and conceptual problems. On the level of scriptural discourse, the notion of an angelic role in creation is never explicitly articulated, nor is the notion of an angelic fall applied directly to the violent elements of the natural world.[67] Although there are hints towards a fall of nature in Scripture (e.g., Gen 3:17–19; Rom 8:20–23), it is never specifically linked with the angels in any clear way. On the contrary, while some passages possibly recognize nature's violence as a type of deviation (e.g., Gen 1:30; 6:11; 9:3), many praise nature's sublime form (including its predatory aspects) as evidence of God's providential wisdom (e.g., Ps 104; Job 38–41). While there is scriptural evidence that contributes towards the notion of a *contingent-fallenness* narrative, these passages

---

66. By connecting the concept of sin to the notion of personal agency, it is not my intention to flatten all evil to simply the outworking of creaturely freedom. While I affirm personal and volitional dimensions to the idea of sin, the biblical and theological character of sin is not always so straightforward. Simply put, the notion of original sin (in both its Western and Eastern configurations) generally trades upon the inheritance of some type of defect, whether it be death, guilt, or concupiscence. Thus, while sin might be a reality ontologically derived from creaturely agency and freedom, the way it is manifested in Scripture, tradition, and human experience suggests that it is also a type of "bondage" or "sickness" that attaches itself to persons irrespective of their volitional freedom. See Duffy, "Our Hearts of Darkness," 597–622.

67. At best both notions are inferred from passages that imply some type of angelic governance of the world, both with respect to the nations (e.g., Deut 32:8–9; Dan 10:10–21) and nature (Rev 7:1). Moreover, much of the case for cosmic fallenness is tethered to an array of passages that refer to the spiritual elements of creation that stand opposed to God (e.g., Col 1:16; 1 Cor 2:8; Eph 1:21; 3:10; Gal 4:3; 2 Cor 4:4; 1 John 5:19). Thus, while not explicit there is some basis for cosmic dualism within the Scriptures, but how this cosmic dualism manifests itself in view of the natural world is not clear.

stand in tension with others that seemingly admit the world's present form as divinely determined. This one-sided connection to Scripture's figural landscape recapitulates the interpretive problem associated with both the *eliminativist* and *instrumentalist* theodicies. The sheer range of scriptural perspectives, with their connective tensions regarding the shape of the natural world, fails to fully materialize in such narrow theodical narratives, partly explaining their interpretive limitations. Because these theodical perspectives grasp only a limited fraction of Scripture's layered discourse, they inevitably mute the interpretive combustion that occurs when all the diverse elements are drawn together. The mysterious character of Scripture's testimony concerning nature suggests that the figuralist approach may more adequately engage the disparate and tensive elements of Scripture in view of the mysterious form of creation.

In terms of conceptual problems, it also appears that *contingent-fallenness* theodicies—whether Adamic, cosmic, or angelic—inevitably fail to sufficiently explain the inherent *fragility* of the creaturely world. One must ask, why is the universe established with a frangible ontological structure open to the perverse manipulations of secondary agents? In describing the problem of fragility, the philosopher Michael J. Murray concedes that, despite appearing to rescue God from direct fault for nature's violence, "we are left with the still more vexing question of why God would create a universe that was subject to such catastrophic corruption on the occasion of a Fall of this sort." Indeed, as Murray concludes, "Such a universe seems defective indeed."[68] Under the auspices of this type of theodicy, it is not clear why the spiritual and physical dimensions of the creaturely world possess a morally integrated link in which a part may functionally corrupt the whole. By implication, a theodicy of fallenness presents a moral economy in which the injuries and effects suffered by sin's presence reverberate beyond the specific agents of sin. The suffering of innocent (non-sinful) creatures seems to challenge the direct Augustinian linkage between sin and suffering. Ultimately, any variation of the *contingent-fallenness* theodicy drives the problem of nature's violence into the murky depths regarding evil's mysterious role within creation.

---

68. Murray, *Nature*, 101.

CONCLUSION

This chapter provides a survey of the primary ways the Christian theological tradition has engaged nature's ontic violence, from its premodern traditions to its subsequent transformation in the modern epoch. In this transition, what I have called the major and minor traditions have been transposed into modern variations. By this, I mean that the broad explanatory structure of each tradition has been preserved, even amidst the shifting scientific and moral landscape of modernity. In their modern forms, these basic interpretive structures are recast into *eliminativist*, *instrumentalist*, and *contingent-fallenness* theodicies. In my view, these three interpretative types represent the explanatory reach of rational reflection concerning natural violence and creaturely death in view of the claims of classical theism. While these approaches offer some reasonable insights, the interpretive force behind such renditions is relatively limited insofar as they remain profoundly underdetermined, both scripturally and philosophically. These approaches tend to both elevate and suppress different aspects of Scripture's figurated landscape and are conceptually open-ended. There does not appear to be theological criteria by which one might adjudicate the probability of one such account being a true representation of reality. These theodicies are also relatively inadequate from a theological perspective insofar as they do not sufficiently engage the determinative Christological form of revelation. On the contrary, these modern theodicies, while profoundly attendant to philosophical resources, operate in relatively tangential terms with respect to the God revealed in Jesus Christ.

Because of these limitations, I would like to examine whether the figural principle that informed the premodern perception of creation might provide a more substantial theological ground for engaging our theodical perspectives. The figural hermeneutic takes in all of Scripture's referents as they pertain to the natural world—including things disparate and contradictory—and weaves them into a narrative that makes sense of the world. Such is the advantage of figuration: it can take up and fruitfully engage the referential network of the Scriptures in view of our desire to interpret nature's *agon* theologically. In this way, the recovery of traditional figural theology might unlock a way of developing and adjudicating theodical perspectives in accord with the Christological axis of the Bible and the natural world. This retrieval of the figural disposition will not succeed by simply transferring and applying the specific content of premodern figurative models (especially in its tropological focus). Rather, a renewed figural engagement of creation must attend to modern scientific and moral concerns. Bringing the Christic form of Scripture to bear upon the universe as described in our late-modern culture necessitates a deepening and extension of the conceptual resources latent in the Christian theological tradition.

3

The Figural Shape of Creation

THE MORAL PROBLEM OF nature's *agon*—that is, that the divinely *created* world is characterized by endemic strife, suffering, and death—beckons for a fresh theological interpretation attuned to the present state of the question. The contemporary context for the problem is conditioned by the combustive union of modern scientific description and late-modern ethical demands, which have gradually effaced the plausibility of the Christian tradition's main lines of interpretation. In large part due to their underdetermined character, theological attempts to retrieve and update these approaches have not fared well. In view of such limitations, our project now turns to developing a compelling natural theology directly shaped by the Christological form manifested in the Scriptures. By engaging the problem of creational suffering within the encompassing scope of scriptural revelation, we will provide a sufficient theological basis to faithfully explore the character of the world, bringing it under the disclosive fullness of God's self-interpretation in Christ and the Spirit.

To attain this objective, we are compelled to adopt the hermeneutical and metaphysical stance that characterized premodern Christian natural theology. The pervasive view that figural interpretation is not a legitimate option for late-modern Christians is largely conditioned by an insufficient appreciation of the radical ontological implications of the Christian doctrine of *creatio ex nihilo*.[1] Whereas premodern theological discourse

---

1. Scriptural figuration appears implausible to many Christians primarily due to the conceptual purchase of historicism's metaphysics, which implicitly rejects the divine shaping of reality. As noted in chapter 1, there appears to be a major link between the thinned-out accounts of the doctrine of creation with its limited view of nature's theological meaning and the literal-historicist accounts of Scripture's reference. From the literal-historicist perspective the Bible's depiction of the creaturely world is of limited

viewed nature as interpretively bound to Scripture's verbal order, modern theology operates under an attenuated ontology where the natural world appears only accidentally (or extrinsically) related to Scripture's layered discourse. Consequently, the *revelatory* significance of nature is obscured in view of such an enervated ontology. In effect, the troubling wonders of the natural world—things like the liver-fluke worm, the ichneumon wasp, and the wider predatory order—are *theodically* reduced to a thinned-out manifestation of divine Wisdom, portrayed abstractly as the mathematical order and causal arrangement of the universe. Under such a vision, the disquieting forms of the world's creatures are interpretively isolated from the mystery of the incarnate Christ—the fullness of divine and created wisdom. This obscures their disclosive significance. At best, modern theology's correlationist[2] approach only reinforces the conceptual hiatus between the *revealed creation* of Christian belief and the *natural world* of modern description, with the result that creation's theological reference is sharply curtailed.[3] Thus, the task of developing a

---

value vis-à-vis nature's ever-shifting landscape because the Bible is strictly bound to its historical referents found "behind the text" which do not directly address our speculative concerns about the shape of nature. One might add that this perspective rightly acknowledges that the Bible displays nature at a literal level in a diversity of ways that resist simple assimilation to any explanatory narrative. For example, the depiction of the predatory economy appears fragmented as it is displayed in Scripture in diverse (or antinomic) ways. At the literal level of interpretation, nature's predatorial form is both divinely established *and* the result of some primordial declension. Thus, from the perspective of modern historicism, which remains the dominant form of interpretation, the accumulation of disparate scriptural texts concerning nature leaves the interpreter in the same interminable deferral of adjudication as displayed by modern theology. The attempt to interpret the theological meaning of creational suffering by means of a literal-historicist approach to Scripture merely recapitulates the same aporetic tension that prevails in contemporary theology. I submit that only a figural apprehension of Scripture can engage the diversity of Scripture and delineate a comprehensive picture in view of exegetical antimonies. For a helpful discussion of the antinomic character of figuration, see Radner, *Time and the Word*, 205–19.

2. As a theological method, "correlation" typically involves conceptual reciprocity or integration between Christian self-description internal to the church's discourse and extrinsic criteria determined by other theoretical structures. The mediation of theology and extrinsic criteria usually takes two distinct forms: either presupposing some transcendental philosophical structure that binds the two together, or a procedure that admits ad hoc forms of mediation. For discussion of theological method see Frei, *Types of Christian Theology*, 1–55.

3. This conceptual hiatus typically limits Christian natural theology to some form of discernment of God based on the world's actuality (*actus essendi*). There are compelling renditions of this type of approach inferring the existence (*esse*) and attributes of God based the world's contingent character. Such an approach operates by abstracting the constitutive principles and properties of being (*esse commune*) and then arguing

natural theology that avoids the limitations of the correlationist approach begins with the traditional Christian supposition that Holy Scripture, as the Word of God, is a vital source for engaging the world *theologically* in all of its enigmatic aspects.[4] This recognizes Scripture as the mysterious divine speech that encompasses and discloses the immense depths of the world's being in time. To put it another way, all things are narrated in some way by the divinely ordered discourse of the figurated Scriptures.[5]

In light of the modern prejudices against figuration, our engagement of the natural world in view of Scripture's reality requires reordering our theological perception of the objects in question. Our implementation of this reordered faculty for natural theology is shaped by the figuralist thought of Hugh of St. Victor, whose integrated vision of the "two books" establishes a way of interpreting the juxtapositional tensions that characterize both natural being and scriptural reference. Thus, the Christocentric theological ontology grounds and guides the probing of Scripture's figurated content vis-à-vis the agonistic properties of the world. This engagement of Hugh's figuration is not simply a descriptive exercise to retrieve his conclusions regarding creation's physical character. Such a limited historical task would leave us in the twelfth century with his

---

for the conceptual necessity of a transcendent source by virtue of the conditions of intelligibility. Nevertheless, such a limited form of "natural theology," while compelling to a certain degree, avoids addressing the concrete character of created being. Here, the thickness of the created world as it is manifested in its specific phenomena is abstracted away. Thus, the abstract world of being discerned by the perspicacious mind might point to God, yet under such a program the concreteness of things—including the history of biotic life—is strikingly silent. For an abstract natural theology concerning finite being's radical insufficiency see Clarke, "Is a Natural Theology Still Viable Today?," 150–82. See also Blanchette, *Philosophy of Being*.

4. This is both a methodological and metaphysical claim. The task of theological reflection as a spiritual discipline and intellectual enterprise is constitutively and historically bound to and determined by the revelatory force of the Scriptures as connected to the life of the church. Of course, this priority of scriptural revelation does not exclude the integration of other sources, whether that of philosophy, magisterial tradition, or scientific description. Indeed, the probative task of theology—and especially figural theology—necessarily engages these realities, all of which fall mysteriously within Scripture's comprehensive reach.

5. This interpretive approach logically derives from the ontological implications of Christian belief in creation. The doctrine of creation (*creatio ex nihilo*) is not a form of cosmological speculation but derives from the Christian doctrine of God, which recognizes the *absolute distinction* and mutual integrity of God and the world. Historically, the doctrine appears as the metaphysical implication of the appearance and act of God in and as Jesus Christ. For a thorough historical study of the metaphysical genealogy of the doctrine of creation in view of the incarnation see May, *Creatio Ex Nihilo*, and the more recent McFarland, *From Nothing*.

rather Neoplatonic interpretation of natural violence and death. On the contrary, our task follows and constructively engages Hugh's interpretive perception to develop a fresh theological description of the natural world. This task is both dialogical and creative insofar as it proposes to construct a theological narrative by exploring Scripture's figurated structures in light of Hugh's theology.

We will begin by rehearsing the Christological foundation for figuralist thinking and then proceed to engage nature according to Scripture's layered connections. Hugh of St. Victor's figuralist interpretation of Noah's ark provides the theological goad that guides our entry into the Bible's networked character, which subsequently discloses a set of interpretive patterns that will structure our theological perception of the natural world. Hugh's ark was chosen as the source for our theological reflection because of its sweeping comprehension of the world and its connection with a host of other scriptural figures. Specifically, Hugh's ark points to the creational significance of the *temple form* as it is manifested in multiple ways throughout the Bible. In its all-encompassing reference, the ark figure and its cognates fittingly advert to the unique Christological "relation" that obtains between God and the world, which forms the conceptual setting for our theodical inquiry.[6] Insofar as the problem of nature's *agon* is bound up with the underlying conditions of created existence, our theological inquiry pursues the wider metaphysical principles that make possible such things as the liver-fluke worm and the broader predatory economy. Thus, our exploration of the ark is animated by its comprehensive reference to the world's being *as a totality* in view of God's infinite agency. Following Hugh's reasoning, we will press into the extended reference of this network of figures as it is displayed in the Bible's narrative sequence. The resultant set of patterns derived from this figuralist interpretation, along with their ontological allusions, will then constitute the theological architecture for constructively exploring the mysterious character of the world in the next chapter.

---

6. The object of all theodical reflection ultimately terminates upon the God-world "relation." Even though our interest is primarily concerned with the shape of nature's *agon*—specifically as it is expressed by nature's predatorial economy and the suffering of nonhuman animals—the issue is wrapped up in the wider metaphysical character of the problem as it pertains to the mysterious distinction between God and the world. Thus, to engage in theodical reflection concerning animal suffering invites wider examination of the God-world relation.

READING NATURE ACCORDING TO SCRIPTURE'S FIGURES

The Mystery of Christ: The Form of All Things

The interpretive key that unlocks our project's theology is the epistemic and metaphysical priority of the incarnate Word, who is the eternal foundation and content of all created things.[7] Following the church's traditional trinitarian ontology, Hugh describes Jesus Christ, the eternal Word and Wisdom of God, as the "living mind and sole primordial idea or pattern of all things."[8] As the "living mind" (or, using a different technical idiom, the eternal expression of the Father's self-knowledge), the Word is the infinite divine essence hypostatized as the "Christic pattern" of eternal *filiation* and responsive *self-offering* that comprehends all the primordial causes or ideas of created time and being.[9] For Hugh, the Christological form of divine Wisdom[10] is the ontological fount of finite existence. Christ is graciously manifested in and through the variegated profusion

---

7. While the divine ideas of creation pertain to God's essence or nature, insofar as all God's acts *ad extra* belong to the entire Trinity, there is a sense that the content of creation is bound up notionally with the hypostatic Word. Under the auspices of this trinitarian ontology, the Father's eternal speaking of Himself in the Word (the eternal divine act of filiation) expresses the entire divine nature and all the ways that nature may be shared by creatures via participation. Thus, the Word of God expresses the content of the world of creatures in all their aspects. For a helpful discussion and defense of the doctrine of the divine ideas, see Levering's Thomistic articulation in his *Engaging the Doctrine of Creation*, 53–70.

8. Hugh of St. Victor, *Didascalicon* 1.2.

9. Hugh writes, "He conceived in eternity in his wisdom, which is coeternal with him, the forms of all creatures. These forms are coeternal with that wisdom and are called the 'reasons' (rationes) of things in the divine mind, or 'ideas,' or 'notions'" (Hugh of St. Victor, *Sententiae de divinitate* 2). Hugh also describes the comprehensive form of hypostatic Wisdom that comprehends everything: "Simultaneously, because She [Wisdom] embraces every essence, form, place, and time; once-and-for-all, because She admits no interrupted vision, nor does She interrupt a vision once begun, because what She is all at once She is always, and what She always is She is totally. She sees all things, She sees all things about all things, She sees always and She sees everywhere" (Hugh of St. Victor, *De tribus diebus* 20.8).

10. With respect to the creaturely world's Christic form Hugh follows the prevailing tradition, identifying the divine creativity as appropriated by the distinct hypostatic relations of the Trinity, expressed by the triad "Power, Wisdom, and Goodness" (Hugh of St. Victor, *Sententiae de divinitate* 3). The actual *content* of the world's being—its diverse entities and temporal manifestation—is related to the property of the hypostatic Word as divine Wisdom. It is the second hypostasis of the Trinity—the Word or Wisdom of God—who functions as the exemplar of all created being "because to its likeness all things have been formed" (Hugh of St. Victor, *Didascalicon* 2.1).

of creatures that constitute the content of the contingent world. In some real sense, the image of the divine Son interprets the concrete entities that comprise the world. Hugh writes, "the Word made what can be seen and is seen through what He made."[11] If we follow the tradition's *sacramental* perception of the universe wherein Christ is the Word "through whom all things were made" (1 Cor 8:6b; Col 1:15–17) and in whom all things are gathered and summed up (Eph 1:10) then it follows that the Christological form is essential to any speculative theology that would move beyond the surface appearances of the phenomenal world. More to the point, this also implies that the specific problems we are addressing, namely, the dissipative structure and ontic violence of nature, somehow converge upon the very being of the crucified and exalted Lord.

The process or method for discerning the Christic form of nature is no straightforward task. Tradition holds that human perception of nature's sacramental depth is profoundly distorted by the exigencies of the human condition in the fallen world. In essence, it is the speech of God in Scripture that performs the rehabilitation of one's perception of the natural world as creation. Hugh adverts to this when he writes, "Just as when an unlettered person sees an open book and notices the shapes but does not recognize the letters, so stupid and carnal people . . . see on the outside the beauty in these visible creatures, but they do not understand its meaning."[12] According to Hugh, the meaning of natural phenomena is rendered opaque to the human mind because of the deforming consequences of original sin. In describing the Hugonian perspective of creation's revelatory character, Grover Zinn writes that fallen humanity "is now deaf and blind . . . and no longer perceives the world as a symbol revealing the Creator . . . [fallen humanity is] unable to read the book of creation."[13] Consequently, the comprehension of the natural world is limited to patterns of thought that are unable to discern the divine form that draws all things together. Such interpretations, whether philosophical, scientific, or artistic, maybe probative inasmuch as they reveal genuine aspects of the world's surface appearance. However, they cannot elucidate the whole of reality in its spiritual depth, that is, in terms of its divine significance. Without a coherent theological-metaphysical foundation,

---

11. Hugh of St. Victor, *De tribus diebus* 1.1.
12. Hugh of St. Victor, *De tribus diebus* 4.3.
13. Zinn, "De Gradibus Ascensionum," 61–79.

the world's being disintegrates into a diverse array of disciplines and fragmentary truths that resist reintegration.[14]

In order to read the natural world rightly—to see the world transparent to its divine meaning—requires the renewal of Christocentric metaphysics that perceives the world's depth through Scripture's theological language.[15] The revelatory form of Jesus Christ, the eternal self-utterance of God, is manifested through the implicit metaphysical grammar of Scripture, which in turn encompasses the world within its referential reach. Thus, the textual landscape of the Bible, in the interior connections of its figures, interpretively displays the whole world in all its complexity. Hugh's figural reading of Scripture opens the natural world up *epistemically* to its divine significance. Boyd Taylor Coolman describes the Hugonian hermeneutic as follows:

> From Hugh's perspective, then, God has interposed Scripture between fallen human beings and the uncreated Beauty they should perceive in created things. The "sacred eloquence" points to and thus mediates the divinely instituted subset of *res*

---

14. To use a contemporary example, the human explication of nature is now rendered almost exclusively in the theoretical terms of the natural sciences. This has yielded enormous success with respect to practical utility. However, while this form of apprehension is legitimate in its methodological distinction, the approach trades upon a type of reduction incapable of making sense of the world's being. Insofar as some practitioners of the natural sciences mistakenly suppose that reality is *entirely* reducible to abstract mathematical description, such accounts display an incoherent metaphysics (and theology) that inevitably distorts what the world actually *is*. Under the interpretive auspices of natural science, the theophanic world of creation is often violently reduced to a form of brute facticity whose meaning is limited to the pragmatic notion of truth, which is ultimately incoherent. Supposition of nature's brute facticity along with an epistemic reduction of knowledge of being to functionality is not simply an abandonment or bracketing of theology and metaphysics as some claim; rather, as Michael Hanby has effectively argued, such a perception of nature is configured by a latent metaphysics and theology that are fundamentally deformed insofar as they fail to sufficiently grasp the ontological structure of the universe's being according to the Christian doctrine of creation. Modern science operates under a series of distorted theological assumptions regarding God's creative act and the nature of the created world which ultimately undermine the enterprise itself. For Hanby's argument, see *No God, No Science*, 107–34, 334–64.

15. In its traditional form, natural theology was the interpretive rendering of the world's creatures in view of the truths given by divine revelation via the Scriptures. Specifically, in view of Scripture's *Christological* disclosure of God, the world's being was rendered in terms derived from the figures given in Scripture. This intellectual and spiritual discipline located the world and its beings within the encompassing truth of Christ's revelatory form. For a description of this interpretive practice, see Meer and Mandelbrote, *Nature and Scripture*.

(persons, objects, places, and events) that have revelatory significance. Scripture is the lens through which God is perceived in created things.[16]

This interpretive stance expresses the reality that scriptural figures—narrated persons, objects, and events—possess meaning that potentially extends to the farthest reaches of the created world. To put it differently, Scripture's verbal forms intersect with the creative unfolding of the world in time.

The approach of this project can thus be distilled into two interrelated principles related to our theological metaphysics. *The first principle asserts that the crucified Jesus Christ, as the revealed Word of God, serves as the interpretive axis of creation, which dynamically encompasses the realities that shape the entirety of natural history.* This entails that the world of nature—including its tangled history of biological development shaped by violence, suffering, and death—is somehow unveiled, gathered, and summed up in Christ. This interpretive apprehension of nature's complex character in view of the comprehending form of the Son opens onto the *second principle: a theological interpretation* of *creation requires reading it in light of the interposed figures of Scripture.* Because of its Christic grammar, Scripture not only *figures* the life of Jesus, but it also outlines the world's existence within the mystery of divine providence.

This figural extension of reference, again, is the logical outworking of the implications of the metaphysics of creation *ex nihilo* with its radical divine comprehension of reality. The theologian Ephraim Radner captures this forceful metaphysical logic of figuration: "Having known Christ in his scriptural figures, one was not only able but also morally compelled to see these figures within the teeming waters of the marsh and lake. The world was a 'book' written by God and speaking about God."[17] Accordingly, as divine discourse, Scripture speaks the very world of contingent being as it is found in the divine mind. This also requires that creation's "groaning" (Rom 8:22) be somehow explicable in view of Scripture's narrative articulation, which orders all things around the paschal mystery. To explicate creation theologically thus requires entrance into the landscape of scriptural discourse where God orders all things in Christ.

---

16. Coolman, "Pulchrum Esse," 182.
17. Radner, *Chasing the Shadow*, 6.

Figuring the World: The Hugonian Ark and the Temple Form

Our stated objective of discerning the world's being in Scripture leads us to consider the primary figures that unveil the world through Scripture's canonical span. If the Christocentric ontology articulated above obtains as our fundamental stance, then it follows that the entire world of created being, including the vast epochs of animal life, are somehow included within the figures represented in the words and sentences of the Bible. In order to engage the conceptual breadth of Scripture's figures, our task begins with Hugh of St. Victor's perceptive reading of Noah's ark, which he presents as the primary figuration of created existence.[18] The Hugonian ark thus provides our project with a theologically expansive figure through which we are able to peer into the networked connections of Scripture itself wherein the divine speech about created life in time becomes discernible.

In his exegetical treatises on Noah's ark, *De arca Noe morali* and *De arca Noe mystica*, Hugh engages the ark's creational reference to develop a set of theological meditations concerning the human condition. The application of this figure to the human traversal of time establishes the *raison d'être* for the occasion of his ark treatises. However, it is not so much this theological agenda that engages our interest but the layered figuralist perception that underlies his interpretation. For Hugh, the ark takes up and enfolds all of creation's reality and displays it as under the condition of eternity (*sub specie aeternitatis*). Hugh writes:

---

18. Hugh's ark possesses an extensive interpretive reach. It goes well beyond that which was typically proffered by the church's traditional exegesis. Since the time of Tertullian in the second century CE, Noah's ark was almost exclusively construed in relation with an ecclesial and sacramental typology (following 1 Pet 3:20) whereby the ark signified the church, the flood waters the baptismal font, and Noah the typological Christ, the righteous one who leads the old creation into a newly re-created world. For a description of the prevailing strand of interpretation of the ark according to an explicitly sacramental and ecclesiological typology, see Daniélou, *From Shadows to Reality*, 69–112. For Hugh, these ecclesial and sacramental motifs are well known and make an appearance within his reflections. Nevertheless, the overall context of his exegetical exploration is conditioned by a different thematic, whereby the ark functions as a cognate (or figural instantiation) of the biblical motif of the divine house of God, i.e., the abode of God's presence within creaturely reality. Grover Zinn writes: "The difference which sets Hugh's treatises on the ark apart from earlier reflections on the same theme lies in the introduction of the motif of the house and accompanying orientation toward the concerns with which the traditional house-texts from the biblical material were associated." See Zinn, "History and Contemplation," 273–85.

> What then is this ark, about which we have said so many things, and in which so many different paths of knowledge are contained? ... There all the works of restoration are contained in all their fullness, from the world's beginning to its end. ... There the sum of things is displayed, and the harmony of its elements explained. There another world is found, over against this passing, transitory one; because the things that go through different times in this world exist in that one simultaneously, as in a condition of eternity.[19]

In Hugh's theology, the ark functions as an exemplar of created time and being insofar as it is structured and governed by the Word's eternal Form. Boyd Taylor Coolman describes this as a theological "synthesis of reality" that fuses scriptural forms with a participationist ontology, which expresses the pattern of God's infinite agency in the works of creation and restoration.[20] In this sense, creaturely existence (macrocosmically in the universe and microcosmically in the human soul) is Christologically structured by the ark, which orders all things according to a pattern internal to the scriptural narrative. This interpretation of the ark explicitly thematizes the metaphysics that grounds Hugh's understanding of the profound interrelation between Scripture and nature, as both are patterned according to the disclosive form of the eternal Word. By engaging Hugh's interpretation of the ark, we pass into a network of scriptural images that will structure our theological explication of the world's being, especially as it pertains to nature's violent and destructive phenomena.

In regard to the interpretive connections of the ark figure, Hugh apprehends both the *Christological* and *creational* reference of the structure according to Isaiah's vision of God's presence inhabiting the temple in Jerusalem (Isa 6:1–13).[21] In this passage, the image of the divine glory filling the temple expresses the manner in which the infinite form of God surpasses, fills, and governs the universe.[22]

---

19. Hugh of St. Victor, *De arca Noe morali* 4.21.
20. Coolman, *Theology of Hugh of St. Victor*, 17–21.
21. Grover Zinn observes that the treatises are "most accurately understood as Hugh's unfolding of the mysteries of Isaiah's theophanic experience for those who wish to be initiated" (Zinn, "Hugh of St. Victor," 103–4).
22. Hugh further identifies the ark with the figure of Mount Zion, a metonymic form of the temple (Isa 2:2–4; cf. Mic 4:1–3). Hugh writes, "This is the mountain of the house of the Lord established in the top of the mountain, unto which all nations flow, and go up from the ark's four corners, as from the four quarters of the earth" (Hugh of St. Victor, *De arca Noe morali* 2.9). The ascending four sides of this *cosmic* mountain converge to a central cubit the "true simplicity and everlasting changelessness, that is

He therefore is rightly represented as sitting upon the throne of eternity since, as there is neither beginning nor end to His being, so is there none either to his omnipotence. He always was, He always was omnipotent. Full ever in Himself and of Himself, He was at once perfect, and yet never overflowed. Well then may the prophet say, "I saw the Lord sitting upon a throne, high and lifted up," for the might of the Godhead at once precedes all creatures in eternity, surpasses them in excellence, and orders them by power.

Next come the words, "and the things that were beneath it filled the temple." The temple may here be understood as meaning the cycle of the ages and revolutions of the centuries. For as the ages in their course return upon themselves, they seem by their cycles to mark out as it were the enclosure of a temple, "the things that were beneath it filled the temple," is to be taken, therefore, as meaning that all the periods of time are full of the works of God.[23]

Hugh interprets the Christic form of the ark figurally with the image of divine glory filling the temple in Jerusalem, which itself signifies the divine comprehension of "heaven and earth" in Scripture (Jer 23:24). This figural collation underscores the referential exchange of the ark and the temple as it appears in Scripture and adverts to its profound creational significance. With respect to this referential exchange, Hugh's interpretive elaborations correspond with the temple form as it manifested throughout the Bible's canonical span. This textual manifestation is not limited to any single iteration (e.g., Solomon's temple or the wilderness tabernacle); instead, it embraces a network of structural images that are bound to Scripture's primary reference to Christ.[24] Thus, Hugh's ark

---

in God." The ark represents the *temple* and the *creaturely world* that ascend towards a central point of culmination that forms the center of the ark and the apex of the mountain. This apex is the incarnate Jesus Christ, represented as the slain Lamb in Jerusalem, who is the central axis point that holds the entire structure together. The ark as temple mountain also conceptually overlaps with the temple as the primordial Garden of Eden. The central axis of the ark, figuratively described as the Lamb of God, is represented by the tree of life in Eden. Thus, there is considerable imagistic overlap between the ark, the temple, the mountain, and Eden. This concatenation of images has primary reference in both Scripture and tradition.

23. Hugh of St. Victor, *De arca Noe morali* 1.8.

24. Hugh's conflation of the ark and the temple does not derive from an excessive allegorism but authentically resides in the texts themselves. Biblical scholars Joseph Blenkinsopp and Stephen Holloway have identified a textual link that lends critical support for Hugh's figural perception of the overlapping meaning of these structures. Holloway and Blenkinsopp argue that internal elements of the texts (linguistic and

theology takes up the extension of the temple form as it simultaneously signifies the person of Christ (John 2:19), the cosmos and history (Gen 1–2; Exod 25–31; 35–40; Rev 21–22), the church (Eph 2:21–22), and the human person (1 Cor 3:16). This extended reference animates Hugh's interpretive engagement of the ark insofar as it outlines the expansive Christological form that structures created existence in all its aspects.

Hugh's interpretation of the ark, based on Isaiah's temple theophany, evokes a tradition that perceives the world in the divinely designed structures of the Bible. For instance, in the theological orations, Gregory of Nazianzus describes "the Tabernacle of Moses" as a "figure of the whole creation . . . the entire system of things visible and invisible."[25] This figural intuition concerning biblical structures reflects a trend that was followed by many Christian and Jewish interpreters[26] from antiquity to the early

---

thematic aspects) and a comparative assessment of the ark-deluge narrative with Mesopotamian parallels is at the very least indicative that the Bible's depiction of Noah's ark possesses some corresponding function with the scriptural temple. Blenkinsopp notes that formulaic correspondence between the description of the wilderness sanctuary's construction (Exod 39:42) and the description of Noah's completion of the ark (Gen 6:22) along with various forms of temple imagery applied to the Noachic narrative indicate identification of the ark with the temple. This includes invocation of cultic elements (clean/unclean animals, and post-deluge sacrifice) and the description of both ark and temple as three-tiered structures, reflecting the prevailing cosmology of the Ancient Near East. Blenkinsopp, "Structure of P," 283; Holloway, "What Ship Goes There," 328–54.

25. Gregory of Nazianzus, *Second Theological Oration* 31.

26. For a general survey of the interpretive use of the temple figure among Jewish and Christian interpreters, see Holder, "Mosaic Tabernacle," 101. The remarkable range of Jewish and Christian interpreters include Philo of Alexandria, Flavius Josephus, Clement of Alexandria, Theodoret of Cyrus, Cosmas Indicopleustes, et al. The interpretive trends concerning biblical structures within early Christian exegesis finds its most systematic manifestation in the exegesis of the eighth-century theologian Venerable Bede, who composed two entire commentaries dedicated to the figural significance of the wilderness tabernacle and the Jerusalem temple. In both *De Temple Salomonis* and *De tabernaculo et eius vasibus*, Bede masterfully weaves together the various interpretive elements embedded within early Christian exegesis, including tropological, Christological, and ecclesiological elements. While there is an implicit cosmological element in the Bede's commentaries, such an interpretation is quite reserved with respect to previous exegetical forays into cosmology (e.g., Cosmas Indicopleustes and Theodoret et al.). Nevertheless, the densely layered allegorical interpretation exhibited by Bede is echoed by Hugh's figural interpretation of the ark. Like Bede, Hugh's exegetical exposition places great emphasis upon the moral or spiritual dimensions of the structure; yet Hugh's interpretation displays a more pronounced emphasis upon the temporal dimension of the church's existence, which, for Hugh, corresponds to the unfolding intervals of the creaturely world's history from creation to eschaton. Hugh's unique conflation of the temple "house of God" interpretation with the ark more vigorously takes up the cosmological strand of interpretation found in early Christian exegesis.

modern period. Furthermore, this creational perception is not merely a historical oddity born from traditional interpretive practice. On the contrary, the notion that biblical structures map the universe is substantiated throughout the Bible by verbal and thematic motifs.[27] This includes salient linguistic and subject-matter parallels between the hexaemeron and the construction of the wilderness tabernacle in the book of Exodus (25–31, 35–40)[28] as well as the story of Solomon's construction of the Jerusalem temple (1 Kgs 6; 8).[29] In light of these parallels, it is evident that creation is manifested in highly textured ways in Scripture's deployment of these structures. The divine pattern of creation is scripturally articulated through an accumulation of texts, which include, among others, the protological hexaemeron (Gen 1:1—2:3), the Eden narrative (Gen 2:4—3:24), the deluge narrative of Noah's ark (Gen 6:11—9:17), the tabernacle-temple narratives of Israel, Ezekiel's apocalyptic temple (Ezek 40–48), the imagery of Christ's atonement in the Letter to the Hebrews,

---

27. Recognition of the temple's cosmic significance is evinced in current biblical scholarship in the works of Blenkinsopp, "Structure of P," 275–92; Walton, *Lost World of Genesis One*, 77–84; Elnes, "Creation and Tabernacle," 144–55; Kearney, "Creation and Liturgy," 375–87; Beale, *Temple and the Church's Mission*; Levenson, "Temple and the World," 275–98; Anderson, *Genesis of Perfection*.

28. According to this argument, the descriptive accounting of the creation of the universe and the tabernacle conform to a seven-fold structure. In the Genesis narrative the world's formation is brought about over a seven-day duration. Within the Exodus narrative, after the glorious divine presence inhabits Mt. Sinai for six days, God calls Moses to the mountaintop on the seventh day to reveal a vision of the divine sanctuary. Subsequently, the instructions for the tabernacle are divided into seven blocks of material in which six sections describe the revealed plan and its actual construction and the seventh describes the Sabbath rest that follows. See Elnes, "Creation and Tabernacle," 150.

29. The temple was constructed over seven years (1 Kgs 6:38b) and dedicated during the festival of booths in the seventh month, accompanied by Solomon's seven petitions (1 Kgs 8:31–55). Jon Levenson remarks: "Can the significance of the number seven in this Temple dedication be coincidence? In light of the argument on other grounds that temple and creation were thought to be congeneric, this is improbable. It is more likely that the construction of the temple is presented here as a parallel to the construction of the world in seven days (Gen 1:1–2:4)" (Levenson, "Temple and the World," 288–89). The second text that Levenson proffers as indicative of the cosmic significance of the Jerusalem temple is the Isaianic theophany wherein the prophet perceives the divine glory filling the temple. According to Levenson, the seraphim chant, "Holy, holy, holy is the Lord of hosts: The whole earth is full of his glory," ought to be rendered, "Holy, holy, holy is the Lord God of hosts: the fullness of the world is his glory." Levenson maintains that if his translation is correct, "the seraphim identify the world in its amplitude with this *terminus technicus* of the Temple cult" (Levenson, "Temple and the World," 289). In light of this reasoning, the divine presence that fills the tabernacle and temple is extended to include the entire world in Isaiah's vision. This fortuitously forms a nuptial fit with Hugh of St. Victor's use of the Isaianic vision as the basis for his ark reflections.

and the eschatological celestial Jerusalem in the book of Revelation (Rev 21–22).[30]

Before we engage elements of Scripture's figuration under the auspices of the Hugonian ark, it is necessary to describe the structure's creational content. As mentioned above, Hugh's ark unfolds Isaiah's vision, wherein the Lord's presence fills the temple, which is the "earth full of his glory" (Isa 6:3b). In visual terms, the cosmic ark is both coextensive with and surpassed by the divine presence—which, for Hugh, is the eternal Word of God. Christ establishes the ark-cosmos by speaking the six-fold act of creation (the hexaemeron) that terminates with the Garden of Eden at the bow of the structure, signifying its temporal foundation. The stern of the ark represents the eschatological end of history (*last judgment*).[31] Descriptively, the bow and stern form the metaphysical boundaries of the created world, beyond which lies the mystery of the Word's eternal being. Hugh describes the form of the Word, "The head and the feet are covered,

---

30. For example, G. K. Beale documents the microcosmic function of the temple both in the figure of the New Jerusalem of the book of Revelation, which represents the eschatological new creation, and the Garden of Eden in Genesis 2–3, the primordial beginning of the creaturely universe. Beale attempts to empirically correlate each aspect of the temple's architectural structure with a distinct aspect of the creaturely universe with varying degrees of success. Beale finds his biblical interpretation of the temple structure to accord with traditional interpretation, especially that of Flavius Josephus. See Beale, *Temple and the Church's Mission*, 31–50.

31. In Hugh's ark the eschatological final judgment is descriptively rendered in the images of the sheep and the goats of Matthew 25. Describing the temporal limits of the cosmic temple, Hugh writes, "The arc of the circle that extends to the east on the bow of the Ark is Paradise, like the lap of Abraham. . . . The other arc, which extends to the west, holds the resurrection and final judgment of all: on the right are the chosen, on the left, the condemned" (Hugh of St. Victor, *De arca Noe mystica* 14.28). Although Hugh clearly includes some variation of the *telos* of creation within the scope of the ark—signified by the last judgment—his interpretation only tacitly touches upon the figural texture of Scripture's description of the eschatological age, described in the image of the cosmic temple of creation. In this respect, Hugh's ark, which is described in some instances as the cosmic mountain with Christ at its apex, appears to mirror the description of the New Jerusalem, which is also a mountain with the throne of God and the Lamb at its center. Hugh writes, "This is the mountain of the house of the Lord established in the top of the mountain unto which all nations flow, and go up from the ark's four corners, as from the four quarters of the earth. . . . Let us go up with joy, for we are going 'into the house of the Lord.' Let us lift up our eyes to see the bright paths strewn along the flanks of the eternal mountains and the footpaths that lead upwards to the gates of Jerusalem. There, on the summit, the standard of the cross, shining with rosy light, makes foes afraid and comforts friends. The doors of the city are open, and in its broad places are the voices of them that sing Alleluia" (Hugh of St. Victor, *De arca Noe morali* 2.9).

therefore, because we cannot discover either the first things or the last."³² However, the structure of the ark represents a type of theophany of the eternal Son as it contains the epochs and ages of history, depicted both geographically from East to West and temporally from creation to the eschaton. The ark's structure is comprised of the entirety of scriptural history, which Hugh designates as the divine "works of restoration."³³ This span of time is ordered around the central figure of the paschal lamb in Israel's temple (*the sacrificial temple*), which forms the conceptual axis of the structure.

> And so, this band, which extends from one side of the ark to the other, signifies the course of time from the beginning of the world until the end of time. The first half of this band, moreover, which goes from the bow of the ark up to the column, signifies all the time from the beginning of the world until the Word was made flesh; the second half signifies all the time from the incarnation of the Word until the end of time.³⁴

In figural terms, the paschal lamb in the temple unites the historical span of cosmic time that exists between the beginning and the end of history insofar as all the figurated persons and events are directed towards the atoning act of Christ's self-offering, which comprehends and fulfills the temple's figuration (Heb 9–10). Christ, as the "Lamb . . . slain from the foundation of the world," guides all things "through Himself unto Himself."³⁵ Remarkably, Hugh's figural ark offers a profound Christological theology that simultaneously captures the Word's form as encompassing and being encompassed by creation in a perfect coincidence of infinite and finite reality. The Christological form, which structures created time, reveals itself as a constituent of the world through the cruciform life of

---

32. Hugh of St. Victor, *De arca Noe morali* 1.10.

33. Spatially speaking the ark contained the earth, which was visually represented by an ancient *mappa mundi* that contained places significant to scriptural time. These included the known continents, nations like Egypt, Babylon, and Israel, and the traditional forty-two stopping places of Israel's sojourn through the wilderness. Above the earth are depicted two concentric circles: the outer ring, the *aether*, represents the visible cosmos with the zodiac and the twelve months; the inner ring, the *aer*, represents the sub-lunar atmosphere with the four seasons and four winds descriptively represented. This vision of cyclical time is linked with the keel of the ark, which represents the linear sequence that makes up the biblical order of history, beginning with the six days of creation and culminating with the last judgment.

34. Hugh of St. Victor, *De arca Noe mystica* 3.7.

35. Hugh of St. Victor, *De arca Noe morali* 1.14.

Jesus. As Hugh puts it: "He it is who rose from the earth and pierced the heavens, who came down to the depths, yet did not leave the heights, who is Himself both above and below, above in majesty, below in compassion, above that He may draw our longings thither, below that He may offer us help."[36] Following Hugh's figural logic, our task leads us to consider this highly textured network of figures. We will use the Hugonian ark to discern and outline the character of the Christological form of creation as it is described by Scripture's figurative display.

THE FIGURAL EXPLICATION OF CREATION

In order to grasp the divine shape of creation, we must read the phenomenal world in view of Scripture's divinely articulated speech. Following Hugh's figural perception, our engagement with the *revealed* form of nature proceeds by means of the ark's figural connections. Our interpretive process will involve passing more deeply into Scripture's networked cognates to apprehend the theological texture of existence as it is given through the content of the temple form. Under this figural lens, distinct patterns emerge that will subsequently inform the development of a theological narrative of creation's suffering in the next chapter.

Our interpretive use of the figural dimensions of creation will not be fixed to a modern chronology of the natural world in a straightforward or literal way. By straightforward or literal, I refer to a type of interpretation that fuses a temporal framework with the scriptural narrative to the point of identity. On the contrary, our metaphysical stance assumes scriptural figures are primarily atemporal forms that stand in a potential relationship with all times created by the triune God. These figural images thus present multiple aspects of creation without being tied to a literal chronological framework. Taken together, they present a varied and seemingly inconsistent picture of the world's existence. However, within this diversity and its unique ontological implications, a coherence emerges that unveils the nature of God's creative action. Before we attempt to discern the symbolic order that supervenes through this juxtaposition of images, we will first outline the scriptural presentation of the world as discerned through the Hugonian ark.

---

36. Hugh of St. Victor, *De arca Noe morali* 2.8.

Nature's Traversing Form: The Ark and the Hexaemeron

As a form of the Bible's cosmic *templum dei*, the Hugonian ark displays the world as mediated through Scripture's narrative structure. According to Hugh's theological vision, the ark takes on the form of Isaiah's temple theophany, symbolizing the paradigmatic shape of God's creative and redemptive agency from eternity. Hugh's interpretive perception also underscores the networked character of the temple as it reveals the theological patterns of creation's manifestation. Accordingly, the eternal Word fills and surpasses creation as its underlying principle and content, which is enfigured as the divine presence, encompassing the Bible's divinely designed structures. The Hugonian ark particularly unveils the divine agency in creation through the temple narrative found in Genesis 1, the hexaemeron. Hugh's figural identification of the *templum dei*, the narrative of the six days of creation, and the ark point towards an embedded ontological narrative that describes the character of the world as it is formed by God in Christ. Under Hugh's enfigured theological guidance, we perceive a theologically thick description of creation that passes beyond the literal sense and connects to our theodical concern. Thus, we must trace the ontological implications of Hugh's reading of the hexaemeron in view of Scripture's figurated connections. The key interpretive insights that we shall uncover will pertain to creation's *unfolding* character between its protological foundation and eschatological *telos*. The cosmic temple of the hexaemeron, with its figural connections, reveals the universe as constituted by an *ontological movement or traversal* that progressively unfolds from imperfection toward greater realization.

According to Hugh's figuralist thinking, God's infinite agency is revealed through the narrative pattern of the hexaemeron. In his description of the ark, the six days of creation emanate from the mouth of the same divine presence that fills and surpasses the temple. This creative action, imaged as six disks, terminates in the global structure of the ark-cosmos, which contains the extended history of the universe within its form. For Hugh, this account reveals the remarkable pattern of God's creative wisdom that illuminates the structure of the universe. Boyd Taylor Coolman regards "Hugh's discussion of God's creative activity" as providing the "pattern for things to come,"[37] as the shape of the narrative reveals God's way of acting in all things. This narrative rendering of

---

37. Coolman, *Theology of Hugh of St. Victor*, 40.

God's infinite agency as a developmental process provides a metaphysical paradigm that is revelatory of the character of God's *being* and *action*.[38]

In Hugh's reading of Genesis 1, creation *ad extra* is a progressive or developmental act that begins with the founding of heaven and earth (Gen 1:1). These two figures represent the interpenetrating poles of created existence: the angelic/spiritual creation and the largely unformed *materia* of the sensible world that is to be brought into progressively deeper form as the universe. "Therefore all things were founded simultaneously, since we believe that equally at one and the same time the matter of all visible things began, and the nature of the invisible, both unformed according to something and formed according to something."[39] Subsequent to the founding of the two ontic dimensions of creation, Hugh reads the Genesis account of the first three days as describing a gradual separation and formation of time and space from the initially confused, chaotic, and minimally formed state.[40] This was followed by days of progressive, beautifying formation represented by the profusion of creatures that fill all dimensions of the cosmos. "On the first three days God created everything in matter and ordered it, and on the last three days He adorned it."[41] In this respect, Hugh's reading emphasizes the hexaemeron's unfolding character as it displays the creative transcendence of the divine act as temporally distended through successive gradations of increasing form and progressively manifested beauty.

---

38. Hugh's exegesis of the hexaemeron engages a twelfth-century debate concerning the temporal dimensions of the divine act of creation. This debate concerned Augustine's conception of the creative act in view of the six days of creation, namely, whether God created all things simultaneously or whether things were created through a temporal distention. Augustine affirmed that all things were timelessly created, thus rendering the successive shape of Genesis 1–2 as a figural explication of the angelic creation's apprehension of created entities. Hugh attempts to affirm both the timeless aspect of the creative act along with its temporal form. Hugh affirms that God created the noetic creation and the raw material of the physical creation all-at-once (in a state of limited form) while affirming his ongoing creativity in bringing creation to greater form through time. See Hugh of St. Victor, *De sacramentis Christianae fidei* 1.5.5. For a discussion of this debate in the twelfth century, see Gross, "Twelfth-Century Concepts of Time," 325–38.

39. Hugh of St. Victor, *De Sacramentis* 1.5.5.

40. Hugh writes, "Therefore, before form matter was in a broken state, yet in form—in a form of confusion, before a form of disposition" (Hugh of St. Victor, *De Sacramentis* 1.1.5). According to Hugh, the "broken state" still possessed some form insofar that it existed. To be absolutely unformed is to not exist.

41. Hugh of St. Victor, *Adnotationes*, 66.

Regarding the actual process of creation, Hugh correlates the unfolding character of the world's being with the discursive understanding of the spiritual creation. For Hugh, the celestial heaven of Genesis 1:1 is the angelic sphere made in "the likeness of the divine idea" of the sensible world, which is then concretely actualized into being through the spiritual sphere's mediative apprehension. Hugh writes, "The other creatures, however, first existed in the Idea of God; next, they were made in the knowledge of the angels; and finally they began to subsist in themselves."[42] The spiritual creation's perception of the divine ideas is manifested as the temporal and ontological pattern of physical existence given through the narrative of the six days. Accordingly, the unfolding form of the sensible world was intended as a divine pedagogy through which the spiritual creation—comprised of both angels and human beings—was to be brought to their divinely intended *telos*.

> For just as the matter of all visible and corporeal things at that beginning of primary creation had the form of confusion and did not have the form of disposition . . . so spiritual and angelic nature at its own creation through wisdom and distinction was formed according to disposition of nature; yet it did not have that form which it was afterwards to receive through love and conversion to its creator.[43]

This underscores a fundamental dimension of Hugh's reading of Genesis: the hexaemeral formation of the cosmic temple is grounded upon a metaphysical pattern that orders the universe through an unfolding interval from an initial state of *imperfec*tion towards an ever-increasing crescendo of divine *perfec*tion and beauty.[44] Hugh states: "God did not

42. Hugh of St. Victor, *Didascalicon* appendix C.
43. Hugh of St. Victor, *De Sacramentis* 1.5.5.
44. This foundational pattern of created existence reflects the dynamic structure that inheres within all rational creatures of the created world, both human and angelic. In Hugh's words: "Just as he first fashioned all things in a good state but not the highest state, namely by creating formless things from nothing, and afterward he brought formlessness of things into the highest state by bringing them into form and order, so God did not immediately place the rational creature, that is, men and angels, in the highest state but in a good state" (Hugh of St. Victor, *Sententiae De Divinitate* 1). This is not to suggest that Hugh proposes some type of proto-evolutionary conception of creational development by transmutation of species (or even something akin to it); on the contrary, Hugh's account conforms to a strictly literal rendition of the hexaemeron along with an implicit acceptance of the stability of the essential forms of all creatures. Nevertheless, his articulation of divine creativity takes seriously the sequenced character of time as divinely established structure of the created world. This is grounded upon

want to create the world at once but successively. He did not want to create it at once with form, but he first brought it from non-being into being and afterwards into a beautiful being."[45] In this sense, Hugh's metaphysical reading cracks open a neglected aspect of the narrative contours of the six days, which sees movement (*motus*) or traversal as a constitutive part of the divine shape of creatures. The notions of *process* and *movement* express something of the revelatory form upon which all things are patterned.

Not only does the Hugonian ark reveal the creative act as an ontological pattern of traversal, but the figural details of the ark's span, which signify the layers of cosmic time, human history, and the human soul, recapitulate the same underlying dynamic. The shape of time and being is thus sacramentally infused with the divine pattern articulated in the hexaemeron. Hugh perceives an unfolding pattern of increasing form and complexity in the six days, which culminates with divine rest on the seventh day, and he reads Scripture's historical span from Eden to the eschaton as corresponding with the same developmental ontology. Here, the six ages of the world—the entire span of creation and redemption—are figurally anticipated and signified by the specific content of the six days, which together reveal the singular character of God as both creator and redeemer.[46] According to this figural perception, the scriptural description of the creative act is not limited to a set of events

---

the hexaemeron's successive depiction of creation. Hugh perceives that the created world, summoned from nothingness in God's eternal utterance of his divine Word, as governed by an arc of temporal succession towards an ever-deeper condition of divine beauty. For discussion of Hugh's understanding of creation's succession, see Coolman, *Theology of Hugh of St. Victor*, 38–40.

45. Hugh of St. Victor, *Sententiae de divinitate* 1.

46. Hugh adopts the Augustinian conception of salvation history structured by to six ages, which is figurally conflated with the six-days of creation. Hugh writes, "Therefore, the works of foundation, as if of little importance, were accomplished in six days, but the works of restoration can not be completed except in six ages. Yet six are placed over against six that the Restorer may be proven to be the same as the Creator" (Hugh of St. Victor, *De Sacramentis* 1. prol. 2). In his treatise on the mystic ark, Hugh writes, "The first age of the world, from Adam until the Flood lasted 1656 years. The second, from the Flood until Abraham, lasted 292 years. The third, from Abraham until David, 942 years. The fourth, from David until the emigration, 475 years. The fifth from the migration until the advent of Christ, 585 years. The sixth age, now in progress, has no certain progression of years: it is a feeble age that will be consumed in the death of the whole world. Those who conquer these wretched, toilsome ages of the world with a blessed death, will be taken up now to the seventh age of eternal Sabbath, and there await the eighth age of the blessed resurrection, in which they will reign eternally with the Lord" (Hugh of St. Victor, *De arca Noe mystica* 4.10).

in the past but is an overflowing reality that continuously frames and configures the entire sweep of created time. For Hugh, the formal pattern of the creative act is recapitulated by the ordered shape of historical time. This is signified in Scripture through multiple figures, whether by the relational movement from the Old Covenant to the New (Gal 3:23–29) or the unfolding form of God's revelation as given through the natural law, the written law, and the age of grace (cf. Rom 1–3).[47] Furthermore, this ontology of formation is reiterated within the life span of the human person, who is subjected to the same traversal of form. Hugh writes: "even the rational creature itself was made unformed in a certain mode of its own, afterwards to be formed through conversion to its Creator; and therefore matter unformed but afterwards formed was shown to it, that it might discern how great was the difference between being and beautiful being."[48] In this way, the hexaemeron's ontology of movement appears inscribed and recapitulated throughout creation, inasmuch as the entirety of time is given and shaped by the Word of God.

This developmental span of time in the Hugonian ark (the six ages) is also encompassed by an ontological horizon that is scripturally narrated as iterations of the cosmic *templum dei*. Specifically, the figurated boundaries of creation are respectively given in the Bible as the Garden of Eden and the celestial Jerusalem, both of which are directly linked to the temple form. Notably, the relationship between these two figures in Scripture underscores the Hugonian perception of the unfolding character of creation's traversal between its beginning and end, albeit in a different modality. While the hexaemeron enfigurates the cosmic temple through a threefold progression of deepening form, the narrative connection between the Garden and the celestial Jerusalem recapitulates the

---

47. See Hugh of St. Victor, *De Sacramentis* 1.11.1; *De arca Noe morali* 1.14.

48. Hugh of St. Victor, *De sacramentis* 1.1.3. Hugh depicts creation's narrative of development as implicitly tethered to the human vocation insofar as Adam mirrors the creative act itself. Thus, Adam functions as a microcosm of the universe, summoned to a process of fulfillment that recapitulates the hexaemeron's ontological structure. For Hugh, the human person was created dynamically ordered towards a glorification that was to be realized through the traversal of time. Hugh writes, "lastly on the sixth day man was made . . . and he was placed in paradise, first to abide there and to work, so that after his work was finished and his obedience fulfilled, he might be transported from there to that place where he was destined to abide forever" (Hugh of St. Victor, *De Sacramentis* 1.1.29). This Irenaean-like perspective on the human vocation recapitulates and extends the culminating movement of creation's temple as signified by the hexaemeron. This figural tether between the two cosmic temples of Genesis 1–2 reconfigures the climactic seventh day of creation as an incomplete reality, figurally denoted as the garden.

same progression through the threefold spatial cosmography of Israel's sacrificial temple.

To foreground this recapitulative form, it is helpful to supplement Hugh's figural reading with insights drawn from modern scriptural scholarship. Hugh clearly identifies an unfolding pattern as the prevailing structure of God's action. This scriptural form is brought out more clearly by attending to the intratextual connections of the Bible. These connections, yielded by modern exegesis, enable us to grasp the expansive nature of creation's ontological traversal.

For instance, the Eden narrative presents the protological creation of Genesis 1–3 as structured according to the temple's threefold form of descending degrees of holiness from the garden (the holy of holies), Eden itself (the inner court), to the outside world (the outer court).[49] According to the garden's scriptural cosmography, with its mountain and outflowing rivers (Gen 2:10; cf. Ezek 28:13–14), the divine presence within the cosmos is implicitly delimited to a narrow aspect of the world where the first humans dwell in prelapsarian innocence, signified by their nakedness and lack of shame (Gen 2:25).[50] The world *beyond* the garden appears thus as a distinct mode of reality—a space and time of creaturely exile where sinful humanity is subsequently driven after the fall (Gen 2:8; 3:24). Significantly, this layered pattern corresponds with Israel's *sacrificial* temple and thus appears inscribed upon the world both at its foundation (Gen 2–3) and through its traversing span (Heb 9:9). Yet, it is noticeably absent from creation's eschatological completion (Rev 21–22). In this way, the application of the temple's sacrificial pattern to the world reveals something of the properties of creation's passage between its beginning and end.

In particular, the threefold dimensions of the Edenic world appear tied with Israel's sacrificial movement from the outer court, where animals

---

49. Beale, *Temple and the Church's Mission*, 73–75.

50. According to the biblical theologian J. R. Middleton, the juxtaposition of the garden temple narrative with the cosmic temple of the six days indicates an aspect of creation's foundational character. Where one would expect the explicit descent (or manifestation) of divine glory on the climactic seventh day of creation (thus fulfilling the temple-building narrative), the text instead configures this expectation around a limited dimension of the creation, signified by the human presence in the garden. Middleton writes, "Whereas Genesis 1 draws on the conceptuality of heaven and earth as a cosmic temple, with humanity as God's image or cult statue in the temple, meant to mediate God's presence and rule from heaven to earth . . . the garden in Genesis 2 is the locus of divine presence on earth, where YHWH God 'walks' in proximity to humanity" (Middleton, "From Primal Harmony to a Broken World," 149).

THE FIGURAL SHAPE OF CREATION 99

are slaughtered, to the heart of the temple—the holy of holies where the divine glory dwells (Lev 16). Ontologically speaking, the correlation of the world's structure according to Israel's temple underscores the implicit significance of sacrifice as part of the world's foundational character. Specifically, the sacrificial form of the temple reveals a spectrum of distinct ontic modalities concerning the world's character in time, from the reality of the "outer court," the place of creation's traversal, to the holy of holies, which anticipates creation's eschatological transformation.[51] The Letter to the Hebrews describes this sacrificial span, which outlines the dynamic character of the world as bound entirely to Christ's recapitulating traversal (Heb 9:11–12; 10:1–18; cf. Eph 1:10; Col 1:16–17). On this score, the sacrificial pattern is the shadowed expression of the Son's act of atonement, which takes up the world in its fragility and sin and presents it to the Father, healed and glorified.

Discussion of the creational dimensions of sacrifice will be reserved until the next section. Here, we will focus primarily on the spatial ontology of the temple's form, whose span from the outer court towards the inner space of God's holy presence gestures towards the unfinished, imperfect character of creation, especially when considered in light of the celestial Jerusalem of the book of Revelation. Here, the figural traversal of creation between the threefold garden world and the celestial Jerusalem is disclosed by the connection between the two figures, which mark out the beginning and end of the scriptural world.

---

51. The tripartite form of the garden temple indicates that the garden itself is a figure of creation's *telos*. Only it proves to be distinct from the vicissitudes of the outer world, which creates a layered sense to the universe insofar as the outer world is the place of bloodshed, struggle, and exile (Gen 3:23–24). The limited nature of the garden implies that the divine fulfillment of creation is also somehow wedded to humanity's task vis-à-vis the outside world, as indicated by Hugh's exegesis. Biblical scholar G. K. Beale has argued that the priestly language of Genesis 2:15 is linked to the divine command in Genesis 1:26–28 where human vocation was directed to encompass, fill, and subdue the entire created world. Beale writes, "In light of Genesis 1:26–28, this meant that the presence of God, which was initially to be limited to the garden temple of Eden, was to be extended throughout the whole earth by his image bearers, as they themselves represented and reflected his glorious presence and attributes" (Beale, *Temple and the Church's Mission*, 82–83). If this insight regarding the human vocation is correct, it reinforces the scriptural claim that the created world is protologically structured by a real narrative of traversal, where relative imperfection is ordered towards a higher state vis-à-vis the human task. The divine presence of the sanctuary was to be extended to the world outside of the garden. By extension, Beale avers that the narrative also implicitly indicates that the outer world, the place of creaturely sacrifice, is already a "disordered space" characterized by "spiritual chaos" (Beale, *Temple and the Church's Mission*, 85).

In Revelation 21:1—22:5, John describes the glorified creation, a new heaven and earth (a biblical *merism* for the universe), according to the image of the garden temple. The celestial city, like the garden, is figurally constituted as a holy mountain (Isa 11:6-9; 65:25; 66:22) with precious stones (1 Kgs 5:17; 6:20-22; 7:9-10), rivers of water (Gen 2:10-14; Ezek 47:1-11), and trees of life (Gen 2:9; Ezek 47:7, 12). Most significantly, the equidistant length, width, and height of the city (Rev 21:15-17) mirror the dimensions of the temple's holy of holies (1 Kgs 6:19-20), thus indicating that the eschatological creation is figurally represented as the holiest part of the temple and the garden. The creaturely world lacks the outer dimensions of the sacrificial temple. Instead, the entire universe has passed into the glorious presence of God. Biblical scholar J. R. Middleton writes, "In the context of the new creation, the new Jerusalem is a mega-sized analogue of the holy of holies in the tabernacle or temple; it is also directly parallel to the garden of Eden in the original creation."[52] Like the river that flowed from the Edenic sanctuary into the outside world in Genesis 2:10, the city also displays a river flowing from its center, identified as "the throne of God and the Lamb" (Rev 21:22-23). The outflow of this river evokes the eschatological vision of the temple in Ezekiel 47 (cf. Zech 14:8), from which a river of living water flowed into the desolate creation, bringing new life.

> Then the angel showed me the river of the water of life, bright as crystal, flowing from the throne of God and of the Lamb through the middle of the street of the city. On either side of the river is the tree of life with its twelve kinds of fruit, producing its fruit each month; and the leaves of the tree are for the healing of the nations. (Rev 22:1-2)

In figural terms, the celestial Jerusalem signifies creation's liberation from its bondage to decay by the sacrificial offering of Christ, the God-man, who takes up the world's being and presents it to the Father (Eph 1:7-10; 2:28; Col 1:19-20; Heb 7:27; 9:11-12) In this manner, the pattern of the original creation—which corresponds with the sacrificial form of the temple—is overcome and completed as the entire creation is refashioned as the garden temple of God.

> Behold, the dwelling of God is with men. He will dwell with them, and they shall be his people, and God himself will be with them; he will wipe away every tear from their eyes, and death

---

52. Middleton, *New Heaven and a New Earth*, 171.

shall be no more, neither shall there be mourning nor crying nor pain anymore, for the former things have passed away. (Rev 21:3b-4)

A major implication of this remarkable figural tether is that it depicts existence as constituted by a passage from the sacrificial division of the cosmic temple towards the eschatological harmony of the holy of holies. The scriptural connection between these two figures recapitulates the ontological dynamic that Hugh discerned within God's creative action in the hexaemeron, reflected in Hugh's cosmic ark figure. Thus, all of creation's being and history in Scripture is divinely shaped by the same unfolding movement or pattern from "non-being into being" and "being into beautiful being."[53]

If we follow Hugh's figural understanding of the ark, which reflects the textual dimensions of Scripture's temple form, an implicit story emerges regarding the narrativity of creation: the overarching form of the world is entirely given through a metaphysical movement from incipient being to glorified being. In other words, the ultimate form of the creaturely world is not present in its initial state; it is realized only through the mysterious distension of time. Hugh's theology thus responds to Scripture's figurative density, articulating a specific pattern (or way of being) behind God's infinite agency. From this point of view, all divine actions *ad extra* are patterned according to this principle motion. Hugh writes, "That the sun was made from the light mentioned above may be inferred from the fact that the Gospel was somehow made from the Law of Moses, like wine was made from water at the marriage {at Cana}."[54] This dynamic ontology of traversal reflects God's way of acting in the larger scriptural frame of reference. Scripture reveals the Word's shaping of all things, characterized by a metaphysical movement from an initial

---

53. Hugh of St. Victor, *Sententiae de divinitate* 1.

54. Hugh of St. Victor, *Adnotationes*, 64; cf. *De arca Noe morali* 1.3: "Our bridegroom . . . offers the good wine last when He allows the heart, which He intends to fill with the sweetness of His love, first to pass beneath the bitter harrow of afflictions; so that, having tasted bitterness, it may quaff with greater eagerness the most sweet cup of charity." This mirrors the pattern Hugh applies to *all* the divine works of creation: "Just as he first fashioned all things in a good state but not the highest state, namely by creating formless things from nothing, and afterwards he brought the formlessness of things into the highest state by bringing them into form and order, so God did not immediately place the rational creature, that is, men and angels, in the highest state but in a good state" (Hugh of St. Victor, *Sententiae de divinitate* 1).

imperfect state of limitation and becoming toward the mysterious perfection of divine glory.

By accepting this scriptural insight concerning the shape of created existence, we are confronted with the question of the origin and meaning of nature's agonistic economy within this narrative ontology. In Hugh's interpretation, the mortal economy of nature is established as part of creation's foundational shape and is comprehended by a universal order that yields higher dimensions of created beauty. Hugh writes, "Just as the good of the whole is more beautiful because the good of a part is less, so it should be more beautiful because some part suffers a defect of good."[55] In this respect, Hugh's theology reflects both the major tradition and the modern instrumentalist theodicy inasmuch as he interprets the natural properties of dissipation, death, and conflict as part of the ordered perfection of the universal whole. Hugh writes, "For everything that God made for the sake of man he made for change and mortality, but man alone for immortality."[56] For Hugh, all creatures are divinely created with intrinsic limitations and imperfections so that "through this the universe appears more beautiful because in some part of some good a defect appears."[57]

In terms of Scripture's figures, this portrait of ontic violence as part of nature's foundational structure corresponds with the layered cosmography of the temple, which intimates an instrumentalist interpretation inasmuch as the existence of imperfections in the natural order is related to the comprehensive good of the whole. Moreover, the fact that the universe is figurated as the *sacrificial* temple implies that the formal structure of sacrifice is somehow located within the interstices of creation's traversal. However, this sacrificial form, which presupposes death as part of nature's foundational character, appears incommensurate with the hexaemeron's implicit depiction of nature's peaceful economy. With respect to the hexaemeron's ontology, ancient and modern interpreters have offered different perspectives concerning natural violence vis-à-vis God's purpose. These perspectives diverge over the Lord's speech found in Genesis 1:26–31:

> And God said, "Let the earth bring forth living creatures according to their kinds: cattle and creeping things and beasts of the earth according to their kinds." And it was so. And God made

---

55. Hugh of St. Victor, *Sententiae de divinitate* 2.
56. Hugh of St. Victor, *Adnotationes*, 66.
57. Hugh of St. Victor, *Sententiae de divinitate* 2.

> the beasts of the earth according to their kinds, and everything that creeps on the earth according to its kind. And God saw that it was good . . . *And to every beast of the earth, and to every bird of the air, and to everything that creeps on the earth, everything that has the breath of life, I have given every green plant for food.* And it was so. And God saw everything that he had made, and behold, it was very good. And there was evening and there was morning, a sixth day. (Gen 1:26, 30–31)

The minor tradition's interpretation of this passage, represented by Irenaeus of Lyon and Ephrem the Syrian, portrays the world's foundational economy as one of harmony and peace in which the consumption of flesh was forbidden for both human beings and animals. This type of interpretation broadly corresponds with the intuition of the modern contingent-fallenness theodicy, which interprets the destructive relations of created existence as the outworking of some metaphysical divergence. Such an interpretation is affirmed by the biblical scholar Gerhard von Rad, who claims that the six days posits a remarkable theological vision where "killing and slaughtering did not come into the world . . . by God's design and command." On the contrary, "the shedding of blood within the animal kingdom" and the "murderous action of human beings" are both fundamentally alien to God's creative purpose.[58] This vision of nature's original peace is also underscored by scriptural references concerning the eschatological renovation of the created world according to Isaiah (11:6–7; 25:6–9; 65:25; cf. Hos 2:18). Accordingly, these passages depict the final world in images that intimate something akin to a primordial harmony: "The wolf and the lamb shall feed together, the lion will eat straw like the ox. . . . They shall not hurt or destroy in all my holy mountain." For Isaiah, the "holy mountain," which refers to both the temple and the creaturely world, is defined by an inherent peacefulness altogether lacking in the present world of historical experience. This final ontology of peace at the world's end is further underscored by the figure of the celestial Jerusalem in which the threefold cosmography of the temple with its sacrificial pattern is transcended and fulfilled. Scripture presents that final world in its entirety as the holy of holies—a world saturated with the divine presence.

Other biblical interpreters, representing both the major tradition and modern instrumentalist theodicy, have not regarded the six days as speaking directly of an original non-predatory state of creation. In their

---

58. Rad, *Genesis*, 61.

view, the world includes destructive relations among creatures as part of its foundational character. Modern exegetes like Claus Westermann and Gordon Wenham have emphasized that the positive character of the divine provision of vegetal life does not necessarily prohibit carnivorous behavior. Westermann states: "An assignment or conveyance does not imply any prohibition; it is an action of the creator who is making provision for his creatures."[59] This interpretation of the economy of Genesis 1 accords with the Lord's positive affirmations of the natural world's violent ecology indicated by Psalm 104 and Job 38–40. These passages characterize the economic relations of the animal world (and the wider creation) as an outworking of divine Wisdom.

These two interpretive positions highlight the open character of Scripture's depiction of nature's economy, which can conform to either ontological interpretation. On the one hand, the hexaemeron describes the act of creation according to an unfolding metaphysics, which may be ultimately determined by an original desire for ontological peace, thus signifying that creation's violence is outside the divine intention. This interpretation corresponds with the modern contingent-fallenness theodicy that views the reign of death as the world's alienation from its divine source. On the other hand, along with the hexaemeron's indeterminate ontology, the protological world of Genesis also appears inscribed with the form of the sacrificial temple as part of its principal character. This indicates that the world is in some way determined by the theme of sacrifice as part of its original constitution. Again, this position is supported by scriptural passages that seemingly confirm nature's violence as expressive of Wisdom's providential order. According to this account, the original inscription of the universe as a sacrificial order would also indicate that the natural world, with its endemic strife, is instrumentally related to the universe's coming-to-be so that it might be transposed towards some deeper perfection.

When interpreting the hexaemeral narrative in isolation, I am inclined to affirm the text's portrait of ontological peace in the original creation. However, this affirmation must also be configured in view of the temple form of Genesis 2–3 and Scripture's wider figuration of the natural world, which appears to subvert the claim of nature's original peace. Thus, we are thrust against the antinomic character of the theological problem of creational violence as it is displayed in Scripture. Interpreters

---

59. Westermann, *Genesis 1–11*, 161–62.

typically resolve this antinomy by stressing one aspect of the tension in order to present a coherent picture of nature's economy vis-à-vis God's creative purpose. For example, one could stress the instrumental character of nature's destructive economy by viewing it as part of the divinely intended coming-to-be of the universe, even while acknowledging that it is also mysteriously ordered towards an eschatological transformation. By contrast, the same figural span of traversal could also be interpreted as the metaphysical foundation for some provisional *divergence* within creation. Here, the motif of creation's traversal would supply the conceptual space for reading a modern theodicy of contingent-fallenness into the world's phenomenal form.

By virtue of the figuralist disposition, our reading of the world will attempt to maintain the juxtapositional portrait given by the Scriptures to grasp the deeper meaning that supervenes through its tensions. By stressing the diversity of nature's ontology in Scripture, we can also see that this tension is encompassed by the wider figural pattern of the world's traversal insofar as both the modern instrumentalist and contingent-fallenness theodicies are interpretively comprehended by the same metaphysical structure. As such, our adjudicating the theological meaning of natural violence will not be resolved by marshaling tentative reconstructions of the purported intentions of each human author or redactor. Instead, the ambiguity will be ordered by its placement within the accumulated field of the temple form's figural web.

In view of Scripture's forms, our figural reading is now compelled to explore the theological significance of the sacrificial cosmography of the temple, which is manifested through creation's principal movement. This pattern of sacrifice is inscribed upon the world's temporal span in view of its eschatological horizon and corresponds with the central figure of the "immolation of the spotless lamb"[60] in the Hugonian ark. This examination of the principal form of the universe in the sacrificial temple will be ordered by its figural connection to the self-offering form of the divine Son. In this respect, the sacrificial temple—as a figure of the world's traversal—will disclose the *paschal character of the universe* between its beginning and end.

---

60. Hugh of St. Victor, *De arca Noe morali* 1.14.

The Paschal Character of Nature: Christ and the Sacrificial Temple

In the previous section, we saw that Hugh's ark depicted the figural connections between the hexaemeron, the garden, and the celestial Jerusalem and disclosed creation as constituted by a traversing principle from an incipient imperfection towards a more perfect realization. This pattern of being, revealed through the temple form's scriptural shape, reflects our first major figural claim regarding the divine Word's creative and providential shaping of the world. Namely, all created entities and events are enfolded by a gradualist narrative teleology, wherein all things are ultimately created *through* time and summoned to a mysterious glorification *beyond* time. This insight regarding creation's ontological form is the first of two metaphysical patterns disclosed in Scripture through the Hugonian lens. The second metaphysical pattern, which is the subject of the present section, concerns the *character* of this movement as it is manifested through the scriptural temple's orientation towards its eschatological divinization. Significantly, the figurated relation between the hexaemeron, the garden, and the celestial Jerusalem—which corresponds with Hugh's developmental metaphysics—evokes the sacrificial pattern of the temple as part of this movement. As such, the practice of sacrifice in the temple's atonement liturgy alludes to a set of cosmic realities that connect with our theodical concern. That is, the divinely mandated destruction of animals in Israel's temple speaks something of the origin and meaning of nature's *agon*.

To guide our reading, we return to Hugh's Christological figuration of the ark as the cosmic *templum dei*, which presses into the figure's sacrificial form inasmuch as the structure is oriented towards "the immolation of the spotless lamb"[61] at its center. Grover Zinn writes,

> As a symbol of Christ the central square represents the Mediator between the divine and the human. It becomes a point of transition from one mode of existence to another. The Incarnate Christ is also the point of cosmic and temporal order, for he is symbolically the center about which the seasons rotate and the central ordering point in history.[62]

The disclosure of the universe's character through the temple's reference is figurally bound to Christ's fulfillment of its sacrificial dimensions.

---

61. Hugh of St. Victor, *De arca Noe morali* 1.14.
62. Zinn, "Mandala Symbolism," 338.

THE FIGURAL SHAPE OF CREATION 107

Ultimately, the scriptural temple's sacrificial pattern speaks of creation as it is grounded upon and enfolded by the crucified and risen Jesus. This comprehensive reality is signified in Hugh's Christic reading of the ark insofar as the structure is foundationally ordered by the Word's transcendent inhabitation, which structures both the creative act (*opus creationis*) and the redemptive shape of history between the beginning and end (*opus restaurationis*).

In the Hugonian ark's conceptual and visual description, both the cosmos and history culminate with the figure of the "immolation of the spotless Lamb"[63] which stands upon the central altar in Jerusalem within the structure.

> What else does it tell you, if not to say that this cubit signifies the same person as the pillar of fire and cloud that preceded the people of Israel in the desert, illuminating them through the fire, and that protected them, overshadowing them through the cloud—he who was both awesome to the former [chosen] people in punishing sins through the fire of divine majesty and who appeared gentle to the later [chosen] people in forgiving sins through the cloud of humanity. For the sins of men, he was sacrificed on the cross like a gentle lamb, not opening his mouth; and for the righteousness of men, he was exalted by arising and ascending above the heavens.[64]

The central position of the paschal lamb, a figure of the Word's crucifixion, is indicative of Christ's thematic comprehension of the temple. The sacrificial form functions as the interpretive axis of the structure's multilayered reference. In his extensive study on the Hugonian ark, art historian Conrad Rudolph describes the paschal lamb as the interpretive key that unlocks the ark's densely layered figuration of history. He writes, "The cross or sacrifice of Christ is the 'center' of both time and space in that it is the focal point of the history of salvation for both humankind and all physical creation."[65] The structural span of the ark, which is the narrative span of scriptural time, is theologically inscribed or patterned according to the eternal Word's revelatory form as the crucified one. Boyd Taylor Coolman sums up the principle of the ark's span: "Both cosmos and history are thus Christologically structured and

---

63. Hugh of St. Victor, *De arca Noe morali* 1.14.

64. This translation of Hugh of St. Victor, *De arca Noe mystica* 1.2, is provided in Rudolph, *Mystic Ark*, 402–3.

65. Rudolph, *Mystic Ark*, 399n12.

governed—embraced by, proceeding from, flowing through, and ordered toward the incarnate Christ. In a sense, He is the formal structure of the world and history."[66] In terms of its scriptural framework, the central position of the paschal lamb provides the interpretive key through which all things are comprehended. The sacrificial form of the crucified and exalted Jesus gathers and determines the *character* of creation's movement in time. According to the inner connection of these figures in Scripture, the same Christ who upholds the cosmic temple "by his word of power" (Heb 1:4) is the "paschal lamb" (1 Cor 5:7), whose body takes up the temple's sacrificial themes and brings them to their eschatological fulfillment (Heb 10:1–10).

The scriptural understanding of sacrifice in the Christian tradition, both in terms of the temple structure and its animals, finds its comprehensive fulfillment in the paschal lamb of God whose death is the sacrificial act by which all things in heaven and earth are reconciled and brought to completion (Eph 1:10). Additionally, the paschal mystery itself is interpretively given in Scripture as bound to the cultic rituals and patterns of Israel's being. Thus, Hugh grasps the multivalent character of Israel's sacrifices as distinct temporal manifestations of the one primary reference in Christ. "For all those sacraments of earlier time, whether under the natural law or under the written, were signs, as it were, and figures of those which now have been set forth under grace."[67] Here, Hugh assumes the figural logic of the Letter to the Hebrews, where the sacrificial themes of Israel are referentially mapped and fulfilled by the revelatory life of the incarnate Word, who traverses our history and carries creation in his person to the Father. This interpretive rendition of animal sacrifice is standard traditional Christian exegesis. However, by virtue of its Christological reference, animal sacrifice is thematically connected to the pattern upon which the universe is created while also being ordered towards eschatological non-existence. In this way, the Levitical figures themselves, particularly the spilled blood and death of creatures (viz., animals), speak of created existence before the end of time insofar as they are the shadows of the crucified one, who stands as the foundation, form, and end of all things. In metaphysical terms, to the extent that these sacrificial figures are in Christ the Word, "through whom" and "for whom" all things are made, the attached meanings of the sacrifices

---

66. Coolman, *Theology of Hugh of St. Victor*, 97.
67. Hugh of St. Victor, *De Sacramentis* 1.11.1.

proliferate and extend to the farthest reaches of the created world. Thus, the animal sacrifices of Scripture—particularly as expressed in the book of Leviticus—*describe* something of the universe as it is created and shaped by God in Christ and the Holy Spirit.

This aspect of our figural venture represents a deepening of the Hugonian perception of the intersection of creation and the scriptural world. For Hugh, the natural world was read in a relatively abstract fashion in view of Scripture's discourse. For instance, in his *De tribus diebus*, he explores the sacramental character of created existence primarily under the abstract properties of God's divine life. Hugh perceives "visible things" as "representations of the invisible," wherein the sheer profusion and strange diversity of creatures—both predator and prey—testify to the glory of God's infinite Wisdom.[68] Under Hugh's conception, both text and world are wide semantic fields that outline the divine Word that stands behind all things. Yet, this outlining is relatively unidirectional insofar as the two realities interpretively converge upon the divine Word, with limited interpretive interaction between the two aspects. Our approach intends to explore the interpretive overlap between the two in a more direct way. By virtue of our prioritization of the Christocentric creational ontology, we can pursue this connection in a way that reads scriptural figures as an index of the theological character of the natural world. For instance, Scripture displays the temple's primary antitype as the incarnate Jesus Christ (John 2:21; Rev 21:22) while simultaneously extending the temple's reference to the universe's existence in time. Likewise, the figures of sacrifice find their primary antitype in the crucified and exalted Christ (Heb 10:1–10) while also pointing towards the shape of the world between its beginning and end. Therefore, these sacrificial figures are lodged within the temple's figural span, which speaks of its unfolding character. We will now explore the descriptive breadth of these figures as theological signs of created existence in time.

To pursue the creational implications of sacrifice first requires an examination of the textual shape of the temple's sacrificial properties. A survey of the Bible's depiction of sacrifice reveals levels of distinction that underscore an important ontological ambiguity. Sacrifice is not a univocal reality in Scripture but is subjected to a diversity of meanings that verges upon conceptual antinomy or contradiction. The practice

---

68. Hugh of St. Victor, *De tribus diebus* 16.1. For a discussion of the sacramental perception of *De tribus diebus*, see Nieuwenhove, "Retrieving a Sacramental Worldview," 539–48.

of sacrifice is divinely willed (Exod 12:23–24; Lev 1:1) and divinely displeasing (Ps 40:6; Hos 6:6; Matt 9:13), given in view of sin and guilt (Lev 4:1—6:7; Rom 3:25; Heb 9–10) and required irrespective of sin's presence (Lev 1–3). By virtue of our figuralist thinking, one would expect this fragmented depiction of Scripture's sacrificial ontology to reveal something of the world's life precisely in its diversity.

In terms of the specific character of scriptural sacrifice, the Bible displays about fifteen types of ritual offerings presented in the outer precincts of the temple or tabernacle.[69] These sacrifices were divinely commanded as the means by which Israel approached the mysterious presence of the living God. These sacrifices were defined by the Hebrew term for gift or offering (*qorban*), and they embody a sense of passage or "drawing near"[70] as part of their theological shape. At the center of this passage or traversal is the body and blood of the divinely created animal whose life is offered up to God by the high priest as he passes through the veil of the temple. "He shall slaughter the goat of the sin offering that is for the people and bring its blood inside the curtain, and do with its blood as he did with the blood of the bull, sprinkling it upon the mercy seat and before the mercy seat" (Lev 16:15). Remarkably, neither Leviticus nor the rest of the Old Testament provides an exhaustive rationale for these sacrificial offerings of animal and vegetal life. The metaphysical logic of the sacrificial ceremonies is passed over in relative silence. As Gerhard von Rad puts it: "While the Old Testament is very full of allusions to the divine activity wherever it becomes effective among men, and full too of the most intensive address and of 'revelation,' there is a realm of silence and secrecy in respect to what God works in sacrifice."[71] The practice of killing and offering certain animals is simply a theological given woven into Scripture's layered discourse concerning Israel's approach to God.

Despite this laconic presence, Scripture does provide a clue to its theological meaning in the figure of the "blood." Blood is the life (*Nephesh*) of creatures, which belongs exclusively to God (Gen 9:3–5). This figure of animate life is interpretively bound to the temple's layered distinctions,

---

69. Among the fifteen variations there are five main classes of offering that may be divided into two overarching categories: sacrifices that appear to *restore* the covenant—the sin offering (*hattat*) and guilt offering (*asham*); and sacrifices that *express* Israel's communion with God—the burnt offering (*olah*), the cereal offering (*minah*), and the peace offering (*shelamim*). See Fretheim, *Pentateuch*, 127–31.

70. Milgrom, *Leviticus*, 17.

71. Rad, *Old Testament Theology*, 260.

which display the shedding and offering of blood in the outer court as the means of creation's passage to God beyond the veil. The blood of Israel's animals signifies the divinely given form of life's passage in that it is both graciously given and demanded by God. In this sacrificial movement, the shedding of blood appears as both the way of life's destruction and the possibility of its renewal through atonement. In this way, the scriptural shape of blood sacrifice in the cosmic temple maps the enveloping mystery of creaturely existence as life given, offered, lost, and renewed—all in God's creative providence.

The Bible's overarching Christological coherence reinforces this creational or cosmic meaning of blood. Here, the creational dimensions of the temple, the priesthood, and its sacrifices converge upon the self-offering form of the crucified Jesus, whose shed blood (life) both establishes and defines the extended reference of the temple and its sacrifices.[72] This vision rests upon the foundational claim that the entire span of Israel's Law, including the temple and its sacrifices, find perfect fulfillment in the paschal mystery. This underscores the significance of these figures as metaphysical markers of the Christic character of the universe. The accumulated figures of the cosmic temple, the priesthood, and the sacrificial "blood" are articulations of the creative principle from which all things proceed and toward which all things converge.

In its most basic ontological reference, the sacrificial forms of Scripture present a different ordering of reality from that displayed in other figurations of the temple form. Unlike the celestial Jerusalem, the world implied by the sacrificial temple with its outer court assumes ontic violence as part of its existence. To apprehend the theological depth of this distinction, it is necessary to pass into the specific character of animal sacrifice as it is given in its scriptural context. In particular, we must analyze sacrifice under two key aspects: first, animal sacrifice enfigurates the world under the mysterious presence of sin and evil, respectively depicted by the sin and guilt offerings (Lev 4:1—6:7; 16–17); second, animal sacrifice also enfigurates the world's being irrespective of sin's encroachment, respectively displayed by the burnt offerings and the peace offerings (Lev 1–3). These two distinct modalities of the sacrificial form indicate a world

---

72. Mary Douglas writes, "Sacrifice invokes the whole cosmos, life and death . . . and it so happens that Leviticus focuses its metaphysical resources on that very point between life and death. With sacrifice Leviticus expresses its doctrine of blood, of atonement, of covenant between God and his people. If we read the instructions for sacrifice and try to imagine them being carried out, we can see it as a form of philosophy by enactment" (Douglas, *Leviticus as Literature*, 66–67).

fraught with ambiguity, as the violence of nature—figured by animal sacrifice—appears both as a declension from God's creative purpose *and* as a divinely willed reality. This dual-aspect depiction of the sacrificial form mirrors the wider scriptural tension concerning nature's ontic violence. By interpreting the scriptural shape of the universe according to the figural dimensions of the sacrificial temple, it seems that both a contingent-fallenness interpretation and an instrumentalist interpretation serve as fitting descriptions of its mysterious form.

According to the contingent-fallenness interpretation, the cosmic temple's inclusion of animal bloodshed and death as part of Israel's restorative passage towards God reveals something of the character of sin and evil within the universe. It presumes sin's deforming and effacing presence. On this subject, the research of Jacob Milgrom is especially noteworthy. According to Milgrom, the sweep of Israel's sacrificial actions, especially in their expiatory form, have in view the reparation of the temple as the place of divine inhabitation. According to Milgrom's thesis, the various sacrificial forms are enacted to purify the temple of a type of spiritual pollution that attaches itself by means of sinful actions. Milgrom writes:

> Why the urgency to purge the sanctuary? The answer lies in the postulate: the God to Israel will not abide in a polluted sanctuary. The merciful God will tolerate a modicum of pollution. But there is a point of no return. If the pollution continues to accumulate the end is inexorable: "The cherubim lifted their wings" (Ezek 11:22). The divine chariot flies heavenward and the sanctuary is left to its doom.[73]

Put differently, the ontic presence of sin deforms the figural world, rendering it deformed and inhospitable to the divine presence. Only by the offering of blood through a variety of rituals is the cosmic temple repaired and made fit to its purpose. Why does animal death have this effect? Or, for what reasons does God require this sacrifice? Milgrom attempts to reconstruct the origin of this practice as a holdover from Israel's ancient Near Eastern background. The scriptural text itself, however, offers no theoretical accounting of this type of sacrificial metaphysic; instead, the rituals are presented without comment. Yet, when perceived within the wider figural (and canonical) perspective of the Christian tradition, the animals offered in these rites enfigurate the sacrificial form of Israel's

---

73. Milgrom, "Israel's Sanctuary," 396–97.

Christ, whose death gathers and redeems the world. The destruction of the sacrificial animal thus appears as a shadowed articulation of the Word's suffering and dying in view of creation's bondage to sin and death (Heb 10:1–10). This Christic interpretation of sacrifice is well-attested in the tradition. For instance, Hugh of St. Victor perceives the sacrificial "blood of the lamb" as a figure that encompasses the historical "passion of Christ."[74] Nevertheless, the *creational* implications of expiation have not been as fully explored in this connection. We must foreground the scriptural *distinction* that marks animal life to draw out the creational breadth of sacrifice.

The scriptural ontology of the sacrificial animal, like the practice of sacrifice in general, is presented in the Bible with little theological explanation. Instead, the ceremonies and accompanying ritual distinctions appear as assumed realities already embedded in Israel's covenantal encounter with the living God. Nevertheless, despite its laconic form, the sacrificial animal itself, in its scriptural manifestation bespeaks a web of figural relations that express something of the fundamental nature of the world. Most significantly, Israel's practice of sacrificing animals in the temple court is conditioned by the principal *distinction* made between clean and unclean creatures. Under the terms of the Mosaic covenant, God commanded Israel to sacrifice (and eat) only those animals that were considered *clean*, which by implication eliminated all creatures except those from their own flocks and herds.

> This is the law pertaining to beast and bird and every living creature that moves through the waters and every creature that swarms upon the earth, to make a distinction between the unclean and the clean and between the living creature that may be eaten and the living creature that may not be eaten. (Lev 11:46–47)

The text's relative silence concerning the precise rationale for the distinction—which stretches beyond nonhuman animals into the human social sphere—has led to a proliferation of interpretations, both premodern and modern, concerning its root meaning.[75] Whereas traditional exegesis

---

74. Hugh of St. Victor, *De sacramentis* 2.8.5.

75. It is unlikely that the categorical divisions of animals in Leviticus presuppose a moral quality as if animals designated unclean are somehow intrinsically disordered; rather, the Leviticus text presupposes God's concern and compassion for all that God has made. Mary Douglas has argued that the negative designations for certain creatures (e.g., "unclean" and "abomination") served as protective laws instructing human beings

perceived the distinction as a tropological reference to the virtues and vices pertaining to the soul's condition, modern interpreters have tended to view the distinction in terms of aesthetic or ethical concerns. Although there is no consensus regarding the original meaning of the distinction, there is no question that this distinction came to embody Israel's election among the surrounding Gentile nations.[76] Such is presupposed by Scripture, which delineates Israel's identity in terms of covenantal obligations centered upon the distinction between clean and unclean (Lev 18:3, 24; 20:24–26).

This theme of elective distinction is brought forward with considerable force in the book of Acts, which announces the beginning of the church's mission to the Gentiles in terms of an abrogation of the ritual distinction between clean and unclean creatures (Acts 10:9–16). Thus, insofar as the clean animals are bound to Israel's covenantal relationship, they figurally represent the *form* of Israel's election, given for the sake of the nations. In this figurative sense, the clean animals embody the shape of Israel's life as one given up (or called) for the many in a sacrificial offering. In Christian terms, this vocation of Israel's election is perfectly embodied and summed up in the mysterious form of the Son of God, who takes up the figural threads of Israel's sacrificial being and fulfills them. Here, Scripture implicitly sketches the sacrificial distinction of the clean offered for the unclean onto the wider frame of history.

In its scriptural articulation, it is significant that the notion of distinction is not bound exclusively to the Mosaic covenant but appears embedded in the divine ordering of the world at its very foundation. Noah's inclusion of seven of every clean animal as opposed to two of every unclean animal highlights the structural distinction in the primeval narrative (Gen 2:2–3; 8:20). In terms of its delineation, many scholars have noted that Leviticus 11 also elucidates the distinction among animate creatures in terms of the foundational categories of the hexaemeron.[77] Accordingly, the book of Leviticus frames the distinction against

---

to avoid such animals in "a demonstration of God's compassion." I agree with this interpretation as it accords these designations with the notion of God's status as the good creator of all things great and small; however, such an "ecological interpretation" cannot limit the text's import, and thus I propose a wider figural application. See Douglas, *Leviticus as Literature*, 134–75.

76. For discussion of the clean-unclean distinction, see Fretheim, *Pentateuch*, 131–36.

77. Mary Douglas writes, "Notice that the language and classifications of Genesis are the same as those on which Leviticus 11 has laid out the dietary laws. In each

the wider scriptural background of creation as divinely desired, ordered, and loved. One might even argue that the emphatic affirmation of God's creative love for all creatures, which echoes throughout the canon (Gen 1:1–31; cf. Wis 11:24; Pss 104; 145), is implicitly manifested as the sacrificial distinction given to the created world at its founding. To put it another way, the revelation of the distinction unveils an implicit ontology of sacrifice as a part of the formal structure of the world. This reading of Israel's sacrificial ontology in view of the entire sweep of time corresponds with the way Hugh grasps the nature of scriptural figures in view of history's Christocentric coherence. Accordingly, Hugh perceives the sacrificial patterns of the scriptural Israel as manifestations of a real participation in their fulfilled referent, the eternal Word's saving passage in created time. The animal sacrifices "under the written law" were "a kind of image or figure" of the "body of truth" that is the manifestation of Christ's visible form in history.[78] Thus, the pattern given through the scriptural distinction between creatures is interpretively bound up with the creative form that constitutes the wider shape of creation. In this regard, the sacrificial distinction of Israel enfigurates the *Christological* pattern of the creaturely world at its metaphysical origin.

The theological implication of the sacrificial distinction as constitutive of the world's being is emphasized by Ephraim Radner, who suggests that Leviticus 11 provides an outline of a sacrificial dynamic whereby "clean animals exist for the sake of all the others, sacrificing themselves, as it were, in the world newly restored and in the place of the unclean."[79] For Radner, the cosmic reference of the sacrificial animal, based upon its distinction, intimates the reality of "offering" at the "basis of creation." This assessment follows the logic of animal distinction in terms of its creational import. The sacrificial form thus appears lodged in the interstices of creation irrespective of sin and evil. Here one might perceive the universe's sacrificial structure, which undergirds nature's violence, as granted to the world at its foundation in order to manifest something of its divine character and purpose. From this vantage, it is relevant that Scripture

---

environment teeming swarmers complement a range of more differentiated creatures: in the waters, fish with fins and scales; in the air, birds with wings and two legs; and on land the various four-legged animals, and finally the whole series crowned by the ruminants with proper hooves, the domestic flocks and herds set apart for consecration" (Douglas, *Leviticus as Literature*, 158). See also Fretheim, *Pentateuch*, 125–27.

78. Hugh of St. Victor, *De sacramentis* 1.11.8.
79. Radner, *Leviticus*, 108.

displays the sacrificial animal in non-expiatory contexts—namely, the peace offering (*shelamin*), the burnt offering (*'olah*), et al.—which seem to indicate *something* concerning the relational form of the finite world. In terms of figurative import, it points to the underlying significance of relationality and costly offering as a constitutive theme of creation's unfolding span. This type of depiction, in turn, seems to confirm something of an instrumentalist vision of nature's ontic character, inasmuch as the interactive relational order of nature, including its violence, is scripturally inscribed upon the world as it unfolds with time.

In sum, the scriptural character of the universe displayed through the threefold pattern of the temple testifies to the mysterious presence of violence and death as part of creation's phenomenal order. However, in the wider scriptural landscape, the distinction between the scriptural temple's sacrificial form and its eschatological referent unveils a striking ontological disjunction lodged in created existence: a disjunction that mirrors wider tensions concerning nature's economy. Accordingly, the scriptural presence of animal sacrifice—an intrinsically violent and destructive form—becomes a cipher revealing the underlying shape of creation's passage, inasmuch as it is a property of the cosmic temple. Here, nature's *economia* of violence is scripturally rendered as a mysterious reality ordered towards an eschatological transformation and fulfillment. The temporal span of created existence, constituted by the tempestuous surges of life's history, is defined by the distinct properties of the sacrificial temple, with the bloodied bodies of animate creatures slaughtered and offered. In this respect, the animal body speaks of a different ordering of the world insofar as it appears to conflict with the divine peace of its final denouement.

Yet, even with these important claims, the precise origin of nature's ontic strife remains obscured by the same web of figures. Indeed, the sacrificed animal—a figural indicator of nature's being—appears in Scripture as both a divinely ordered form and a form at odds with the ultimate *telos* of creation. Thus, the scriptural shape of the sacrificial animal is displayed both in reference to sin's incursion into creation (sacrifices of expiation and atonement) and as part of creation's foundational order (presumed by the created distinction of clean and unclean animals). It appears that this sacrificial ontology mirrors the juxtaposition of creational realities found elsewhere in Scripture. Creation's economy of violence appears as both a fallen reality (Gen 1:30; cf. Isa 11:6–9) and as the unfolding of God's providential wisdom (Ps 104; Job 38–41). This leads to our second major figural claim: the sacrificial pattern of the cosmic temple reveals the universe as constituted by an ontology of offering; creation's passage to God, irrespective of sin's encroachment, is founded upon the reality of the sacrificial form. The scriptural concept of sacrificial offering, displayed as an intrinsic property of nature, indicates a remarkable relational ontology at the center of created existence.

This relational ontology outlined by the sacrificial figures brings us back to Scripture's primary referent: the crucified and exalted Christ who interprets creation's being. This Christological form, explicated by Scripture's sacrificial logic, will frame our exploration of the triune God's creative agency in view of the unfolding ontology of the finite world. Both the sacrificial pattern of the temple and its animals are thus the shadowed patterns of the Word's revelation of both the eternal character of the divine nature and the unfolding content of the created world. Taken as a figural description, the scriptural pattern of sacrifice sketches creation as ordered by a relational ontology of offering manifested and fulfilled in Christ's movement through history. The sacrificial form of Christ's being *is* thus the key image of this world's unfolding span in all its aspects.

CONCLUSION

In this chapter, we began developing a natural theology grounded upon Scripture's figural ontology. We used Hugh of St. Victor's profound Christological metaphysics, which grounds and authorizes the interpretive coinherence of the world and Scripture to discern the shape of creation in view of the divine Word's textual embodiment. To see how creation was enfigurated by Scripture, we followed Hugh's symbolic exegesis of the ark which unveiled the universe through the juxtapositional presence of Scripture's three-tiered structures. Through this Hugonian lens we abstracted the ark-temple's referential contours within Scripture and discerned figural connections through which we were able to engage creation's ontology. Three of these figures—the hexaemeron, the garden, and the celestial Jerusalem—outlined the metaphysical shape of nature's traversal. The fourth figure, the sacrificial form of the temple, underscored the character of creation's movement. In view of our theodical concern, these scriptural figures intimate a series of theological claims concerning the divine shaping of the world. This juxtaposed arrangement of images and content will form the basis for our theological exploration in the next chapter.

In review, the hexaemeron, Eden, and the celestial Jerusalem outline creation's imperfect foundation as it anticipates its eschatological fulfillment. The intrinsic relation between these figures indicates that the natural world's being was given through an ordered passage, temporally and metaphysically, that corresponds with the temple form's scriptural reference. Namely, the figures outline the finite world as intrinsically constituted by a narrative of traversal, from relative imperfection towards an incomprehensible eschatological fullness transparent to the divine presence. In conjunction with this narrative passage, the sacrificial pattern of the cosmic temple illuminates the ontological character of this unfolding traversal. The sacrificial temple's animals and bloodstained altar present a range of figures that are ostensibly absent from creation's ultimate *telos*. By taking the sacrificial temple as a figure of the universe, the distinct images associated with sacrifice thus present the theme of creation in its temporal passage between its beginning and end. The figured content of animal sacrifice leads us to conclude that nature is both subject to some type of deviation and constituted by an ontology of sacrifice irrespective of sin's presence.

This accumulation of creational figures, with their expansive referrals, provides a range of perspectives concerning creation that challenge any straightforward construal of the origin and meaning of nature's violence. Thus, our figural exploration brings us back to the same tensions concerning creation's *agon* that exist at the surface of the biblical text. Nevertheless, even in their continuity and divergence these figural images outline something of the comprehensive order of the natural world as created by God in Christ and the Spirit. This scriptural array reveals the parameters by which we will begin to sketch our theological interpretation of the phenomena in question. Our task now compels us to develop these figural patterns as the primary interpretive structures for our theological narrative.

4

The Figural Coherence of Christ and the Suffering World

ONE DAY IN THE Egyptian wilderness a hyena approached Abba Macarius (300–391 CE) while he was praying silently in his cell. Observing the presence of the hyena outside, the monk opened the door and saw the animal gently holding a newborn pup in her mouth. He took the pup into his hands, diligently examined it, and discerned that the creature had been born with a congenital blindness. Abba Macarius then prayed over the pup and placed his spittle in its eyes, which immediately restored its vision and assured its survival. The next day, the mother hyena returned to the cell, this time bringing with her the hide of a recently killed animal and presented it to Macarius as a type of thanksgiving offering for the healing of the pup. Upon seeing the slaughtered animal, Macarius reproached the mother hyena and enjoined her to kill no longer and to feed only upon those creatures that had already died. He further offered to feed her if she could not find enough carrion to eat. The hyena assented to Macarius' instructions, and throughout her life, the hyena would return to him for food.[1]

This brief depiction of the encounter between the saintly Macarius and nature's predatorial character, represented by the hyena, manifests the world's theological identity as given in Scripture. Within the narrative, the natural world created by God with its sickness, bloodshed, and death is transformed by the mediation of the holy man, whose objection to nature's present form appears as a proleptic manifestation of the

---

1. An English translation of "St. Macarius and the Grateful Hyena," can be found in Waddell, *Beasts and Saints*, 12–14.

eschatological kingdom of God. There is an implicit aporia unveiled by the tension between the world's present dissipative form and its eschatological fulfillment that reflects the complex articulation of the world's life as disclosed in Scripture. This tension expresses the incomplete character of our theological understanding of creation's unfolding in time. The world seems to point in two different directions ontologically: its coming-to-be is shaped by endemic strife and destruction, yet its end surpasses its traversing form. The unfolding universe, with its ontic violence and suffering, is God's creation, yet that very divine creation is summoned beyond its temporal limits towards an eschatological transformation stripped of all metaphysical violence. These narrative parameters imply the need for further exploration of the meaning of nature's *agon* in terms of scriptural revelation. Thus, it is in accord with the Christological form manifested in Scripture that we seek to sketch a fuller theological understanding of the narrative shape of the divinely created world, replete with creatures like the liver-fluke worm, the ichneumon wasp, and the hyena.

By speaking of the eternal mystery of Christ, whose being and action creates and redeems the world, the creative figures of Scripture convey God's incomprehensible nature and the metaphysical theme of the created world. Because of this referential tethering of Scripture to the visible form of the crucified and exalted Jesus, who concurrently reveals God and the life of the world, it follows that the illuminating patterns of Scripture's figural order operate in the same conceptual space as that of theodical reflection, treading along the mysterious terrain that negotiates the world's being in view of the almighty love of God. Seeing that we have already unearthed certain figurated structures in Scripture through engagement with Hugh of St. Victor's mystic ark, we can now explore these structural patterns further in terms of their revelatory extension.

For this task, we will constructively engage these figural patterns in terms of their mysterious reference to God and the world. This will provide a way of narrating the form of God's infinite agency, which is centered upon the disclosure of Christ's sacrificial life as given in Scripture. Furthermore, these same patterns, again in their Christic reference, will also speak something of the world's passage through time with its fragile beauty and endemic limitations. From within the revelation of the paschal mystery of Christ, we can begin to more faithfully grasp the nature of the world's existence with its disturbing magnitudes of creaturely violence, suffering, and death.

This undertaking admits the scope of the world's suffering as it is manifested according to the scientific and moral configurations of the late-modern period. By this, we assume that the entropic character of the universe makes the dissolution and death of creatures an intrinsic feature of the world's coming-to-be. Moreover, our constructive reflections refuse to sidestep the severity of the problem by recourse to what I have previously designated as the eliminativist theodicy, a categorical approach that seeks to recast the ostensible suffering of animals as a morally neutral feature of the world. My refusal of the eliminativist perspective is broadly conditioned by several theological and philosophical objections, along with my concern to address the question of nature's suffering in its most obdurate form.[2] This concern entails rejecting any position that negotiates the problem away by denying the reality of animal suffering. The following set of reflections will pursue an interpretation that admits the problem of nature's suffering in its most intractable state.

This search for a theological narrative of nature's *agon* presupposes the figural insights of our previous investigation. They provide the *revealed basis* for developing a set of theological-metaphysical elaborations that explicate creation's agonistic history in light of God's revealed form. Based upon this investigation, our project will expound a theological narrative of creational suffering that operates as a type of *argumentum ex convenientia*, an argument that is "fitting" or compatible with our figural claims. By cultivating the disclosive pressures exerted by Scripture concerning the nature of God and the world, an implicit narrative will emerge that fits the accumulated set of theological notions derived from the inquiry. This theodical exploration is not intended as the definitive logical explanation of what *must* be the case vis-à-vis God and the world; rather, our task sketches a fitting narrative that captures the textured contours of Scripture's figural landscape.

In pursuit of this fitting theological narrative, our chapter will be divided into two parts: first, we will briefly recapitulate the patterns

---

2. Both early and late modern articulations of this type of interpretation trade upon highly contentious theories of perceptual consciousness in animals. The eliminativist approach, in my judgment, lacks a sufficient empirical basis to overturn our commonsense apprehension of the suffering of nonhuman animals. Additionally, from a figuralist perspective there is a limited theological basis for assuming the eliminativist interpretation and it is subject to countervailing evidence. For instance, animals in Scripture both "praise" (Pss 148:10; 150:6; Dan 3:57–59) and "cry" (Joel 1:20; Job 38:41) to God. This is, at the least, suggestive of a more textured view of animals' inner-lives. See my previous discussion of eliminativist theodicies in chapter 2.

discerned through our engagement of Scripture via the Hugonian ark and map out its depiction of the world's being; second, we will interpretively move beyond Hugh's theology and our figural exegesis, and engage these structuring insights in a more theologically speculative manner. This will entail interpreting the figures as bound to the form of the crucified Jesus, who simultaneously unveils God and the world. As a work of constructive theology, our figural approach will creatively take up and configure some of the conceptual and thematic resources of the Christian theodical tradition as previously described in chapter 2. Ultimately, this theological exploration will furnish a narrative framework rooted in the revealed life of Christ that envisions nature's *agon* as a fallen reality that mysteriously reflects the form of the Son of God in his sacrificial traversal.

THE FIGURAL STRUCTURES: TRAVERSAL AND SACRIFICE

In our engagement with Hugh's figuration of the ark we discerned within Scripture two interpretive patterns that appear to straddle the mysterious distinction that obtains between God and the world. The first figured structure was a pattern of traversal, metaphysically described by Hugh of St. Victor as the unfolding transition of created being from an incipient "formlessness to highest beauty."[3] Hugh engaged this pattern of traversal as a description of God's action in Christ, both in the work of creation and the work of salvation. For instance, Hugh interprets the creation story of Genesis 1 (the hexaemeron) as a developmental process whereby the finite world receives greater form only gradually through intervals of time. Besides structuring God's creative action, the figurated structure in its scriptural recapitulation also reveals the character of the universe in terms of an overarching narrative trajectory. Notably, the scripturally described horizons of the created world (the garden and the celestial Jerusalem) reveal creation to be ordered by a type of movement (*motus*) from protological imperfection towards an eschatological glorification characterized by a definitive ontological peace.

The second figurated structure discerned was the pattern of sacrifice centered upon the paschal mystery of Christ, which in its scriptural articulation encompassed the temple form with its bloodied altar and animals. This figural display of Scripture's sacrificial forms reveals the

---

3. Hugh of St. Victor, *Sententiae de divinitate* 1.

world as founded upon an intrinsic relational structure patterned according to the suffering form of the Son of God. This sacrificial ontology is expressed primarily through the scriptural notion of *distinction*, which, when interpreted in its cosmic reference, indicates a field of receptivity, exchange, and offering as part of creation's fundamental order. In other words, the being of the world appears foundationally shaped by a sacrificial form that reflects the underlying Christological principle, which is the "primordial cause of all things; that is, God Himself."[4]

As an index of divine truth, these figures defy the interpretive constraints assumed by a historicist ontology, which submerges scriptural meaning within a positivistic ontology of time. In contrast, our approach assumes that these figurated patterns, as the inner discourse of God's Word, speak of *the finite world* as it is creatively posited from nothingness. The abstracted patterns of traversal and sacrifice are thus akin to *a priori* ontological forms that disclose the revealed truth about God and the created world. These forms are extended and recapitulated across the vast expanse of creaturely existence in its profuse multiplicity and diversity. As Ephraim Radner writes,

> It is not the case that Scripture "documents" the created world, such that there is a world in its historical forms that Scripture "documents," like a witness who gives a recorded statement of testimony with respect to this or that event. It is just the opposite: the world in its temporal appearance is a record of Scripture, that is, the created trace of God's own creating Word.[5]

Rather than treating the patterns of traversal and sacrifice as a limited set of historical referents, our approach instead affirms their revelatory density as overarching principles of the mysterious act of creation.

I want to stress that the act of reading scriptural figures as a divine disclosure is not an idiosyncratic interpretation but rather one that formally represents the prevailing exegetical disposition of the Christian theological tradition.[6] This tradition interpreted the natural world in light of the textual forms and patterns of the Scriptures, which are grounded in the mystery of God's trinitarian self-revelation. When Hugh of St. Victor interpreted creation as a type of sacramental "book" that signified the

---

4. Hugh of St. Victor, *Sententiae de divinitate* 2.
5. Radner, *Chasing the Shadow*, 20.
6. See the collection of essays in Meer and Mandelbrote, *Nature and Scripture*.

"invisible wisdom of God,"[7] which is Christ Jesus, he was performing an action that was carried out by many Christian theologians in both the East and the West. Conceptually, this scriptural hermeneutic was enacted and animated by the implicative force of the church's theological metaphysics. Under this ontological vision, the scriptural world functions as a revelation of creation's temporal form as it is divinely shaped according to the visible disclosure of Christ's incarnate life. Our approach takes up this traditional perception as a way of searching out the mysterious "discourse" of nature's suffering in light of its Christological principle.

In terms of this interpretive disposition, the truthful description of divine creation appears through the figurated patterns of traversal and sacrifice precisely in their Christological significance. To recap, the patterns that we have discerned among Scripture's figural connections seem to indicate the following about the finite creation: (1) That the finite world is structured by a metaphysics of traversal wherein being unfolds successively through increasing degrees of form; (2) That the finite world is comprehended by an ultimate eschatological horizon beyond history, which abjures ontic violence; and (3) That the finite world's traversal into subsistence is foundationally inscribed with a sacrificial ontology that intimates limit, exchange, and offering as essential aspects of creation's manifestation through time.

While not strictly contradictory, this set of theological claims possesses a certain degree of tension that is mirrored in Scripture's wider discourse concerning the natural world. Namely, nature's economy appears in Scripture as both divinely ordered (Ps 104; Job 38–40) and deficient with respect to its eschatological fulfillment (Isa 11:6–9; Rom 8:18–25). In terms of figural theology, we cannot grasp and elevate one aspect of the world's being and cancel out the others without obscuring its revelatory fullness. Thus, our interpretive stance assumes that the revealed truth about God and the world in Scripture emerges through these jointly posited truths. The multiple perspectives of Scripture belong together as theological goads to structure our theoretical exploration. This constructive theological task will engage the figurated structures in their Christological comprehension to discern something of the revealed shape of God's creative action and the character of creaturely existence.

---

7. Hugh of St. Victor, *De tribus diebus* 4.3.

THE FIGURAL FORM OF JESUS: THE DIVINE WORLD AND THE CREATED WORLD

The Sacrificial Traversal: The Being and Act of God

The theological reach of figuration ultimately depends upon the Christocentric metaphysics that frames all things. Insofar as Scripture is the way God utters the world into being through Christ, all the words of Scripture in their clustered connections narrate something of the divine truth of the world in God's creative providence. This traditional theological vision is aptly expressed by Maximus the Confessor, who writes that Christ "ineffably concealed himself in the logoi of beings" and "consented to be embodied through letters, syllables, and sounds" of Scripture.[8] The first aspect of our interpretive exploration will therefore trace out the theological implications of the figurated structures of traversal and sacrifice in terms of their *divine* reference in the mystery of Christ. The revealed patterns will evoke something of the eternal form of God's *Being* and *Action*. This initial venture into the figural revelation of God's character engages the divine term of the theodical question, which, as previously mentioned, straddles the mysterious distinction between the uncreated and the created. Once we have gathered some key metaphysical insights into the Christological shape of God's being and action, we will subsequently take up this emergent portrait with our figural exploration of the created term, that is, the natural world's agonistic form.

The Divine Being: Trinity and Sacrifice

In its primary *divine* reference, the scriptural forms of traversal and sacrifice are ultimately anchored to the incarnate revelation of Jesus Christ, who encompasses the breadth of Scripture's verbal order (Luke 24:27, 44–46). As Hugh of St. Victor describes it: "the whole of Divine Scripture is one book, and that one book is Christ, for the whole divine scripture speaks of and is fulfilled in Christ."[9] The disclosive fullness of these figural patterns is given exhaustively in the life and death of Jesus of Nazareth, whose temporal existence defines the character of Scripture's sacrificial traversal. Scripture narrates Christ's eternal form as he who is sent by the Father in the traversal of creation (Gal 4:4–5; 1 John 4:9) and he who

---

8. Maximus the Confessor, *Ambiguum* 33.
9. Hugh of St. Victor, *De arca Noe morali* 2.11.

offers himself in divine sacrifice for the sake of creation's reconciliation and fulfillment (Eph 5:1).

When perceived as the visible icon of the divine nature (Col 1:15), the figurated patterns of the scripturally described Christ possess an analogical depth that discloses the infinite life and essence of God. This interpretive connection of the scriptural form of Jesus with the mystery of God's infinite life accords with the traditional theological axiom that God's action in the *economia* unveils the immanent shape of God's infinite divine life. As Karl Rahner famously writes, "The Trinity of the economy of salvation is the immanent Trinity and vice versa."[10] Historically, the scriptural description of the crucified and exalted Jesus precipitated the development of the trinitarian dogma, which captured the prevailing intelligibility of the mystery of salvation given amongst Scripture's differentiated claims. Likewise, insofar as the figurated forms of traversal and sacrifice describe the shape of Christ's visible revelation, they also disclose, by analogy, the immanent form of God's eternal subsistence. There are, of course, dangers involved with plunging into an overly ambitious exploration of the intra-trinitarian life of God. In order to avoid the temptation of an excessive narration of God's infinite life, my task here is limited to setting forth a rather traditional articulation of God's trinitarian distinctions in light of Christ's figurated form.

The scriptural manifestation of Jesus of Nazareth is the visible narrative of the eternal Son's hypostatic form, which simultaneously reveals the divine hypostases of the Father and the Holy Spirit. According to the traditional *taxis* of the immanent Trinity, the Father eternally generates (or begets) the Son, whose property is the eternal *reception* and *sacrificial offering* of all that the Son has received from the Father. The sacrificial character of the Son's eternal form is manifested in history in the visible mission of the crucified and exalted Christ, who is sent to gather and unite heaven and earth in his sacrificial return to the Father. Augustine writes,

> Wherefore the apostle says, that "all things are gathered together in one in Christ, both which are in heaven and which are on earth." . . . And thus, through that single sacrifice in which the Mediator was offered up, the one sacrifice of which the many victims under the law were types, heavenly things are brought into peace with earthly things, and earthly things with heavenly. Wherefore, as the same apostle says: "For it pleased the Father

---

10. Rahner, *More Recent Writings*, 87 (original emphasis).

that in Him should all fullness dwell: and, having made peace through the blood of His cross, by Him to reconcile all things to Himself: by Him, I say, whether they be things in earth, or things in heaven."[11]

This visage of Christ's sacrificial obedience to the Father analogically manifests the invisible property or character of the Son's incommunicable subsistence. The incarnate sending and self-offering of Christ from and to the Father *in time* discloses the way the Son eternally hypostatizes the divine nature as the Father's image. Thus, the paschal mystery not only unveils the Son's eternal property but also narrates the mysterious depths of the Father's divine form. "Jesus said to them, 'Truly, truly, I say to you, the Son can do nothing of his own accord, but only what he sees the Father doing; for whatever he does, that the Son does likewise'" (John 5:19). Commenting on this passage, Augustine writes,

> The reason he does what he sees the Father doing is that he is from the Father. He does not do other things likewise, like a painter copying pictures he has seen painted by someone else; nor does he do the same things differently, like the body forming letters which the mind has thought; but whatever the Father does, he says, the same Son also does likewise. "The same," he said; and also, "likewise"; thus showing that the working of the Father and of the Son is equal and indivisible, and yet the Son's working comes from the Father. That is why the Son cannot do anything of himself except what he sees the Father doing.[12]

In the revelation of Christ's sacrificial traversal there is thus an eternal imaging of the sacrificial form of the Father, who eternally donates the divine fullness to the Son. By extension, the two co-inherent sacrificial relations of the Father and Son together by way of spiration constitute the hypostatic identity of the Holy Spirit. The theologian Michael Hanby offers an apt summary of this Augustinian trinitarian *ordo*, writing:

> The Father is eternally Father precisely as donating his being without remainder to the Son; the Son is Son precisely in receiving himself, which is to say in receiving this act of self-donation from the Father, and thus also as offering the being given in love from the Father back to the Father in an act of mutual embrace (Augustine, *De Trin.*, II.1.2). Because God is what he has and gives what he is, this mutual embrace, this *vinculum amoris*,

11. Augustine, *Enchiridion* 62.
12. Augustine, *Trinity* 2.3.

which is, in a sense, the distance simultaneously uniting and distinguishing the Father and the Son, is no less the divine essence than the Father and the Son are, and thus is wholly a third person.[13]

According to this trinitarian ontology, the Son's *iconic* "sacrificial" property reflects the eternal form of the Father, which together in their mutual donation and exchange are eternally hypostatized as the Holy Spirit, whose identity radiates the ecstatic glory of the sacrificial "traversals" of the Father and the Son.

The point I want to stress here is that the revelation of the Son's sacrificial form in time unveils something of the mystery of the infinite depth of God's being. Namely, the patterns given by Scripture disclose the trihypostatic life of God as an infinite and eternal exchange of sacrificial love, which is narrated in time as the visible form of the incarnate Jesus.[14] By narrating the divine being/nature according to the revealed character of the crucified and exalted Jesus, we gain an important vantage point for discerning the shape of God's transcendent action. Following the metaphysical axiom that action flows from and is expressive of nature (*agere sequitur esse*), the shape of God's *action* appears structured by the same figurated dimensions of Christ's crucified form.[15] The revelation of the sacrificial nature opens up a conceptual re-formation of our understanding of God's all-determining omnipotence, which may illuminate the story of creation.

The Divine Action: Creation and Sacrifice

The interpretive act of negotiating God's being and action in light of Christ's sacrificial form is not foreign to modern theological reasoning. Along with an increased apprehension of the scope and magnitude of human suffering in the modern era there arose a range of sacrificial "kenotic" theologies that pursued a conceptual redefinition of God's engagement with the world. The theological use of the term "kenosis" derives from

13. Hanby, *No God, No Science*, 316.

14. As Maximus the Confessor puts it: "Theology is taught us by the incarnate Logos of God, since He reveals in Himself the Father and the Holy Spirit. For the whole of the Father and the whole of the Holy Spirit were present essentially and perfectly in the whole of the incarnate Son" (Maximus the Confessor, "On the Lord's Prayer," 287).

15. For clear articulation and defense of this principle, see Clarke, "Action as the Self-Revelation of Being," 45–64.

Paul's letter to the Philippians, in which he describes Christ's incarnate form as a type of divine self-emptying that Christians are called to imitate. "Have this mind among yourselves, which was in Christ Jesus, who, because he was in the form of God, did not count equality with God a thing to be grasped but emptied himself" (Phil 2:5–7a). The first expressions of kenotic theology as an interpretive gestalt emerged among German and English theologians in the nineteenth century. They took up the scriptural motif of kenosis as a way to interpret Christ's person in light of the challenges presented by biblical criticism, modern psychology, and the influence of post-Hegelian metaphysics.[16] In the twentieth century, the motif of Christ's kenosis was further explored by a range of theologians who sought to illuminate the trinitarian life of God and the relationship of the uncreated with the created. Among the most influential of these kenotic theologians were Sergius Bulgakov (1871–1944), Hans Urs von Balthasar (1905–1988), and Jürgen Moltmann (1926–2024). Each one of these modern theologians presented a vision of God's nature and agency that prioritized the sacrificial suffering of Christ. This type of approach that emphasizes the divine kenosis has continued to prove attractive to contemporary theodicists in the late twentieth and early twenty-first centuries.[17]

For our task, the creational theology of Sergius Bulgakov provides the orienting basis for our figural exploration of God's sacrificial action. My engagement with Bulgakov's thought is largely due to its remarkable extension of the sacrificial motif which he pursues in a manner that constructively addresses the modern configuration of the world. Other theologians venture to do so as well, but I find the alternative approaches to suffer from conceptual difficulties. For instance, Moltmann abandons

---

16. Dawe, *Form of a Servant*.

17. Creational application of the notion of kenosis resembles the Kabbalistic concept of *tzim tzum*, which describes the divine act of creation as contraction that enables the possibility of the world's being. In modern Christian discourse, the adoption of kenosis (or tzim tzum) as a formal approach to the problem of the evil and suffering has become more prevalent. For instance, Jürgen Moltmann, John Haught, and Christopher Southgate (and many others) have affirmed kenosis as way of engaging God's nature in view of creational suffering. The difficulty with such approaches concerns their implications for a classical understanding of God's divine aseity. Often, these modern approaches (in varying degrees) veer into some type of process thought, which involves significant redefinitions of God's nature. While these redefinitions might prove theodically compelling in certain respects, they suffer from metaphysical problems in view of Christian theistic claims. For some examples of a kenotic redefinition of God's creative act influenced by process thought, see Moltmann, *God in Creation*.

some traditional aspects of God's divine aseity (e.g., divine *apatheia*) while over-interpreting the economic missions of the Trinity in relation within the immanent life of the divine nature.[18] The latter critique could also be applied to Balthasar to some extent. Moreover, Balthasar's kenotic theology, while in many ways more amenable with classical theism, is somewhat less restrained in its claims than Bulgakov's trinitarian thought. For instance, Balthasar seems to interpret Christ's incarnate estrangement from the Father in history as reflective of an eternal dialectic of alienation in God's trinitarian life.[19] More positively, besides presenting a restrained intra-trinitarian kenosis, Bulgakov's thought is also theologically attentive to the problem of creation's *agon* in a direct way. The problem of nature's character through time appears as a significant aporia around which he pursues his creational theology. As such, Bulgakov's reflections concerning God's agency and the nature of the world provide a rich basis for searching out and developing our figural structures. Nevertheless, certain ambiguities in Bulgakov's thought, including his sense of a provisional abdication of God's traditional attributes vis-à-vis the world's "autonomous" being, will not sit well with other claims regarding God's absolute creative priority. Thus, after describing Bulgakov's vision of creation as an act of divine sacrifice that reflects God's trihypostatic life, I will present an interpretation that seeks to address the tension in Bulgakov's theology between God's transcendent creativity and the ontological density of the world's autonomy.

Sergius Bulgakov's searching metaphysical explorations of the creative act describe it as an analogical expression of Christ's form, which also epistemically reveals the character of God's eternal life as sacrificial love. He writes,

> We know that the Trinity's love is mutually sacrificial as a mutual renunciation of the hypostases. Each hypostasis finds itself and realizes itself in the others in this renunciation. Therefore, the Trinity's love can be understood in this sense as a supraeternal kenosis, but a kenosis that is overcome for each of the hypostases in joint trinitarian love, in the all-blissfulness of this love.[20]

---

18. For example, see Moltmann, *Crucified God*.
19. See Balthasar, *Dramatis Personae*, 183–92, 489–521.
20. Bulgakov, *Bride of the Lamb*, 49.

For Bulgakov, the revealed pattern of Christ's exhaustive self-emptying in history manifests the eternal pattern or form of the triune God's being and action. He thus interprets the very act of creation as a type of sacrifice metaphorically grasped as a form of divine self-limitation or separation that allows the world to exist in its own ontic freedom. He writes,

> The creation of heaven and earth, as an act of God's love flowing beyond the limits of the proper divine life into the world, is, in relation to divinity itself, a voluntary self-diminution, a metaphysical kenosis: Alongside his *absolute* being, God establishes a relative being with which He enters into an interrelation, being God and Creator for this being.[21]

According to Bulgakov's theology, the sacrificial form of the divine nature reframes the traditional understanding of God's providential action in relation to creation's temporal realization. Here, he straddles the conceptual tension between classical affirmations of God's creative transcendence and a sense of God's interrelatedness with the world. For Bulgakov, the divine attributes of classical theism are antinomically joined with divine limitations in light of the universe's relative autonomy. He writes, "The relation of the Creator to creation in 'synergism' always remains meek and restrained, the kenosis of God in creation. This kenosis is determined by the union of God's omniscience and wisdom in relation to the paths of the world, but with the self-limitation of His omnipotence."[22] For Bulgakov, in God's *absolute being*, God remains omnipotent, omniscient, and omnipresent; yet, *as creator*, God voluntarily "diminishes" the fullness of the divine nature and engages the world through this limitation.

This depiction of the creative act as a divine self-limitation is metaphysically coextensive with a vision of the world intrinsically shaped by divine Wisdom, which is non-identically recapitulated in the temporal becoming of the world. For Bulgakov, the act of metaphysical separation simultaneously imparts to the world a real participation in divine Wisdom, which is the positive orientation and content of the world's entelechic traversal. "In its creation the world contains the entire fullness of the logos-seeds of being; all is said about it and in it. The theme of the world is fully given and only needs to be developed. In the fullness of its being and in its connectedness as a multi-unity, the world is an image

---

21. Bulgakov, *Lamb of God*, 128.
22. Bulgakov, *Bride of the Lamb*, 234.

of the Logos."²³ Thus, Bulgakov's depiction of God's creative withdrawal is paradoxically connected with the positing of the divine "theme" that governs the temporal manifestation and fulfillment of creation. Both metaphysical aspects, the divine withdrawal and divine participation, inform the incomprehensible character of God's unbounded creativity.

In figural terms, we can relate Bulgakov's understanding of the mystery of creation's separation and participation with the figurated temple. As a cosmic figure, the temple's layered architecture in its historical traversal contracts the divine presence to a single locale (the holy of holies), which signifies the hiddenness of God in view of the world. Likewise, in an almost paradoxical fashion, the cosmic temple in its contracted state also reveals the theme of Christ's incarnate life, which both informs and fulfills the figurated content of the scriptural temple in its temporal extension. The Christic form appears precisely as the world's metaphysical orientation grasped through the limitations and imperfections of its origination (signified by Eden) and in its movement towards eschatological divinization where creation is finally rendered transparent to God's divine glory (signified by the celestial Jerusalem).

Bulgakov's depiction of divine agency, which reflects the Christic shape of Wisdom, provides a fruitful set of metaphors for interpreting the paradox of divine omni-causality and creaturely freedom. On the one hand, Bulgakov's account is beneficial to theodical reflection insofar as it presents God's creative fullness in a way that ontologically grounds the freedom of creation, which can then be used to "locate" the endemic violence of nature as outside God's *direct* intentions for the creaturely world. This means, theoretically, that the specific forms of creatures (e.g., the hyena or ichneumon wasp) and the contingent conditions that give birth to such creatures may not align entirely with God's foundational intentions. Under such an account, the countless evils and sufferings of nature's history are defined as contingent realities born of a fallenness that emerges through creation's ontological separation. This Bulgakovian notion establishes metaphysical space for evil's possibility and avoids some of the conceptual difficulties associated with more compatibilist accounts of the relationship between God and the world.²⁴

---

23. Bulgakov, *Comforter*, 198.

24. Theological compatibilism holds that there is no logical contradiction between God's all-determining agency and the free actions of creatures. For a critique of compatibilism, see Hasker, *Metaphysics*, 33–37.

In traditional forms of theological compatibilism, the presence of moral and physical evil and suffering ineluctably falls within the determining counsels of God. The freedom of creaturely beings exists solely at the contingent level of secondary causation, even though everything that happens in the universe is providentially determined by God's omnipotent creativity. The compatibilist account of divine action thus functions as a type of instrumentalist theodicy, whereby nature's *agon* is instrumentally willed as the direct means for achieving some overarching benefit. For instance, the existence of the liver-fluke worm, with its capacity to feed off another creature's internal organs while still alive, could be construed as providing some mysterious benefit to the world's beauty. In contrast, Bulgakov's account stresses a genuine "interrelationship" between God and the world, where the world's freedom serves as the metaphysical context for creation's agonistic history.[25] This grounds the paradox of nature's ontic violence as both founded upon God's creative action and yet somehow outside of God's eternal desire.[26] Thus, this account in no way entails that God *directly* wills the suffering of creatures as the proper and necessary means to achieve some greater purpose. Rather, according to Bulgakov's interpretation, both the *possibility* and *actuality* of nature's disorders are kenotic realities *permitted* by God's sacrificial love in Christ.

---

25. This variation of kenosis as a relative divine absence is prevalent in contemporary theistic evolutionary accounts of God's creative causality. One of the most recurrent forms of this divine absence is expressed by the physicist turned theologian John Polkinghorne, who develops a variation of God's kenotic agency as a type of "opentheism." His kenotic theology redefines or abandons some aspects of the classical theistic account of God's creative causality in view of created reality. For Polkinghorne, God interacts with the world through his kenotic absence, which allows the universe to realize itself through a free process. This free process of created realities is analogically conceived on the model of rational free agency applied to nonrational entities. See Polkinghorne, *Faith of a Physicist*, 83–85. For a critique of kenotic evolutionary theologies, see Peters, "Extinction, Natural Selection," 691–710.

26. Paul Gavrilyuk describes Bulgakov's constrictions of the divine nature as follows: "Bulgakov's own solution is that the creator bridges the gap between himself and his creation in a voluntary act of kenosis. One can identify three distinct aspects of the divine self-emptying in creation developed by our author: (1) God freely constrains his actions in the world by time and space; (2) God limits his power and (3) gives up his foreknowledge in order to preserve human freedom" (Gavrilyuk, "Kenotic Theology of Sergius Bulgakov," 257). These "revisions" of the divine nature vis-à-vis created autonomy ultimately provide a way of accounting for the ontic density of creaturely agencies as secondary modes of causation. In other words, Bulgakov's submitting all things under the form of sacrificial offering establishes the world with a certain ontic integrity and contingent freedom that provides the conceptual space for apprehending the possibility of evil within creation.

One might infer that the expansive presence of ontic strife in the vast ages of the world is the mysterious outworking of God's creative *absence* from natural history rather than a reality born directly from God's antecedent will for the world.[27]

While the Bulgakovian language provides a helpful way of narrating creational suffering as an indirect possibility born of God's creative agency, this is not without theological difficulties. In spite of the implicit figural basis for the sacrificial form of the creative act, this account appears in tension with other significant scriptural claims concerning God's all-determining providence.[28] For instance, in what way can a divine self-limitation make sense of a God scripturally described as the one who "made heaven, the heaven of heavens with all their host, the earth and all that is on it, the seas and all that is in them" (Neh 9:6), the God who "forms light and creates darkness," who "makes weal and creates woe" (Isa 45:7), and the God who knows every sparrow that "falls to the ground" (Matt 10:29)? The natural world with its disorienting amount of suffering appears in Scripture as comprehended by God's overarching presence. In a similar vein, against a kenotic theology like Bulgakov's, the theologian Ted Peters argues that in Scripture Christ's kenotic life "has the net effect of increased divine presence in the world, not absence. . . . Neither here nor anywhere else in Holy Scripture do we find God withdrawing from creation. To the contrary, we find repeated testimony of God engaging creation with divine presence."[29] Therefore, the idea of creation as a limitation of God's infinite fullness requires further development, especially given the scriptural emphasis on God's creative presence in all things. This necessitates the integration of the sacrificial image of divine agency within a traditional understanding of God's creative priority. The metaphysical narrative I aim to develop regarding divine agency will navigate the conceptual tension given by Scripture concerning the paradox of the

---

27. This vision of the divine absence from the created world is articulated in the remarkable thought of the twentieth-century philosopher Simone Weil. Weil argued that the very act of "creation is an abandonment" and that God's creative act is "all-powerful" only to the extent that God's "abdication of creation is voluntary" (Weil, *Gateway to God*, 48).

28. The force of such passages with their high creational monotheism might be mitigated through interpretive strategies. Yet, in terms of our figural theology, we cannot avoid the import of such scriptural renderings of God's creative agency in accounting for the sacrificial form of divine revelation.

29. Peters, "Extinction, Natural Selection," 703.

world's ontological separation from, and creative comprehension by, the God revealed in the crucified and risen Jesus.

Regarding the divine origin of the world, Scripture clearly affirms that God is the absolute determining author of all things. Therefore, it follows that no contingent reality is ever opaque to divine knowledge and power, contra some of Bulgakov's language. The philosopher Brian J. Shanley writes, "God knows all temporal events in their real existence because God is the cause of that existence; temporal events are present to God's eternal knowledge as the object or terminus of God's eternal creative causality."[30] In other words, God timelessly knows all things in the very act by which they are created and ordered. Hugh of St. Victor expresses this all-determining creative knowledge with the image of the divine mind holding all finite entities and events in a single creative act of intentional consciousness. He writes, "For as in the mind of God the causes of all things exist eternally without change or temporal differentiation, so also in our minds things past, things present, and things future exist together by means of thought."[31] In this traditional understanding, there is no ontological reciprocity or real relation whereby God is metaphysically reactive to or absent from finite beings; rather, all things are creatively posited in divine eternity. God, as the transcendent creative source, exhaustively knows all things through the immediate act of imparting being (esse) to all things. This is all quite traditional vis-à-vis classical theism and makes good sense of some scriptural content. However, this position struggles to account for the existence of evil and suffering in a way that does not ultimately reduce it to God's creative intention. While normally asserted alongside affirmations of creaturely freedom, it is not entirely clear how this rendering of God's creative fullness does not render creaturely agency superfluous and thus become subject to the conceptual problems of compatibilism. Critics of this causal account of omnipotence and omniscience assert that this formulation cannot do justice to the genuine agency of creatures; it instead resolves everything into a form of causal determinism.[32] Without the genuine autonomy and

---

30. Shanley, "Aquinas on God's Causal Knowledge," 451.

31. Hugh of St. Victor, *De arca Noe morali* 2.1.

32. This form of theological compatibilism insists upon the ontic authenticity of creaturely freedom, which *only* obtains in the realm of other secondary causes. By such an account it is hard to see how the subsuming of all secondary free actions under the encompassing determination of God's eternal action can avoid the implication that evil and suffering are directly willed by God. See Tracy, "God and Creatures Acting," 221–37.

freedom of creaturely being, the world and its agonies become a phenomenal edifice of God's absolute creativity. By implication, such an account would inevitably terminate in an instrumentalist theodicy, wherein the elected order of creation, with its fecundity and devastation, is simply the outworking of the divinely willed intention for the world. The primary difficulty with this type of theodicy is its apparent fusing of creation's violent and destructive form with God's eternal idea of the world. Without a proper accounting of creaturely distinction and freedom, the world with its violence becomes reduced to a direct expression of God's creative character, with all its moral and theological implications. This "fusing" of the divine will with the world's form *in toto* fits rather disjointedly with the wider scriptural articulation of God's nature as perfect peace and self-giving love.

Thus, the image of God's sacrificial agency displayed through the temple's layered form provides an important corrective for our interpretation of the divine act of creation. Yet the question arises how the sacrificial form of God's agency found in a theology like Bulgakov's might be squared with a traditional understanding of God's transcendent creativity that accords with Scripture and classical accounts of the divine nature. The tension between God's causal priority and the Bulgakovian notion of sacrifice appears to capture the underlying scriptural antinomy concerning the shape of God's agency in relation to created realities. God is described scripturally as the creative and providential source of all things. All the long ages of creation's history, in its richness and desolation, are enfolded in the single act of God's creative positing of the universe into being. Nothing happens in the realm of creatures apart from God's absolute origination and providence. Yet God so *transcendentally* creates all things that *not* everything that happens in the proximate order of secondary causes entirely accords with God's antecedent desire or intention.[33] Creation is posited in its ontic freedom to realize itself in a metaphysically dynamic way. This paradox between God's causal priority and the revealed sacrificial form is the infinite mystery of God's being and action. While deciphering this mystery exhaustively is impossible, it is worthwhile exploring this tension to gain a deeper apprehension of

---

33. The key element in thinking through the *sui generis* character of the act of creation is the analogical similarity and difference between divine creation and all forms of creaturely causality. While there is a limited sense that one can denote the divine act as a type of "cause," this remote affirmation is analogically freighted with an ever-greater dissimilarity that renders the act incomprehensible.

the mysterious character of God's infinite agency. The philosopher W. Norris Clarke provides a theoretical account of divine action that is helpfully suggestive with respect to this tension between divine omnipotence and the genuine freedom of the world. The following will take up aspects of Clarke's metaphysical speculation to explore the analogical *hiatus* between divine and creaturely freedom.

The basic structure of Clarke's metaphysical position affirms that the actuality of the finite universe—as a diverse communion of beings with their respective actions—emanates entirely from God's infinitely encompassing creative fullness, which he *sacrificially* allows to be determined by creatures. The first aspect affirms God's causal priority: all creatures, entities, and events are gifted with existence through the act of creation. Nothing that happens within the created universe—past, present, or future—is outside the creative presence of God's immediate and eternal knowledge, power, and love. The second aspect affirms the implicit sacrificial form that governs God's creative authorship. This means that the world's creatures participate in the donation of being (*esse*) in such a way that they truly direct it without subverting the transcendent comprehension of God's infinite fullness. Taking the rational creature as the paradigmatic expression of this participation, Clarke writes,

> God knows my choice by knowing his own active power working within me, as thus determined or channeled determinately here and now by me. Hence God knows by acting, not by being acted on, but I supply the inner determination or limit of this power at work—which I repeat is not a new positive being at all but only a limiting down of an indeterminate plenitude.[34]

For Clarke, God's transcendent donation of *esse* can be grasped as a form of "active receptivity" that permits the genuine autonomy of the world insofar as the actions of finite creatures are actively "received in God" as *delimitations* of God's infinite creativity. Creaturely actions are thus "received" in the divine eternity as configurations of God's intentional consciousness (*esse intentionale*), which can be contingently differentiated without altering the infinite simplicity and fullness of the divine nature (*esse reale*).[35] In divine eternity, God comprehends or encompasses all

---

34. Clarke, "New Look," 205.

35. The freedom of creatures (at least, of rational creatures) consists of the negative excluding of all possible avenues of action, whereby the act is less a positive doing than a negation of all other possibilities. This has the advantage opening up the personalist dimensions of the divine nature in view of created realities. Instead of letting the

things in the single transcendent act through which divine power timelessly posits and flows through the entire ensemble of creaturely agents in their distinct temporal orders. Creaturely entities receive their being from God in such a way that they unfold and shape their distinctive existence freely in time. In this way, God incomprehensibly imparts to the world an existence where creatures freely and authentically participate in the divine purpose. While highly speculative, this account provides a clue to how we may sketch the sacrificial image of divine creativity which possesses a donative and participatory form. The image of divine agency in and through created time is the donation of the "permissive space" for creatures to participate in the world's unfolding.

Based upon these considerations, this portrait of divine action provides a way of admitting Bulgakov's sacrificial motif while situating it within a traditional Christian metaphysical framework. This allows us to perceive creation's history as displaying elements that are possibly outside of God's immediate volition yet are further encompassed by God's ultimate purpose. I want to stress that within the transcendent fullness of the Divine Life there is an eternal sacrificial "moment" whereby God actively offers creation its own life to be realized in time. As Bulgakov writes, "The creative 'let there be,' which is the command of God's omnipotence, at the same time expresses the sacrifice of Divine love, of God's love for the world, the love of the Absolute for the relative, in virtue of which the Absolute becomes the Absolute-Relative."[36] This sacrificial theme establishes the world in a type of "natural freedom"[37] which not only pertains to rational creatures (as it does for Clarke) but also applies to the very structure of the universe as an integrated reality that enfolds the entire ensemble of creatures (inanimate, animate, spiritual, etc.).

Following Bulgakov, my understanding of the world's freedom in its traversal *from* God (so to speak) into subsistence is simultaneously conditioned by the divine presence to creation, which is expressed by nature's inner-dynamism and "entelechic character"[38] both in its coming-to-be and in its eschatological fulfillment. Within the creative traversal from

---

immutability of divine transcendence over-determine God's causal knowledge and love of creatures, the distinction between God's intentional being and real being provides a way of conceiving the "mutual relationships of friendship, both giving and receiving love, between God and ourselves" (Clarke, "New Look," 187).

36. Bulgakov, *Lamb of God*, 128.
37. Bulgakov, *Bride of the Lamb*, 131.
38. Bulgakov, *Bride of the Lamb*, 197.

nothingness, the world's capacity to shape itself depends upon the particular modalities granted to creaturely entities. Creatures are empowered to shape the manifestation of the world according to their variegated capacities. However, this freedom is not absolute as if it were absolved of all conditions; on the contrary, the world in its traversal remains tethered and conditioned by the foundational themes given by divine Wisdom, which incomprehensibly *unfolds* the world in its movement from nothingness into being. Thus, both the freedom and determined conditions of the world's traversal are grounded *in* the Christological form of the divine nature, which sets it free in its coming-to-be and conditions its ongoing manifestation and orientation towards its divine end.

By interpreting God's action as an analogical sacrifice that constitutes the world's freedom and content, it reasonably follows that it also enfolds a divine election to "suffer" the distortions and deviations of this freedom, not by denying or annihilating their reality, but by permitting them and providentially ordering them towards an eschatological fulfillment that will finally reveal the splendor and peace of the divine life in the world. Thus, the theme of divine sacrifice comprehends both the *permission* and providential *answer* to nature's ontic violence as it emerges in time. While the devastating contours of the empirical world may not originate in the divine will in a direct sense, the contingent particulars born of nature's modal freedom are made to serve God's transcendent *telos*. This vision is reflected in the scriptural antinomy that affirms God's providential use of creational violence in history (Ps 104; Job 38–40) and the revelation that nature's violence is alienated from creation's end (Isa 11:6–9). Based upon this revelation of the world's eschatological horizon, I would interpret God's providential use of creational violence in Scripture as figuring God's sacrificial forbearance to creatures in a fallen world. This interpretive point is echoed by the theologian Neil Messer, who writes, "In this world, neither we nor God's other creatures can live without violence and struggle, and texts such as Job 38 and Psalm 104 are perhaps best read as expressions of God's patience and grace, making it possible for creatures to live even in this broken world."[39] The sacrificial form of the creative act underscores the antinomic character of nature's history, describing it as both the result of creation's contingent freedom (and open to the possibility of divergence) and creatively enfolded within the mystery of God's transcendent providence.

---

39. Messer, "Evolution and Theodicy," 831.

In comparison to Bulgakov's interpretation, this account understands the sacrificial nature of divine creativity as the gift to the world and its creatures of the capacity to traverse in freedom, ensuring that they are not merely an extension of God's life. This involves a *metaphorical* limitation of God's action in the sense that God transcendently permits the divine theme of creation to be realized by creatures in their respective capacities. This does not involve any provisional diminishment of God's creative presence, however. On the contrary, God *actively* creates and knows the free actions of the universe's creatures as the infinite source of their being and power. In essence, God transcendently acts through creaturely freedom by *permitting* their diverse manifestation without subjecting them to proximate causal determination. As in Bulgakov's account, this vision affirms the metaphysical density of the world as a realm of genuine entities and events that operate in freedom and distinction.

The above sketch of God's being and action revises one of the major terms of the theodical problem by reconceiving the causal nexus "between" God and the world. This interpretation foregrounds the Christological revelation of the divine nature in order to establish conceptual space to navigate the tension between divine omnipotence and omnibenevolence and the reality of nature's ostensive brutality. Specifically, reading the creative act as a sacrificial donation establishes the "permissive space" for the creaturely world to come-to-be in freedom and distinction from God while also being mysteriously bound to God's eternal purpose in Christ. This emerging image of divine agency thus incorporates the antinomic claims of Scripture that perceive the world's agonistic character as both *outside* and *within* the scope of divine providence.

This account relieves our theodical reflection of the immediate burden of making God the direct source of nature's disorders, a problem with traditional accounts of creative omnipotence, especially as expressed in many instrumentalist theodicies. By contrast, the conviction that ontological violence is not positively willed implies that the world is subject to some form of metaphysical deviation, which evokes the interpretive framework of the contingent-fallenness theodicy. In this respect, nature in its empirical form may be defined as a landscape characterized by what theologian Nicola Hoggard Creegan aptly dubs the "wheat and tares,"[40]

---

40. Nicola Hoggard Creegan uses Christ's parable of the wheat and tares as a paradigmatic articulation of the mystery of creation's fallenness. Somehow the world's being is interlaced with disorders that come to it from outside of God's direct will. See Creegan, *Animal Suffering*.

that is, a dense integration of good and evil that remains epistemically indiscerptible until the end of time. Nonetheless, even with the admission of nature's contingent fallenness, the God of sacrificial love remains the metaphysical ground of the world's temporal realization, establishing both the fruitful and dissolving patterns of creaturely existence.

This theoretical portrait of divine agency forms only the first aspect of our theological engagement regarding the tension between God's revealed character and the shape of the created world as disclosed through Christ's scriptural form. The next section will press further into the *Christic* shape of creation's ontological form as disclosed in our figurated structures.

The Sacrificial Traversal: The Created World

The manifestation of the creaturely world in Scripture is ultimately ordered by its comprehension in the eternal Son, whose incarnate life maps the unfolding essence of the world's being in time. The seemingly disparate and obdurate patterns of meaning given through Christ's figural body provide the structuring principles that unveil the world, replete with its physical evil and suffering, as it is sacrificially summoned into existence by God in Christ and the Spirit. In particular, the connected figures of traversal and sacrifice display the unruly nature of the universe as bearing the shape of the Son of God in some way. Hugh of St. Victor describes this from the divine perspective:

> In Him I have eternally arranged whatever I have made in time. And the more perfectly I see each work of mine to be in harmony with that first arrangement, the more fully I love it. Do not think that He is only the mediator in the reconciliation of humankind, for through Him also the creation of all creatures becomes praiseworthy and pleasing in my sight. In Him I consider all the works I do, and I cannot *not* love what I see is similar to Him whom I love.[41]

Our exploration will now sketch a fitting image of the world as interpreted by our figural patterns, which forms the conceptual obverse to the reflections given above concerning God's eternal being and action. Previously, we had interpreted divine agency according to Christ's sacrificial passage: the world appeared constituted by a metaphysical polarity

---

41. Hugh of St. Victor, *De tribus diebus* 24.2.

between divine separation and participation rooted in the sacrificial love of God's infinite nature. The metaphysical identity of the world is thus defined as that which is *not* God and yet manifests the form and content of the eternal Word in its temporal passage. Thus, the shape of the creaturely world in time, both in terms of its teleological traversal and its relational economy, is indelibly stamped with the form of the Son of God.

The World's Teleological Traversal in-and-Beyond Time

In terms of creation's teleological structure, Christ's sacrificial form diagrams the metaphysical polarity of the world's being as it appears from nothingness. These two fundamental aspects—separation and participation—establish the overarching principle of creation's temporal passage, which reverberates with the shadowed form of Christ's figural being. While Christ's incarnate life perfectly narrates the divine Son's eternal receptivity *from* the Father and eternal self-offering *to* the Father, the world bears something of this same divine movement.

The first characteristic of creation's analogical *receptivity* is the form of the universe as it exists according to the metaphorical withdrawal figured by the scriptural temple. The world's essence is constituted by the divine donation that sets the world free from God in order that it might be granted its own ontological density. This separation grounds the traversal of creation in its "negative contingence," to use the phrase of T. F. Torrance. Accordingly, this negative contingence is the basis for creation's developmental character in its *independence* from God. Torrance writes,

> In its orientation away from God, the one self-sufficient being and the creative source of all other being, the contingent universe borders on nonbeing and chaos, so that from that direction there would appear to be a natural threat to the being of the universe if it were left to itself. Contingent reality has thus an intrinsic fragility and liability: without stability of its own, it is evanescent.[42]

The adoption of the qualifier "negative" is intended to indicate creation's constitution in nothingness, which determines its distinction from the infinite fullness of the Trinity and marks the ensemble of creatures within the prescribed limits of finitude. The orienting limits of creatures (and of the universe as a totality) are not evils, but divine gifts, endowing creatures

---

42. Torrance, *Divine and Contingent Order*, 111.

with their distinctive reality that serves as the basis for creation's freedom. This freedom is the relative autonomy and spontaneity of the divine content gifted to the world at its foundation. While supremely manifested in the personal (hypostatic) dimensions of the creaturely world, the same modality of being is possessed analogously within the hierarchies of creaturely existence, from its elemental principles to its diverse expressions in organic life. In recognition of the analogical character of this freedom, Sergius Bulgakov writes,

> The world realizes itself in the evolution of life, obeying an obscure instinct and ascending to higher forms of life *freely*, not as a thing but as a living being. . . . This freedom attains a great height first in the animal world, where the fire of life burns clearly, and then it reaches its peak in man, where nature transcends itself and the instinct of natural freedom passes into personal, spiritual freedom.[43]

This freedom of creation is distinct from the divine fullness. It grounds the possibility of ontic divergence within the unfolding procession of the universe, whether by some mysterious impulsion of life or through the hypostatic (personal) dimensions of rational being. In scriptural terms, the figural contraction of the divine presence vis-à-vis the cosmic temple establishes the world with an "indeterminate range of possibility"[44] that is bound up with the nothingness from which being arises. This notion of separation (or negative contingency) is the first dimension of nature's traversing character and is wedded to the paradoxical enfoldment of the world by the divine Word's creative presence. Nevertheless, the metaphysical "separation" and "distance" of the world from God reveal it as something more than simply an extension of eternal being. It is real, distinct being, free and pregnant with the possibilities that God creatively enacts in the divine Word.

The second aspect of this receptive separation from God is figurally enveloped by the pattern mediated through Christ's creative form, which signals the positive order and teleological orientation of the universe. Because the incarnate Christ is the form of the temple in Scripture, his divine life is the underlying principle that defines the shape of creation's passage in its temporality. By implication, the creatures that make up the unfolding world are enigmatically inscribed with the shape of Christ's life.

---

43. Bulgakov, *Bride of the Lamb*, 131–32.
44. Torrance, *Divine and Contingent Order*, 109.

Both the universe and its creatures bear the impress of the crucified and exalted Christ in some essential way. Remarkably, in Hugh of St. Victor's ark reflections, the history of the universe appears from beginning to end as "an allegorical figure for the human body in which Christ appeared, for it is itself His body."[45] In some of his writings Hugh presses the analogy of creation as the visible "body" of God, whereby God's creative presence to the world is similar to the soul's constitutive presence to a corporeal body, albeit in a way that stresses divine transcendence.[46] Hence, in Hugh's Christocentric ontology, the world in its relative freedom remains paradoxically bound to the creative presence of Jesus who—as the true form of the ark, the temple, and the cosmos—comprehends and fulfills all things. This expresses the positive aspect of creation's movement as ordered by God in its creative fecundity *in* history and in its eschatological transformation *beyond* history.

The universe's foundation in the eternal Word evinces a progressive directionality, a type of "positive contingence," to use Torrance's terminology, by which creatures are dynamically ordered towards fruitful expression. Torrance writes,

> The contingency of the creation as it derives from God is inseparably bound up with its orderliness, for it is the product not merely of his almighty will but of his eternal reason. . . . There is no contingence without order and no order without contingence, for contingence is inherently orderly and order is essentially contingent. . . . Moreover, under the ceaseless creative bearing of God upon the universe, this integration is to be understood not as a static or predetermined programming but as a dynamic functioning of its contingent processes in a mutual involution of form and being, giving rise to ever richer patterns of order which may be understood only in terms of their natural onto-relational structures.[47]

Here, Torrance adverts to the manifestation of "ever richer patterns of order" that may be tethered with Hugh's notion of creation as a process of gradual *formatio*. In its ontological separation, the world is called to realize the divine content of its life, which is manifested freely through the unfolding of time. This divine content corresponds with the traditional notion of the divine ideas or primary causes eternally conceived in God's

---

45. Hugh of St. Victor, *De arca Noe morali* 1.14.
46. Hugh of St. Victor, *De tribus diebus* 19.9.
47. Torrance, *Divine and Contingent Order*, 109–10.

Word. In the creative act *ad extra*, this content is *dynamically* actualized as the unfolding distention of creaturely time and being. Bulgakov writes,

> The becoming world must, in its becoming, follow the long path of cosmic being to the end before it can reflect in itself the countenance of the Divine Sophia, which, being the *foundation* and entelechy of the world's being, is only in a state of *potentiality*, which the world must actualize in itself. This potentialization by God of His proper Divine world into extradivine being is precisely *creation out of nothing*.[48]

The creative content of the world's movement includes the rich developmental sequences of the universe and its individuated creatures, and it constitutes the positive orientation of creation's receptivity of being.

In addition to this depiction of creation's positive contingence, Scripture's articulation of the world's traversing form is not exhausted by the cosmological profusion of creatures in its temporal ages. On the contrary, the figure also possesses a *distinct* eschatological reference that takes up the unfolded conditions of the creaturely cosmos and radically recreates it in Christ through the Holy Spirit. This discrete traversal of being is the divinization of creation, and it is both continuous and disjunctive with the present world. Indeed, as will be later explored, the second horizon of creation's traversal unveils a world markedly different from that which is manifested in its temporal passage. Specifically, the *economia* of the eschatological recreation appears mysteriously purged of all traces of the dissipative character and ontic violence that govern the first horizon of creation's coming-to-be.

In terms of its creational reference, the dimensions of Scripture's figurated movement may be summarized as follows: the first aspect perceives the empirical directionality of the universe by means of the paradoxical separation from and creative participation in God's infinite presence. In Hugh's theology, this may be figurally represented by the sequential character of the six days of creation, which describe the traversal of creation through a developmental process of increasing form that generates the wonder and beauty of the cosmos. In conjunction with this creative traversal, the second aspect depicts the world as intrinsically open to a discrete eschatological fulfillment that presupposes and transcends the historical form of the finite world. In its freedom, the creaturely world's coming-to-be is ultimately ordered towards a distinct

---

48. Bulgakov, *Lamb of God*, 127 (original emphasis).

finality that fulfills and transcends its original separation. This eschatological pattern is revealed through the figurated connection of the garden and the celestial Jerusalem. At its end, the scriptural form of the created cosmos transcends the layered cosmography of the temple with its delimitation of the divine presence; instead, all creation is set aflame with the holy presence of the living God.

The World's Economy in-and-Beyond Time

The comprehensive figure of traversal, which outlines the metaphysical teleology of the natural world in its creational and eschatological orientations, is indelibly informed by the analogical pattern of the crucified and exalted Christ, who reveals the world's life as it takes shape in time. The image of the universe (and its vast array of creatures) appears intrinsically constituted by the sacrificial distinctions of Christ's scriptural comprehension. The accumulated range of figures, especially of animals in their *created distinction*, allude to the foundational principle of the world's being as it is ordered from its origination towards its divinized end. As described in the previous chapter, the sacrificial distinction in Scripture is displayed as part of the world's ontic architecture. This *economia* of sacrifice, of life received and life offered, constitutes the character of creation's movement, both in terms of its protological constitution and its eschatological refashioning. Insofar as Christ structures God's creative and redemptive action, his metaphysical form is recapitulated in both the profusion of creatures that make up the span of the natural world (with its limits and relational structure) and the recreation of that order at its end.

In terms of the world's economic character, the form of the crucified and exalted Jesus, which grounds the referential reach of the cosmic temple and its sacrifices, also outlines the mysterious unity-in-distinction of creation—the relational continuum of the finite world. All things created (spiritual and physical) exist through a field of interaction of donation and reciprocity mirroring the eternal character of the Word of God. The theologian Jonathan Wilson perceptively interprets the relational form of the divine nature as the inscribed "grammar" of the creaturely world. He writes, "Just as God the Father, the Son, and the Holy Spirit live in continual self-giving and self-receiving, so also do all created things live—things in heaven and on earth, visible and invisible."[49] In this way,

---

49. Wilson, *God's Good World*, 109.

the relational dimensions of divine self-offering structure the unfolding constituents of the universe according to the form of life received and life offered. Within such a vision, the world and its creatures analogously recapitulate the pattern of Christ's life, which adumbrates the relational nexus that constitutes the world at the level of secondary causal relations. Something like this relational connection is described in Hugh of St. Victor when he writes: "The order and disposition of all things from the highest even to the lowest in the structure of the universe so follows in sequence with certain causes and generated reasons that of all things that exist none is found unconnected or separable and external by nature."[50] In a way similar to Hugh's ontology, the sacrificial pattern points toward the mystery of offering as an intrinsic dimension of the world's movement through time, both in terms of its creative emergence and in its eschatological transfiguration. This sacrificial form is the enveloping nexus of integrated connections through which all creatures receive existence, grow, decline, and die. This portrait reveals that to be a creature is to be given over to this mysterious sacrificial economy where life exists by means of a costly exchange of life.

This figural description of the universe underscores the logic of creation's sacrificial form. Accordingly, the entire sweep of natural history on the earth from 3.8 billion years ago to the present day appears conditioned by an ontic narrative of distinction and relational exchange, which accompanies the sheer wonder of life's proliferation and diversity. This pattern of distinction and exchange is costly insofar as it is manifested in the violence, wastefulness, and disorder of natural history. Yet it is also, ostensibly, the ontic concomitant of the world's richness in being. The theologian Frances Young summarizes this point well:

> What we perceive as good or bad is so closely intertwined as to belong to a single "geotapistry." This kind of thing is found time and time again: natural disasters arise from characteristics of the earth, like volcanoes and rainstorms, which are vital for its chemical balance; some bacteria may cause ill-health, but bacteria were responsible for oxygenating the atmosphere, so making animal life possible, and without bacteria in guts food would not be digested. . . .

---

50. Hugh of St. Victor, *De sacramentis* 1.2.2. According to Hugh, no aspect of the created world is causally inert in view of other realities, but rather, all things are embedded in mutually interpenetrating relations whereby all things exist through and for the sake of other things.

> Indeed, reflection on the food chain again gives us pause. Life depends on the consumption of other life, the stuff of life constantly being recycled, a process which can either be viewed as death-dealing and destructive or as constitutive of the surging diversity of living growth. Death is part of life, a prerequisite for the constant recycling that produces abundance.[51]

This description of the world aligns with the idea that the sacrificial traversal of creation manifests the cruciform reality of Christ (*mysterium crucis*) because all things fulfill their existence through a threshold of violence and suffering that supervenes through the underlying field of relational limits constituting the structure of the created world.

Nevertheless, the mystery of creation's cruciformity cannot be grasped apart from its divinely intended end. The revelation of Christ's sacrificial traversal through affliction, suffering, and death, which gathers and unites all of creation in its wake, discloses a world re-narrated as ontological reconciliation and peace. Jonathan Wilson writes,

> Today, creation anticipates its peace, but its actual life is cruciform. That is, the violence that we see exposed on the cross of Christ is the story of creation today. So the various agonistic accounts of the world, such as some accounts of evolution or a Nietzschean will to power, rightly describe the contingent nature of creation. . . . Creation is contingently marked by agony, but it is eschatologically marked by peace . . . this peace is the redemption of creation.[52]

This eschatological fulfillment is enfigured in Scripture through a series of images connected with the celestial Jerusalem wherein the economy of sacrificial exchange—with its animals and bloodied altar—is transposed into an ontology of peace that reconciles all creatures in their distinctions.

> The wolf shall dwell with the lamb, and the leopard shall lie down with the kid, and the calf and the lion, and the fatling together, and a little child shall lead them. The cow and the bear shall feed; their young shall lie down together; and the lion shall eat straw like the ox. The sucking child shall play over the hole of the asp, and the weaned child shall put his hand on the adder's den. They shall not hurt or destroy in all my holy mountain; for the earth shall be full of the knowledge of the Lord as the waters cover the sea. (Isa 11:6–9)

---

51. Young, *God's Presence*, 67–68.
52. Wilson, *God's Good World*, 28.

> I consider that the sufferings of this present time are not worth comparing with the glory that is to be revealed to us. For the creation waits with eager longing for the revealing of the sons of God; for the creation was subjected to futility, not of its own will but by the will of him who subjected it in hope; because the creation itself will be set free from its bondage to decay and obtain the glorious liberty of the children of God. We know that the whole creation has been groaning in travail together until now. (Rom 8:18–22)

> And he who sat upon the throne said, "Behold, I make all things new." (Rev 21:5a)

In Scripture's depiction of the *eschaton*, the economy of creaturely distinction is not annihilated but purified of its ontic violence and liberated from its bondage to decay through Christ's sacrificial gathering of all things. The relational structure that forms the identity of creatures as creatures remains, though it is now pacified in Christ and absolved from the endemic agonies that define our world. Remarkably, the world's foundational ontology of limit and exchange is thus transcended in the recreated world.

This scriptural manifestation of the Christic form, which outlines the world's economy and its teleological traversal, also unveils the mystery of the new heaven and the new earth in its eschatological fulfillment. Previously, we saw creation's history marked with the visible life of Jesus in his sacrificial passage. This pattern, defined as the integrated manifold of finite existence, antecedently constituted the relational basis for all creatures and the possibility of ontic disorder. At creation's eschatological *telos*, the same sacrificial pattern is not absolved or overturned but reconfigured, purified, and set on a new basis. This vision of creaturely life, adumbrated by Scripture's figured landscape, outstrips our finite categories. It can only be hinted at through images and symbols: celestial cities, cosmic mountains, living water, trees of life. All these scriptural images coalesce around the risen body of Jesus, whose incarnate life passed beyond suffering and death and entered a new modality of creaturely existence. The reality of this transcendent passage, with its reordered metaphysical logic, is unveiled in the present world by the Lord's mysterious presence in the Eucharistic celebration. For the church, the liturgical action of the Eucharist both re-presents the sacrificial form of Christ and anticipates the final eschatological transformation of the creaturely world. According to theologian Gustave Martelet, the mystery of the Eucharist in the life of the church reveals "to us the true and ultimate destiny of the world."[53] In the church's worship, the sacrificial body and blood of Christ, perpetually offered, unveils the true form of all things.

The mysterious ontology of the Eucharistic celebration, in which the crucified and raised body of Jesus is eternally offered and received, discloses the character of creation's eschatological destiny, liberated from its mysterious bondage to destruction and death. The distinction and exchange of life's traversal appear, finally, without disorder, diminution, or loss. In describing the Eucharistic celebration, Hugh writes, "We eat the flesh of the lamb when by taking His true body in the sacrament we are incorporated with Christ through faith and love. Elsewhere what is eaten is incorporated. Now when the body of Christ is eaten, not what is eaten but he who eats is incorporated with Him whom he eats."[54] While the relational nexus of created existence remains, the materiality of creation is transformed into a new modality that is set free from the dissolving strictures of the old. The perfect self-offering that is Jesus Christ—life eternally sacrificed and yet eternally beyond destruction—embodies the mysterious shape of this new world as it is raised up beyond the traversal of creation's veil. In this vein, Rowan Williams writes,

> This is the sense in which the Eucharist is a sign of the end of all things, the consummation of Christ's kingship: here is part of the material world wholly and unequivocally given over to the significant being of Christ, embodying his culminating gift on the cross. . . . The Eucharist demonstrates that material reality can become charged with Jesus' life, and so proclaims hope for the whole world of matter.[55]

In the figuration of the Eucharist, the risen Christ gathers the old creation with its distinctions, relational structure, and epochs of suffering and creates it anew. The divinized body and blood of the risen Jesus is a cipher revealing the final cosmic redemption wherein the agnostic order is taken up into the very life of God. The Eucharistic sacrifice is the concrete figuration of the mystery of creation's ultimate glory, which is life given and received without ontological destruction.

At this point in our study, we can sketch the emerging theological narrative. By engaging the figural structures of traversal and sacrifice

---

53. Martelet, *Risen Christ and the Eucharistic World*, 195.
54. Hugh of St. Victor, *De sacramentis* 2.8.5.
55. Williams, *Resurrection*, 103–4.

in terms of their Christological reference, our analysis has explored the disclosive potential of these figures in view of the metaphysical analogy that exists between God and creation.

In terms of its divine reference, the revealed form of Christ's sacrificial traversal unveils the character of God's creative action. Specifically, the sacrificial form of the triune God is manifested through the paradox of God's omnipotent priority and God's mysterious withdrawal. This depiction of God's sacrificial agency underscores the incomprehensible nature of the divine act of creation as it is expressed through the world's metaphysical separation and participation.

In terms of its creaturely reference, the sacrificial traversal of Christ's form also frames the world as integrally constituted by two orientations, which inversely mirror the sacrificial form of divine action. The first orientation reveals the world as constituted by a metaphysical separation, which established the world in contingent freedom defined by its emergence in time. This freedom also mysteriously grounded the metaphysical *possibility* of creation's deviation. The second orientation of the creaturely world concerns the character of creation's traversal *in-and-beyond*-time, as revealed through the figurated life of the crucified and exalted Jesus. This form reveals the world's freedom as governed by a mysterious sacrificial ontology that binds the entire universe together in a relational nexus of giving and receiving. This relational ontology has manifested itself in empirical history as an agonistic order of violence and death. And yet, the sacrificial traversal of Christ also reveals that the creaturely universe, despite its suffering character, is ordered towards a final Eucharistic peace that reflects the glory of God's trihypostatic nature.

These revelatory images, which disclose the space "between" God and the world, lead us to consider the question of the exact origin of nature's strife. The revealed theological disjunction between the world's eschatological finality absolved of all violence and the world's traversal through time, marked by suffering, compels us to pursue the significance of nature's *economia* in the context of its redemption and divinization. In short, what is the metaphysical disposition of nature's concrete existence in view of God's eschatological purpose?

The Origin of Nature's Agon *and The Mystery of the Fallen World*

Having explored the figurated Scriptures in terms of the God-world relation, the question of nature's destructive economy now arises in terms of its precise origin vis-à-vis the world's eschatological *terminus*. Given creation's eschatological reconciliation, whence comes the agonistic order of life? If all things are divinely intended to finally manifest peace, why are creatures endowed with properties intrinsically connected with ontic violence and suffering? For example, if the spotted hyena is eschatologically ordered towards peaceful reconciliation with the wildebeest, what are we to make of its innate properties that seemly require the violent pursuit and consumption of other sentient creatures? So far, our interpretation of figurated realities has provided a theological image wherein we might discern something of the conditions for the world's phenomenal character. However, even with these important conditions concerning the nature of God's sacrificial action and the world's ontic freedom, the question of the world's violent form escapes a clear and definitive explanation.

The figural theology articulated above only provides some of the sufficient conditions for creation's dissipative properties. It does not "add up" to a total explanation of its material actuality. One could assert that the violence of the world is just the mysterious outworking of God's creativity. According to this approach, God might positively will creation's *agon* as part of creation's emergence in time, while also willing its eschatological transformation. This type of narrative corresponds with the broad shape of the instrumentalist theodicy, wherein physical evils are the proper and necessary means for achieving some divinely desired end.

For instance, the theologian Christopher Southgate builds his instrumentalist theodicy according to the revelation of creation's distinct metaphysical horizons: one characterized by necessary violence, and another characterized by eschatological peace. According to his account, the world's creatures are divinely enacted through an evolutionary process intrinsically bound up with endemic violence and suffering. Hence, the world evinces "the values of beauty, diversity, and ingenuity" along with certain "disvalues" in a process that is the "only way" for God to create.[56] Note that despite Southgate's insistence on an intrinsic constraint placed upon God's creative omnipotence, he also wants to affirm God's eschatological power to transform the frustration and failures of evolutionary history definitively. Thus, Southgate's approach presents

---

56. Southgate, *Groaning of Creation*, 16.

us with a remarkable bifurcation of God's creative power. It appears to possess two distinct modalities vis-à-vis creation: one where ontological violence is an inescapable necessity and another where ontological peace is both divinely desired and divinely fulfilled. This is difficult to justify in metaphysical terms. If God can liberate and recreate the world that God originally made, then why did God not make it so from the beginning? To assert that this was the "only way" for God to create necessitates accounting for why the constraint disappears with respect to God's redemptive desire. Indeed, his invocation of an intrinsic constraint in God's action does not fit the wider scriptural portrait concerning God's incomprehensible power and love. It would seem more parsimonious at this point for Southgate to invoke divine inscrutability rather than a disjunction in God's creative omnipotence.[57] According to such an "inscrutabilist" account, the positing of an original ontology of violence that is ultimately ordered towards divine transformation would simply be offered as the manifestation of God's mysterious elective will, which cannot be subjected to rational interrogation.

It is certainly possible to invoke divine inscrutability with respect to the disjunction between nature's ontic violence and the revelation of its eschatological redemption. Nevertheless, invoking inscrutability at this point appears to link God to violence in a morally direct way.[58] Indeed,

---

57. More recently, it seems that Southgate is moving towards the inscrutabilist position under the conceptual auspices of "divine glory." He writes, "Here the inscape of the event includes long evolutionary histories of predator and prey. . . . It includes the power and expertise of flight of the eagle, its extraordinary visual acuity that picks out its prey at a vast distance, the quickness and agility of the hare, the twists and turns of the hunt, the hunger of the predator, and the fear and pain of the victim. It includes (I venture to suggest) God's delight in all those creaturely skills, and God's closeness to the suffering hare, in a particular and peculiar relationship of love and praise in extremis. So the search for those signs of the divine that constitute glory again involves a complex discernment, with elements of the counter-intuitive. It is emphatically not a way of saying that everything is lovely when seen in a big enough perspective. The world is complex and troubling, and yet charged with the grandeur of God" (Southgate, "Divine Glory in a Darwinian World," 803).

58. One might affirm that these two distinct horizons of creation, each shaped by distinct ontologies (of foundational violence and of eschatological peace), are simply the mystery of God's creative wisdom, which refuses our push to understand and explain. In this sense, the reality that God orders creation through its violent traversal in view of eschatological transformation is just the way of God's love, as God transcends all explanatory frameworks. Although this is a live option for some, the assertion involves us in series of claims that are difficult to reconcile. For instance, the positing of two distinct ends for creation appears to bifurcate the divine will so that it points in two directions: one where violence is directly willed, and one where it is not willed

one wonders if the inscrutabilist account, where violence and death are mysteriously willed by God, can fit with scriptural claims that God is "love" (1 John 4:8), and that God "did not make death" and "does not delight in the death of the living" (Wis 1:13). The question is about theological and moral fitness. That is, can the inscrutabilist's portrait of a God who mysteriously wills creaturely violence and suffering be adequately framed alongside other scriptural claims concerning God's nature and creative purpose? Perhaps more needs to be said. Our emerging theological narrative based on figural elaborations grants us a tentative framework through which we can press on to a deeper theological coherence. The mysterious nexus between divine creativity and creaturely agency admits the possibility of deviations within the comprehensive divine order. This indicates that the world does not align entirely with God's creative desire. On the contrary, it appears that the positive character of the divine will is only perfectly enacted in creation's eschatological transformation, wherein suffering is dissolved in the light of divine glory. This promise of an eschatological fulfillment of nature's brutal history invites the inference that the world is somehow estranged from God.

The Mystery of the Fallen World

The inference of the world's estrangement from God orients our figural theology toward elaborating some variation of the contingent-fallenness theodicy in its broad contours. This theodical framework interprets the world as somehow manifesting elements alienated from God's positive will. The remarkable juxtaposition of the ages of creation with inescapable and unremitting agonies and the revelation of creation's eschatological peace points toward the need for retrieval of the language of "deviation" and "fallenness" as a theological description of the world as it appears through time. While this terminology functions as shorthand for the theological and moral problem of nature's *agon*, the language by itself

---

to exist. This way of framing creation's two orders might possess clarity in locating ontological violence and its concomitant suffering directly within God's creative will. However, such a vision raises significant problems concerning traditional claims of God's perfect goodness and love. The issue largely trades upon the distinction between direct willing and permissive willing of evil and suffering. In both cases we might say that God is ultimately responsible inasmuch as God is the creator, and God elects to be the creator and God of all; yet, it makes considerable difference whether God directly *elects* violence in order to achieve the divine purpose or God *permits* violence in order to achieve the divine purpose.

cannot dispel the obscuring haze surrounding its origin. This presses us to consider the grammar of fallenness implied by our figural theology and speculatively engage the interpretive options regarding its origin.

Set forth as a theological description of the world, the grammar of "fallenness" requires a narrative framework that can make sense of its reference. This necessitates the uncovering of implicit theological structures that can account for such language and its referential application. If God's creation is laced with some inveterate corruption or wound in its ontological depths, there must be a way to somehow grasp its concrete actuality, at least within the realm of reasonable speculation.

Some contemporary theologians have adopted the grammar of fallenness by recasting the notion in a manner that reflects a late-modern ordering of reality. In such cases, the mythic primordial fall at the dawn of history is largely abandoned in favor of a narrative that stresses a deviation rooted in creation's contingency. Such an account interprets both the possibility and concrete manifestation of deviation as entirely bound up in the metaphysical character of the world as signified by its separation from the divine nature. Not only does the world's ontological distinction from God provide the basis for evil's possibility, but by some mysterious impulsion it also drives nature's physical brutality.

Following the Augustinian notion that the potentiality of evil emerges from the fact that "nature was made from nothing," the theologian Robert J. Russell, in dialogue with Reinhold Niebuhr's understanding of original sin, suggests that the physical universe retains a "universal contingent" whereby all natural evils, and their adjoined suffering, are both metaphysically *unnecessary* and *inevitable* in any finite world. This extension of the Niebuhrian interpretation of the underlying structure of sin recasts nature's *agon* as deriving from the intrinsic conditions of the finite world. Russell theorizes that the principle of entropy is such a universal contingent woven into every aspect of the world's physical structure. He writes:

> Whether cast in classical or modern metaphysics, God creates all that is through processes aimed at a dynamic peace. Evil is likened to a disorder, a dysfunction in an organism, an obstruction to growth, or an imperfection in being. Entropy refers to such disorder, measuring the dissipation of a system, the fracturing of a whole. In religious language, sin is universal, and it inevitably leads to despair, war, and death. Even though we grow in our relationship with God and each other, evil thwarts us.

> Similarly, our wasted energy scars our world and pollutes our environment. More generally, we need only to think of the pain and cost of natural disasters like famines, hurricanes, earthquakes, lightning, tornadoes, accidents of all kinds, or plagues and diseases to recognize the extent of suffering in this world. All these are rooted in the press of entropy, the relentless disintegration of form, environment, and organism; all are an affront to hope and peace.[59]

Nature's dissipative character flows from its entropic form and is affirmed as "ontologically contingent and thus not necessary," and yet the presence of natural evil and suffering "holds in all cases and thus is inevitable."[60] This vision of the *contingent inevitability* of suffering operates as a creational analogue for "original sin" insofar as all creatures are subjected to the obdurate consequences of existence without any prior personal determination.

Celia Deane-Drummond echoes a similar sentiment in her account of theistic evolution. She maintains that creation's fallenness is nonhypostatic—that is, not based on any type of *personal* agency but rather bound to the contingent regularities of the universe. Creation, in its contingency, possesses a mysterious potentiality open to the disorders and deformities of natural history. According to Deane-Drummond, the actualization of creational deviations is not the work of a satanic figure[61] but the manifestation of properties connected to creation's *ex nihilo* character. Here, the universe is construed as an impersonal reality whose diverse impulses lack intelligence and will yet remain ontically "free" to manifest properties at odds with the divine intention behind the world.[62]

These explanations of creation's fallenness rightly perceive the moral ambiguity of nature but suffer from a series of difficulties. Making physical strife an *inescapable* aspect of contingence appears to fuse the two concepts whereby the divine act of creation is bound up with the

---

59. Russell, "Entropy and Evil," 457.
60. Russell, "Groaning of Creation," 129–30.
61. Deane-Drummond, *Christ and Evolution*, 187.

62. One might conceive the nonhypostatic fallenness of creation as an expression of creation's contingent freedom wherein divergence is a statistical probability accorded to creation's elemental character. The freedom of creation would then be defined as non-personal ontic *indetermination* which God sacrificially grants to the world's principles at its foundation. Under this vision, God grants the world an elemental freedom expressed through certain divinely given necessities. However, it is not clear how the divinely given non-personal principles of creation, if acting according to their natures, could "freely" manifest divergent properties at odds with the divine will.

manifestation of violence and suffering. This is similar to Christopher Southgate's "only way" theodicy, which is subject to the same objections. It is unclear how the universe's contingent character, structured with God's divine Wisdom and power, could lead *inevitably* to evil by means of an impersonal instinct. If creation's principles operate invariably according to divinely determined natures, then describing their interactions as "free" is largely vacuous insofar as the production of the positive and negative dimensions of existence are the outworking of divinely determined properties. Thus, the image of nature's liability towards deviation is inherently undifferentiated from God's foundational intention for the universe. The assertion that creation is intrinsically endowed with properties that inevitably deviate works against the fitting theological narrative developed in our figural exegesis; this is especially so concerning the claim that God does not directly will or desire the world's ontic violence. Apart from some form of creaturely self-possession or personhood, metaphorical accounts of creation's freedom cannot fully illuminate the character of nature's divergence. Indeed, the lack of personal volition makes such a claim conceptually nebulous, wherein evil is either a direct intention of the divine will (making God the author of violence) or else God is subjected to some limiting principle where the possibility of suffering is the inevitable concomitant of creaturely existence. Either option is discordant with the prevailing theological understanding concerning God's nature and attributes—namely, infinite power, love, and peace. Deane-Drummond concedes as much when she claims that her understanding of fallenness is largely metaphorical in that it does not provide a causal framework that explains how creation might deviate from God's intentions; it merely asserts that this is the case. This idea of fallenness amounts to a re-description of the problem at hand. To speak of the world's contingent fallenness without some notion of personal self-possession or agency seems to recapitulate the conceptual tension of our theodicy in a different idiom without deepening our understanding.

If creation's contingent character by itself cannot account for the manifestation of physical suffering in the pre-human cosmos, we are led to consider the mysterious notion of a hypostatic fall connected to the structures of the world. Only those creatures capable of some form of rational self-possession can introduce real divergence into the world that God creatively wills. While all forms of impersonal agency are reducible to the divine impetus that creates and sustains them, only the ontic solidity of personalized spirit can render the language of deviation and fallenness morally intelligible in view of God's creative providence.

However, the traditional form of the fall narrative—the story of the primordial sin of the first human pair—does not lend itself easily to an explanation of the reality of creational strife. The reality of biological violence and death prior to the temporal emergence of human beings severely complicates the applicative force of the traditional doctrine. Possible solutions might abandon the modern scientific chronology of natural history, or perhaps refashion a pre-mundane fall as sketched by Origen in the third century. One could also explore the animal creation itself as the source of fallenness, as proposed by the philosopher Joshua Moritz.[63] While rejecting contemporary scientific chronology is, to my mind, untenable, the suppositions of a pre-mundane or animal fall have a degree of conceptual coherence that could be explored. Both positions, however, appear too thinly tethered to the world given in Scripture. In view of these limitations, the Christian theological tradition also provides an additional avenue worth exploring in terms of creation's contingent fallenness. This position links the brutal *agon* of the physical world with those mysterious beings that constitute the spiritual or angelic dimension of the universe.

63. Based upon his study of cognitive ethology and developmental biology, Moritz makes a sophisticated case that animals possess the incipient elements of conscious intention and volitional freedom (diversely instantiated) which, in turn, influenced the unfolding dynamics of creation's evolutionary history. Moritz writes, "Animals are not merely the passive objects of evolution but rather the active executive subjects who significantly determine the paths which their own—and their descendants—evolution will take" (Moritz, "Evolutionary Evil," 181). Even while conditioned by phylogenetic contingencies, animals exercise a degree of choice in their diverse subjective capacities, which affords a type of "protomoral" freedom diversely manifested within the natural world. For Moritz, the upshot of this account lies in opening up the possibility that the sufferings of nature may be subjected to an extension of the "free will" or "free process" defense, where at least some of the ontic violence among animals is conditioned by the volitional freedom latent within creaturely subjectivity. Moritz's theodical account makes a strong case for recognizing at least some forms of animal intentionality and the possibility of some incipient protomoral dimension. This may accord with scriptural locutions that speak of animals "praying" and "praising" God. However, even if we were to assume this account of animal sentience, the reality of creation's *agon* appears woven into the depths of creation in a way that extends beyond its manifestation in the higher animals, with their purported "rich cognitive lives." The predatory shape of nature is found in forms of life that would hardly count as candidates for a type of volitional sentience (including predatory microbes and carnivorous plants). Moreover, the emergence of nature's violent economy is rooted in the elemental character of the created cosmos. At least, it appears that the predatory shape of nature is etched upon the fundamental disposition of matter and energy in the space-time creation (entropy).

According to Christian tradition, a mysterious arrangement of personal beings constitutes the spiritual envelope of the physical world. Some of these spirits are reported as having decisively rebelled against the purpose originally allotted to them in God's creative act. This deviation or fall of the spiritual creation may be somehow connected to the empirical determinations of the physical world. This theological narrative assumes a mediating connection of the spiritual creation with respect to the visible world as well as the personal rebellion of these beings. Both assumptions can be shown to be present to varying degrees in Scripture and tradition.

In the medieval thought of Hugh of St. Victor, the spiritual creation was perceived as having a mediating function with respect to the outworking of the divine ideas. He writes, "The rational creature was made in first place and in the likeness of the divine Idea, with nothing mediating between them. The corporeal creature, however, was made in the likeness of the divine Idea through the mediation of the rational creature."[64] In this respect, Hugh was simply expressing a widely regarded tradition that linked the function of the spiritual world with the governance of physical realities. For case in point, the fourth-century theologian Gregory of Nazianzus described angels as "ministrants of God's will, strong with both inborn and imparted strength, traversing all space, readily present to all at any place through their zeal for ministry and the agility of their nature . . . different individuals of them embracing different parts of the world, or appointed over different districts of the Universe, as He knoweth who ordered and distributed it all."[65] This traditional vision of the integral unity of the spiritual and physical is connected with Hugh's ontology that describes creation as an enveloping relational nexus wherein all things are "connected causally."[66] By this account, no part of the created world, whether physical or spiritual, remains causally inert with respect to the other. According to this Hugonian ontology, the spiritual cosmos recapitulates and participates in the same figured patterns that are inscribed upon both human beings and the natural world.

In figural terms, this vision of the spiritual world may be perceived in the scriptural form of the temple, wherein the divine presence is withdrawn and veiled by a curtain inscribed with the image of angelic beings (Exod 26:1, 31; 36:8, 35). This figured connection of the temple

64. Hugh of St. Victor, *Didascalicon* appendix C.
65. Gregory of Nazianzus, *Second Theological Oration* 31.
66. Hugh of St. Victor, *De sacramentis* 1.2.2.

with the angelic creation is also described by Gregory Nazianzus, who writes: "Since the Word knows the Tabernacle of Moses to be a figure of the whole creation—I mean the entire system of things visible and invisible—shall we pass the first veil, and stepping beyond the realm of sense, shall we look into the Holy Place, the Intellectual and Celestial creation?"[67] For Gregory, the temple's Holy Place is the celestial or spiritual creation that shrouds the divine glory in the holy of holies. When interpreted in the light of God's sacrificial agency, this textured image expresses the ontic density of the visible world insofar as it is subjected to the mysterious governance of the angels. In other words, spiritual creatures are the ordained intermediaries between the overwhelming fullness of God's infinite glory and the visible manifestation of the finite world in time.[68] This vision of the mediating function of these spirits, although speculative, possesses a fitting coherence with respect to our figural theology. Moreover, such an account intimates a wider narrative framework that could helpfully interpret the brutality of the natural world in terms of our theodical purpose.

In support of this supposition, Scripture's cosmology assumes the presence of some kind of adverse spiritual creature. Specifically, the New Testament displays a collection of passages that allude to the present age as mysteriously subjugated to fallen powers. These creatures are the "thrones" (Col 1:16), the "dominions" (Eph 1:21), the "principalities" (Eph 3:10), and the "rulers of this age" (1 Cor 2:8). The church constantly struggles against these "principalities, against these powers, against the world rulers of this present darkness, against the spiritual hosts of wickedness in the heavenly places" (Eph 6:12).[69] Indeed, Satan is referred to as "the god of this cosmos" (2 Cor 4:4), the "prince of this cosmos" (John 12:31; 14:30; 16:11), and "the prince of the power of the air" (Eph 2:2). Such descriptions imply a provisional dualism as part of the cosmological vision of early Christianity. This dualistic vision of the created world

---

67. Gregory of Nazianzus, *Second Theological Oration* 31.

68. Paul seems to express something of this figuration of the angelic mediation when he refers to angels ordaining Israel's law—including the temple and its sacrifices (Gal 3:19).

69. It is possible to see the New Testament cosmology as antecedently connected to various descriptions of the "heavenly council" that surrounds the divine throne in the Old Testament. For instance, Psalm 82 and Psalm 58 may possibly describe these "gods" as subjected to divine judgment for "partiality to the wicked" (82:2) and for dealing "out violence on the earth" (58:2). One could also advert to the mysterious "sons of God" of Genesis 6, who took the daughters of men for their wives.

is expressed in the scriptural use of the term "cosmos," which in its semantic range simultaneously describes the world as the object of divine love (John 3:16; 12:47) and that which strives incessantly against God (John 15:18–19; 16:33). The world in Scripture is not therefore simply the perfect expression of divine glory; rather, the world possesses, or is possessed by, elements that conflict with God. The scriptural predication of "authority" and "power" to these creatures lends substance to the postulate that the physical world's manifest character is somehow enlaced with the effects of their presence.

One of the primary difficulties with the notion of fallen spirits is that the scriptural depiction of their origin and fall is rather restrained. There are implicit references to these spirits' antagonism towards God's purpose (as noted above), but Scripture is laconic in its expression of their origin. There is no clear, definitive account of the creation and fall of such beings. Indeed, the relative silence of the hexaemeron regarding their origin led theologians like Augustine to discern their presence in Scripture under the figures of "heaven" and "light."[70] According to the Augustinian interpretation followed by Hugh of St. Victor, the separation of created light from darkness on the first day signifies the primordial deviation of the universe's spiritual aspect. This figural inference is legitimately compelled by the wider landscape of figures given by Scripture, alluding to the mysterious presence of such beings.

In terms of this scriptural cosmology, theologians like Hugh of St. Victor have generally affirmed the operative role of angels in connection with physical realities. However, this connection has rarely been explored in view of nature's metaphysical violence. The interpretive potential of such a theological cosmology has become more apparent with the emergence of the modern scientific and moral ordering of reality, which has rendered the moral intelligibility of creation increasingly opaque. Thus, only in the modern period has the notion of cosmic fallenness been *substantially* engaged to relieve the pressure presented by the world's empirical form. To pursue the narrative possibility of fallenness implied by our figural theology, we return to the thought of Sergius Bulgakov, who articulates a vision of the world subsisting through the mediating function of the angels.

According to Bulgakov's theological cosmology, the angelic world's mediating connection with the visible world is bound up with the

---

70. Augustine, *Literal Meaning of Genesis* 2.16–17.

sacrificial form of God's creative act. Thus, the metaphysical freedom of the world is expressed by personal spiritual principles that subsist in close connection with the material content of physical reality. The unfolding emergence of the physical cosmos is shepherded into form by the spiritual world. Bulgakov writes,

> This is a manifestation of God's providential activity with respect to the creaturely world, realized through the angels: The elemental life of the world, in its blind instinct, is protected and directed by the hypostatically conscious guidance of the angels, who can be seen as a heavenly mirror of the earthly creation, the helmsmen of this creation.[71]

According to this cosmology, personal spirits exercise a form of governance over the preconscious nonhypostatic elements of the universe. These spirits are integrally expressive of "the plan of creation sketched out by the Creator."[72]

> In this general sense it must be said that the angelic world contains in itself the ideal analogue of the universe in all its parts: all ideas or creative themes of this world are present in the angelic world and are realized only when it is present. In this the angelic world is really the intermediary between God and the world, the ladder from earth to the heavens without which our world could not endure the immediate proximity of God.[73]

This emphasis upon the relational unity of heaven and earth—of the spiritual and physical universe—explicates the dual-aspect contingence (its separation from and participation in God) in a way that accounts for the divergent shape of nature's phenomenal manifestation.

For Bulgakov, the traversal of the material creation is distressed by the primeval deviation of spirit, which has infected the physical world with a congenital "sickness."[74] He writes, "the fall in the spiritual world could not fail to have repercussions in the natural world, since angels who had formerly been guardians of creation are transformed through the fall into spirits of wickedness in high places, poisoning and perverting

---

71. Bulgakov, *Bride of the Lamb*, 197.
72. Bulgakov, *Bride of the Lamb*, 55.
73. Bulgakov, *Jacob's Ladder*, 34.
74. "The very fall of the angels is already a severe sickness for all of creation, for this sickness does not remain localized but extends to all of nature and to man" (Bulgakov, *Bride of the Lamb*, 159).

creation."[75] This mysterious connection between physical and spiritual creatures provides an interpretive framework that locates the origin of nature's *agon* within the conflicted world of spirit. The empirical manifestations of nature mirror the anterior strife of the spirit world with its mysterious rebellion. Hence, the unfolding ages of natural history are simply "the outer shell" of this unfathomable struggle of the "powers" that form the inner principles of the world.[76] This account might explain the disturbing wonders of nature—things like the liver-fluke worm, the ichneumon wasp, and the wider predatory economy—as the visible form of the invisible world's strife. This speculative vision is shared by the French Catholic theologian Louis Bouyer who argues that both the wastefulness and fecundity of the evolutionary process are visible expressions of this immaterial struggle between fallen spirits, who deform and distort physical creation and the faithful spirits who integrate that disorder into the unfolding traversal of created being. Bouyer writes,

> The remaining forces of life—represented by the faithful angels entrusted with guarding the universe and protecting it against the demonic treason—succeeded in achieving much more than a mere static equilibrium in creation. Supported and nourished by the creative grace to which the angels' fidelity contributed, their struggle was to bring about the consistent triumph in this world of the forces of life over those of death.[77]

Like Bulgakov, Bouyer takes seriously the provisional cosmic dualism of the New Testament and uses it to interpret the ontic violence of natural history.

The advantage of this view lies precisely in its application of the *personal* dimension of freedom to the interstitial fabric of creation, which

75. Bulgakov, *Bride of the Lamb*, 198.

76. While the spiritual powers of the created world are not themselves co-creators with God since they cannot create ex nihilo, they may possess the capacity to influence or shape the unfolding dimensions of the physical creation. Augustine affirms that angels (both good and fallen) can shape material realities by being able to "bring things to birth and accelerate their growth in novel ways." For Augustine, the seminal reasons embedded in creation's fabric are subjected to the influence of secondary spiritual powers. Augustine maintains this position while addressing the issue of whether Egyptian magicians could create frogs or serpents out of matter with the help of the fallen angels. See Augustine, *Trinity* 3.13. See also the discussion of the medieval debates concerning the creative or productive power of angels in Keck, *Angels and Angelology*, 20–22. For a contemporary account as to how angels might influence evolutionary developments in natural history, see Dumsday, "Natural Evil, Evolution," 71–84.

77. Bouyer, *Cosmos*, 212–13.

explains the world's strife in terms of nature's spiritual foundation. This fits with the wider theological sketch concerning God's sacrificial nature and the world's ontic freedom derived from our figural engagement of the Scriptures. God's sacrificial donation is the creative summons to these spiritual principles to unfold the grand themes of creation's temporal existence. For a theologian like Bulgakov, the unfolding character of the world reveals the original theme of creation as it "is written in heaven," while its "execution (of which there are various possibilities) or nonexecution is entrusted to creation in its creaturely freedom."[78] At its core, this interpretive narrative evaluates the brutal conditions of nature's history as intrinsically connected to some moral corruption in these personal beings; this echoes the free-will defense in traditional theodical reasoning. God appears to have created the world with spiritual principles, themselves endowed with a personalized freedom that ineluctably carries the risk of evil. Significantly, unlike other traditional free-will theodicies, the metaphysical form of this account assumes a mysterious relational nexus that provides a narrative framework for describing the shape of nature's strife even while veiling the logic of evil's manifestation in history (more about this below). This position possesses theological viability inasmuch as it coheres with both the sacrificial form of God's creative agency and the contingent dynamics of creation's developmental character. Furthermore, it avoids the problems associated with the notion of impersonal fallenness that too closely binds God's creative action with the reality of evil and suffering. Despite offering a more comprehensible vision of natural evil by resolving it into an expression of personal agency, the notion is not without significant pitfalls.

Putting aside the banal objection to the spiritual world's mythological character, the major difficulty with this theological vision concerns difficulties inherent with the moralization of evil and suffering. First, attributing the brutal reality of creation to fallen spiritual powers pushes the problem conceptually back into the nature of God. As soon as one envisions a spiritual deviation in creation's history—with its long epochs of violence, suffering, and death—the question arises: why did God create the world in such a way that physical life is tied to corruptible spirits? If such antagonistic beings shape the physical world, this can only be by God's directive. Second, this type of theodical narrative also amends the direct causal nexus between moral evil and suffering that is typical of

---

78. Bulgakov, *Bride of the Lamb*, 134.

free-will theodicies. Traditionally, the problem of suffering was causally linked with the sin of rational creatures, whereby only rational creatures were subjected to suffering. In the case of a cosmic fall, one's recognition of the suffering of the *animal* creation because of moral disorder implies an important revision of the Augustinian logic concerning evil and suffering. Accordingly, the material world is dragged downwards (so to speak) by the spiritual creation. This fallenness, with its cascading ontological damage, functions as an analogical expression of "original sin" construed in terms of nature's foundational principles. The world and its creatures come-to-be in the wake of this primordial struggle, which extends to all aspects of created existence. While this narrative provides a fitting account for the origination of nature's congenital strife by locating it in the heart of the spiritual creation, it cannot explain why the world's creatures are enfolded within the participatory consequences of this original distortion.[79] In order to pursue a theological interpretation of the relational character of creation with its intrinsic fragility we must engage the world's economic form in light of the Christological principle.

The Eucharistic Life of the World: Life Deformed and Redeemed

While the figural theology articulated in this project might not solve the problem of creation's fragility, it does offer a way to faithfully pursue the mystery according to God's self-revelation in Christ. Our figural vision posits that the world in its fragility, fallenness, and transformation bears the indelible imprint of the incarnate life of Christ, the Word of God through whom all things are made. This comprehensive vision of the entire sweep of the world's being in Christ conceptually recapitulates Hugh's figuralism wherein all things are the shadowed forms and figures of Christ himself. For Hugh, the Word of God is "seen through what He

79. This is strikingly analogous to the problem of human participation in "original sin." The traditional doctrine refers to the congenital state inherited by all human persons by virtue of their existence and precedes and actualizes all human manifestations of actual sin. This state of being, while authored by some enigmatic event of personal agency, unfolds in history according to an enveloping logic that afflicts all irrespective of their personal actions. This mysterious "participatory affliction" corresponds conceptually with the position articulated here with respect to creation's fallenness. The world's creatures come-to-be in a world conditioned by anterior ontological damage that cascades throughout time. While this deviation is initiated by a mysterious "other," creatures inherit and enact their existence according to what has been given. For an excellent discussion of theological issues concerning the doctrine of original sin. See McFarland, *In Adam's Fall*.

made,"[80] and this is largely expressed in Hugh's theology through abstract ontological categories. Thus, Christ is seen primarily in the manifest order, diversity, and beauty of creatures. By deepening this Hugonian vision of Christ as the animating idea and principle of the creaturely world, we can begin to perceive the natural world's manifestations not only as expressions of the Word's creative plenitude but as a concrete unveiling of the crucified and exalted Jesus. To put it another way, the mystery of the world's vast epochs of suffering, violence, and waste are comprehended through the self-offering disclosure of God's nature as it is given in and through the scripturally described form of Jesus. As such, Christ's life as the innocent one *par excellence* who suffers for the sake of the world appears as the foundational pattern upon which the world's ambiguous manifestations ultimately find coherence. That which is created in Christ is a world where all creatures are etched according to the pattern of the paschal mystery, summoned *in* self-offering and ordered *towards* self-offering.

According to this figuralist logic, the meaning of the world and its creatures is given utterly in the mystery of Jesus, whose incarnate passion, death, and resurrection trace out the world in its temporal manifestation. From this vantage, the figured Scriptures disclose the world's being as protologically oriented towards an eschatological perfection, which is the revelation of God's life in the world. This divinized unveiling of the world at its end assumes the perfected *Eucharistic* form of the paschal mystery, wherein life is given for the sake of life without ontological destruction. This is the glory of creation's being, the culmination of the divine purpose to gather and unite all things in divine peace. By contrast, in the light of the Son's sacrificial traversal, the empirical world appears submerged in an ontology of violence where life is shadowed by the looming presence of conflict, strife, and death. In the passage of the world's ages, all material creatures emerge in a time-space fabric where the exchange of life is enveloped by realities that appear profoundly disjunctive with creation's final revelation in Christ. However, it is not Christ's exaltation alone that speaks of the world's meaning. The concrete form of his paschal suffering unveils something of the mysterious character of the world's form.

By taking the paschal mystery of Christ as our metaphysical starting point, the manifestation of the world in its traversal appears as a type of *deformed eucharist* wherein life is ordered by a narrative of fallen

---

80. Hugh of St. Victor, *De tribus diebus* 1.1.

time that parasitically shadows the original form of the divine Word of God. Accordingly, the narrative logic of fallen time is the mysterious out-working of some primeval deviation, which enacts a cascading set of realities that deform creation in a parody of the divine Truth. This narrative of deviation supervenes the foundational ontological order of the world wherein all creatures are bound together in mysterious participation. In the mystery of the cosmic fall, the ontological theme of the world's relational form is narrated as discord, conflict, and destruction. The deviated, discordant narration of the original theme is traced out along the figurated body of Jesus as he passes through the darkness of the fallen world. Under such a revelation, nature's *agon*, with its overwhelming ontic violence and absurd logic, is unveiled as a kind of improvised distortion that plays along and mocks the underlying glory of the created world. Evil's transgressive presence leaps across boundaries, defies direct causal logics, and renders the world's suffering unintelligible to any explanatory pattern other than that given through Jesus Christ's salvific traversal of fallen time. The Son's *innocent suffering* in this world thus explicates the fallen time of creation as a type of disfigured communion that reverberates with an absolute excess of suffering that defies any moral calculation. This excess is the ruined image of the unconditioned grace and sacrificial love that summons the world into being and recreates the world at its end. In the interval or traversal of creation's fallen time, the reality of creation's suffering is the irrational and encompassing shadow that grows alongside the unfolding divine theme of creaturely being.

From the perspective of the paschal mystery, we can perceive the shadowed form of Jesus within the concrete history of the fallen world. The disturbing wonders of created nature, including the suffering of animal life, speak of the eternal beauty of Christ, who innocently suffers the fallen world for the sake of its redemption and transformation. The revelation of Christ thus discloses the character of creation's distortion as a mysterious simulacrum of the foundational theme given to the world by God in Christ. This speculative claim concerning creation's Christic shape is less an explanation of the *why* of creation's agonistic order than it is an articulation of its mysterious *how*. That is, the figurated revelation of Christ grasped through scriptural forms provides a way of perceiving the shape of the world with its tangled connections as the enigmatic reflection of God's sacrificial love. According to this account, the world's suffering is born from the participatory and relational nature of created being, which mirrors the paschal character of God's trihypostatic nature. From this vantage, we perceive evil's form, with its cascading consequences that defy all causal logic, as the bent expression of the original theme narrated in the world by the Word of God. Ultimately, the innocent suffering of Jesus in history both unveils and restores the true form of the creaturely world, as it exists in the eternal desire of God.

CONCLUSION

The theological problem of the world's metaphysical character is conditioned by a conceptual tension between God's nature, classically understood, and the agonistic character of the created world. Theodical reasoning operates within this tension, seeking ways to negotiate or structure the two aspects in ways that shed light on the mystery of suffering. Our exploration of Scripture's figural landscape by means of the Hugonian ark reveals theological patterns that interpretively engage the distinction between God and the world. The referential reach of the patterns of traversal and sacrifice descriptively articulate the Word's incarnate form, which perfectly inhabits both "sides" of the metaphysical distinction. Thus, Christ's incarnate life, as it is figurally mediated, appears as the conceptual key for exploring the mystery of creation.

In our figural exploration, we interpreted our scriptural patterns as types of a metaphysical disclosure of the divine nature and, by extension, of the divine act of creation *ad extra*. The sacrificial shape of the creative act is a divine impartation through which the world's creatures are called to participate in the world's emergence in time. This participatory existence outlines the shape of the world with the figures of traversal and sacrifice. Here, the scriptural temple's figuration of the world reveals the paradoxical co-inherence of metaphysical freedom and divine participation within the Word of God both in its creative unfolding and its eschatological promise. The natural world, in its autonomy and freedom, is framed by a traversing metaphysical form that constitutes all things *in* time, even as it is further summoned to a transcendent horizon *beyond* history.

The revelation of the ultimate ontological peace of creation at its eschatological fulfillment led us to consider the extent to which the description of fallenness is applicable to the natural world in its present state. We followed both scriptural clues and traditional Christian cosmology to explore the origin of nature's strife in connection with the notion of fallen spiritual powers. We concluded that the mediating role of spiritual principles in the development of the world might be the source of its conflicted character. If the world's separation from God establishes its relative freedom, which is intended to be realized in the relational unity of the spiritual and physical worlds, then this connection may narrate how evil emerges in history. The present world appears subject to a primordial deviation that plunged the visible world into an economy of violence that is both creatively fruitful and ontically disordered. What was intended as the foundational theme of creation, figurated in the pattern of traversal and sacrifice, has thus been perverted. Instead of displaying the peaceful reciprocity of the Eucharistic form of Christ in divinely given limits, the world's relations have become primordially diseased by the presence of spiritual evil.

This set of theological explorations operates altogether under the principle that the figurated patterns of Scripture analogically describe both the God revealed in Jesus Christ and the created world in all its aspects. The mystery of nature's agonistic order in terms of its metaphysical possibility and concrete actuality is bound up with the very character of God making all things in Jesus Christ; his form reveals both the triune nature and the shape of the world as it emerges in time. In view of our theodical concern, the metaphysics of traversal and relational participation illuminate the ontic possibilities of creation's deviation, which appear as the mystery of fallenness. Yet, despite the interpretive possibilities afforded by this framework, the explanatory power of this account, like that of all theodical discourse, ultimately fades into the very mystery of God. In other words, the suffering form of the created universe, even with an acknowledgment of spiritual fallenness, can only be grasped through the impenetrable mystery of the sacrificial love revealed in Jesus Christ.

Conclusion:
Nature's *Agon* in the Shadow of Christ

THIS ESSAY'S PRIMARY OBJECTIVE was to develop a theological understanding of the disturbing wonders of the natural world centrally ordered by God's trinitarian self-revelation. For this task, we embraced the Christian tradition's original mode of natural theology, denoted as the tradition of the two books (*liber scripturae* and *liber naturae*), as the means toward this theological understanding. This constructive retrieval, with its far-reaching metaphysical claims, was in part motivated and conditioned by a general dissatisfaction with contemporary creational theodicies and their limited engagement with Christian revelation. While philosophically based theodicies are compelling in many respects, they are also constrained in their theological significance insofar as the central form of Christian belief—the revelation of the divine-humanity of Jesus Christ—appears more or less *extrinsic* to their interpretive judgments. By contrast, this study's approach to the problem of creation's agonistic existence assumes the conceptual orientation of a traditional natural theology with its profound figuralism to foreground the Christological dimension for our thinking about the natural world. This disposition assumes the scripturally articulated form of the crucified and exalted Jesus as the revealed principle for structuring our understanding of nature's *agon* in view of God's creative and omnipotent love.

In terms of the *status questionis*, the problem of animal suffering (or more broadly, creational suffering) has only emerged as a significant theodical problem for the Christian tradition since the beginning of the modern period. Christian theologians and philosophers have since sought to explain creation's strife in view of traditional claims concerning the divine nature. For the most part, the attention given to the problem of nature's *agon* has produced a set of approaches, which we have designated in this project as the *eliminativist, instrumentalist,* and *contingent-fallenness* theodicies. These theodical categories, broadly construed, capture the essential narrative forms for interpreting the problem of creational suffering from the perspective of Christian belief. All three of these categories also find substantial presence in contemporary Christian discourse, and in my judgment, they represent the limit of rational reflection regarding the issue. Moreover, such abstract renderings with their contrary perspectives appear interchangeable within the broad framework of Christian theistic claims. This indicates that each type of theodical approach could fit theoretically with the Christian narrative insofar as each one possesses some referential basis within Scripture and theological tradition.

This open character of modern creational theodicies vis-à-vis Christian revelation underscores what I consider to be the central limitation of these discussions: they are formulated and evaluated in relative isolation from the primary revelatory form of theological discourse. By contrast, our project emphasizes the absolute priority of God's self-interpretation in Christ as the determinative basis upon which to engage and explore the relationship "between" the infinite nature of God and the finite world. As a methodological gestalt, this theology emphasizes the ontological and epistemic priority of Christ for theological thinking, a position somewhat reminiscent of the theologies of Hans Urs von Balthasar and Karl Barth. However, this project's Christocentric vision of theology is distinctive because it retrieves the practice of scriptural figuration as the operative basis for elucidating the revealed form of Christ in relation to all things. Our figural thinking thus flows from an underlying Christological principle that perceives all things as interpretively encompassed by the mysterious reference of the Holy Scriptures, grasped as God's revelatory discourse.

Within this Christocentric context, the subsequent theoretical exploration of nature's *agon* is structured according to Scripture's figured landscape. Like the conceptual problem of theodicy, the layered reference of the Scriptures pertains to the unique ontological space that obtains "between" God and the world. By examining these scriptural patterns and their extended theological significance, we are able to orient our thinking about the mysterious realities of God's infinite agency and the shape of created existence by tethering them to the exhaustive reach of the world given by the Scriptures.

One of the advantages of a figuralist approach is its provision of a *determinative* point of reference for generating and evaluating theological explorations. Specifically, the development of theoretical structures that flow from and deeply cohere with the principal axis of Christian revelation affords a formative schematic for organizing our theological reasoning about the shape of created existence. By engaging the Bible figurally as God's creative and disclosive speech, we are thus able to integrate the various conceptual elements afforded by modern theodical reflection, configuring them within the disclosive parameters articulated through the scriptural order of reality. This, in turn, provides the ground for developing a type of *argumentum ex convenientia*—a suitable narrative of creational suffering fitted and determined by the underlying Christo-logic of the Scriptures.

According to this account, our figuralist theology represents an approach that does not generate *new* and *distinctive* theodical claims. Rather, it is an approach that provides a determinative theological basis for sifting and discerning what the world *is*—with its endemic violence and suffering—in a way that is anchored to the narrative articulation of Christ's form as given by the Scriptures. In brief, an axiomatic assumption of this project is that only in the light of Christ's divine humanity can the true shape of things—including divine agency and nature's *agon*—come into view. This project is thus distinguished and animated by a theological disposition that trusts in the disclosive efficacy of the Scriptures to orient one's apprehension of the world's being in God's creative providence.

For this task, the figuralism of Hugh of St. Victor with its Christocentric point of departure was examined and used to facilitate our theological reasoning about the created world. Hugh's comprehensive figuralist vision of the intersection between creation and Scripture and his specific exegetical engagement of the scriptural ark provided the epistemic foundation for initiating our discernment of the Bible. In examining Hugh's ark in terms of its scripturally networked cognates (specifically the temple form), we unveiled within Scripture two profound structural patterns that pertain to the principal shape of the universe. In their Christological and creational reference, these scriptural patterns of *traversal* and *sacrifice* formed the conceptual anchors for our theoretical discussion of the world's phenomenal character. Our exploration of Scripture was thus shaped by both Hugh's figuration and his creational theology, which then oriented our theological elaborations regarding nature's *agon*.

In terms of constructive theology, this study has discerned and examined a series of probative structures that determine how we approach the metaphysically mysterious borderland between the uncreated God and the finite world. By delineating the theological import of these figured structures, we have established a type of theoretical architecture for a broad theological narrative of creation that is deeply determined by the revelatory mystery of Christ. These scripturally based theoretical structures cohere to form a "fitting" theological narrative that comprehends the wonder of creation's suffering. Before summarizing the resultant narrative and its implications, we will rehearse the specific theoretical structures that anchor this narrative.

The first theoretical structure reveals the character of God's creative action. The scriptural form of Christ's incarnate life, grasped by the figurated patterns of traversal and sacrifice, unveils an implicit trinitarian ontology that narrates the divine nature as absolute sacrificial love. According to this understanding, the triune nature is analogically expressed according to the *self-offering* form that constitutes Christ's incarnate life. By extension, this disclosure further unveils the character of divine action *ad extra* as structured according to the same pattern. Thus, the mystery of creation, the positing of the whole contingent world, appears under the sign of God's sacrificially determined form. The divine shape of traversal and sacrifice reframes how we narrate the character of divine omnipotence in terms of creation's ontological freedom. The self-offering nature of God's agency includes a "permissive space" for the realization of the world (described as a metaphorical separation or contraction) that is simultaneously (and paradoxically) encompassed by God's patient providence, which is again narrated by the sacrificial logic of Christ's form.

The second theoretical structure is the created obverse to the above Christic revelation of God's being and action as self-offering love. Namely, the unfolding span of the universe is manifested according to Christ's scripturally articulated passage in time. In ontological terms, the world's traversal mirrors the sacrificial movement (*motus*) of Christ's scriptural form in its traversal of coming-to-be, expressed by its evolutionary fecundity and its mysterious openness towards its eschatological horizon. This understanding of traversal as a framing ontology also grounds the contingent freedom of creatures (as immanent secondary causal agents) within the unfolding span of finite existence. The contingent universe was founded upon divine sacrificial love and is encompassed by metaphysical freedom. This sets the interpretive context for recognizing that not everything in creation aligns with God's eternal purpose in all its aspects.

In conjunction with the theoretical form of creation's traversal in-and-beyond-time, the sacrificial form also interpretively frames the universe's span as revealed through the form of Christ's suffering. This formal structure unveils the world as governed by a mysterious sacrificial theme binding all creatures (elements, forces, animals, and events) together in a continuum of relational exchange of giving and receiving. This relational ontology is manifested in empirical time as the agonistic order of violence and death, which encompasses the entire span of natural history. However, within the disclosive light of Christ's temporal traversal—which perfectly narrates this sacrificial theme as one of definitive ontological peace—the temporal manifestation of the world appears disjunctive with its eschatological *telos*. In figural terms, Christ's Eucharistic presence unveiled the sacrificial theme of the world in its eschatological fullness under the form of life exhaustively given for the sake of life *without ontological destruction*. This figured pattern in its scriptural deployment presses us to revise how we grasp the agonistic shape of the world's traversal into being. The Christological theme of the world appears not as one of original metaphysical violence but of self-offering peace. Somehow, within the unfolding movement of creation's temporality, this original theme has been manifested as an economic order of assertive dispossession, ruthless predation, and wasteful loss.

Taken together, the combustive interaction of these theoretical structures outlines something of divine agency and the life and purpose of creation. They also manifest an *implicit* structure as part of our thinking about the world, concerning the fallenness of creation in view of nature's violent history. The figurated disclosure of Christ's sacrificial fulfillment of creation, outlined by our figural reflections, implies that the empirical nature of the world, with its ontic violence, was somehow outside God's ultimate purpose. The precise source for this original deviation is somewhat mysterious in Scripture's figured landscape. We proposed that the origination of nature's metaphysical violence was in some way connected with the corruption of the spiritual creation—that is, with the theological tradition of the fallen angels. According to this narrative, the moral corruption of these spiritual principles cascaded along the interactive structure of the universe and subverted its underlying relational logic. The phenomenal world thus appeared as a type of deformed Eucharist whereby the original relational reciprocity of being, which mirrored the sacrificial love of God at its foundation, was marred by a dark impulsion deforming it beyond recognition.

Within this accumulated set of theoretical structures, an implicit theological narrative emerged, articulating something of creation's mysterious traversal in-and-beyond-time. This vision of God's absolute creativity and nature's autonomous form is relatively traditional since it reworks theological categories regarding divine goodness, infinite and finite agency, and creation's fallenness. This narrative, along with some of its theological implications, may be summarily sketched as follows.

In the mystery of divine love, God sacrificially posited the contingent world in freedom, endowing it with foundational themes reflecting the eternal form of the Word of God. These divinely gifted themes were manifested in the world's traversal into subsistence with its rich profusion of creatures bound together by an intrinsic relational structure. However, the possibility of deviation was also endowed at its foundation because of the world's profound ontological freedom born from divine sacrificial love. And though the precise origin of this original deviation is mysterious, it is plausible that it was somehow connected to the universe's spiritual principles, which, according to tradition, played some role in the unfolding of the world's themes. According to this understanding, the primordial spiritual deviation unleashed a cascading set of realities that deformed the universe's relational continuum. Thus, creation's movement into being is marked by an indiscerptible fusion of divine content and ontic distortions constituting the phenomenal world with its wondrous beauty and harrowing violence. Nevertheless, even with nature's endemic sickness, the unfolding span of time reveals a hidden providence that patiently gathers up all the deviated and deformed elements of the world to bring them to their eschatological fulfillment. This final passage of the world beyond our fallen empirical time is proleptically revealed in the resurrected body of Christ, whose suffering passage re-narrates the world's primordial violence as perfect ontological peace.

According to this account, nature's agonies are expressive of the metaphysical identity of the world, both in terms of its divine foundation and its mysterious corruption. The revelation of Christ's passage in time unveils the suffering of creation to be essentially determined by both the traversing span of the world in its ontological distinction from God and the outworking of its contingent freedom. At the center of this account is the divine reality of self-donating love. This love determines the world's distinctive metaphysical form, which ultimately conditions its beauty, fragility, and fallenness. All the creaturely constituents of natural history, even the liver-fluke worm and its victims, are enfolded by the all-encompassing omnipotent love of God, which suffers their deviations through time in order to gather and judge them all in eschatological glory.

It is only in the shadow of the paschal mystery that we can grasp the manifest character of divine love and gain some understanding of creation's story. In Christ's suffering passage through time, the things of the fallen world are gathered through death and definitively unveiled in the mystery of nature's divinization. And yet what this mystery looks like for the world's innumerable creatures remains unknown, as does the human understanding of what it all means. At most, we can say that the enmeshed character of natural time, with its ontological goods and recalcitrant brutalities, points toward some unspeakable goodness in Christ that defies our comprehension. Until that final unveiling, the desire to understand why God permits the violence and agonies of creation remains eschatologically deferred. On these subjects, we can only confess that the world is not yet what God intends. Yet hope remains. Insofar as Christ has come to restore *all* things, we may hope that the suffering creation, apparently submerged in the dissolving currents of time, will one day shine forth in its vast array as the new heaven and earth, healed and transformed.

This comprehensive narrative, determined by our exploration of the scriptural world *via* Hugh's figuralism, articulates a constructive theology that displays essential continuities and differences with the broader character of Hugh's creational theology. Our theological exploration retains something of Hugh's interpretation of the developmental image of creaturely existence, which, in theodical terms, functions as a type of instrumentalist narrative. Hugh's creational theology describes the economic order of the universe as determined by certain foundational limitations and imperfections that are comprehensively open to some mysterious deepening of form. Our theology is an expansive variation of this structure inasmuch as our understanding of creation's eschatological transformation implies a distinct protological foundation (with its structural limitations) open to a mysterious transfiguration in union with God's infinite life. In brief, the outweighing purpose of creation's receptive divinization presupposes a natural infrastructure ordered through some mysterious traversal of time.

Our narrative also differs from Hugh's instrumentalist vision in a critical way. For Hugh, the divine will directly establishes and affirms the role of ontic violence in creation's coming-to-be. His instrumentalist account depicts the suffering of creatures as the costly price necessary to bring about the divine purpose. And in this, Hugh's position simply accords with the essential sentiments of the major tradition and the vast majority of modern instrumentalist theodicies. By contrast, our narrative of creation's traversal, both in its coming-to-be and in its eschatological openness, is conditioned by the possibility of contingent fallenness. This reconfigures our narrative by defining nature's ontic violence as an indirect reality born from the mysterious self-offering character of the creative act. By its very nature, this act opens up the world to the possibility of corruption. The distinction between direct willing and permissive willing weaves elements of the instrumentalist form into a variation of the contingent-fallenness theodicy, establishing a fitting theological account that reflects the emergent intelligibility of scriptural claims.

Overall, this narrative outlines a theological understanding of the terms of the theodical problem—namely, divine agency and creaturely becoming—determined by the revelatory fullness of Christ, who is both the revelation of the infinite God and the ultimate meaning of *all* that has occurred in time. Our narrative of nature's *agon* is thus a speculative explication of the revealed form of Christ, which casts light upon the whole of natural history, including the sufferings of animals. In this regard, the theological "fittingness" of our interpretation and its interpretive fecundity is bound entirely to its generative connection with the form of Jesus given by the Scriptures. In this way, the truth about the world's suffering is disclosed through the passage of the divine Son, who unveils nature's *agon* as neither divinely desired nor divinely intended. In the light of Christ's eschatological victory *through* suffering and death, the logic of the world and its violence are unmasked as deformations of God's eternal purpose. This purpose is to gather and unite all things with the divine fullness so that in the end, "God may be all in all" (1 Cor 15:28).

In terms of its interpretive implications, the specific content of this study and its methodological orientation indicate some potentially fruitful areas for future theological research. The first area concerns the implications of our theological narrative in terms of its concrete developments. In this regard, our project advances a type of theology that prioritizes Christ as the ground and measure of all dimensions of created existence. In light of this Christocentric perception, our theology, with its theoretical structures, can be explored in relation to the mysterious character of the human condition. The question of human life in time, in terms of individual lifespans and the collective duration of human history, might be opened up interpretively by the theoretical structures fashioned by our theological investigation. This interpretive extension of these structures makes sense insofar as human beings are themselves plotted along the same continuum of creaturely existence. Moreover, the human person—individually and collectively—reflects the underlying Christological form of the universe's being in a concentrated mode. Thus, the figural patterns of traversal, sacrifice, and endemic fallenness possess significant interpretive potential for thinking through the theological shape of human existence in all of its challenging opacity.

Additionally, our theological narrative points towards the need for a deeper consideration of the grammar of fallenness in relation to the natural world. This project's recovery of the interpretive category of fallenness captures something essential with respect to the experiential character of created existence. However, our understanding of the specific nature of fallenness requires further theoretical exploration. How can we understand the ontological relationship presupposed by the claim that natural realities are mediated or governed by spiritual principles? Or, how can we understand the causal relation of spiritual intelligence with material bodies in connection with evolutionary biology? The relational dimension between spiritual principles and evolutionary history represents a fertile area for further speculative study in dialogue with metaphysics and the natural sciences.

A second major implication concerns the broader methodological relationship of constructive theological discourse with scriptural interpretation. This project is a creative retrieval in that it performs a probative demonstration of some fruitful possibilities of figuralism for thinking theologically about God, the world, and everything "in-between." Accordingly, this study develops a theology that responds to the very theological pressures of the Scriptures. In this way, our figural practice affirms the traditional orientation of theology as a scripturally saturated process, driven by the mysterious living world of the Scriptures with its expansive referrals all bound to the revealed form of the triune God.

In conclusion, this study's search for a fitting theological narrative of creation's *agon* ordered by Scripture's figural logic begins and ends with the central mystery of Christ as the one who creatively enfolds all things. Only in light of the disclosure of the crucified and exalted one—the Word of God made suffering flesh—can we perceive the world and its disturbing wonders simultaneously as a divine gift, a fallen reality, and a reality ordered toward some final redemption. This set of theological claims does not in the end provide an exhaustive explanation or rationale for the world's immense suffering. Such a feat is not theologically warranted or epistemically possible in this world. On the contrary, the aim and purpose behind this study with its accumulated claims is more modest. This study's constructive theology was intended to search out the depths of the Scriptures with the hope that it would point toward something of the truth about God and the world. The truth that emerges is that nature's agonistic history is ultimately caught up within the vast mystery of God's paschal love that creates, gathers, and transforms all things in Christ.

Bibliography

Akhtar, Sahar. "Animal Pain and Welfare: Can Pain Sometimes Be Worse for Them than for Us?" In *The Oxford Handbook of Animal Ethics*, edited by Tom L. Beauchamp and Raymond Gillespie Frey, 495–518. New York: Oxford University Press, 2011.

Anderson, Gary A. "Creatio Ex Nihilo and the Bible." In *Creation Ex Nihilo: Origins, Development, and Contemporary Challenges*, edited by Gary A. Anderson and Markus Bockmuehl, 15–36. Notre Dame, IN: University of Notre Dame, 2017.

———. *The Genesis of Perfection: Adam and Eve in Jewish and Christian Imagination*. Louisville: Westminster John Knox, 2001.

Aquinas, Thomas. *Summa Theologica*. Translated by Fathers of the English Dominican Province. Notre Dame, IN: Christian Classics, 1948.

Armstrong, D. M. *A Materialist Theory of Mind*. London: Routledge, 1993.

Arnobius. *Against the Heathen*. In ANF 6:403–543.

Athenagoras. *A Plea for Christians*. In ANF 2:129–48.

Augustine. *City of God*. In NPNF[1] 2:1–511.

———. *The Confessions*. Translated by Maria Boulding. Hyde Park, NY: New City, 1997.

———. *Enchiridion*. In NPNF[1] 3:237–76.

———. *Exposition of the Psalms 33–50*. Translated by Maria Boulding. Hyde Park, NY: New City, 2000.

———. *On Genesis: A Refutation of the Manichees; Unfinished Literal Commentary on Genesis; The Literal Meaning of Genesis*. Translated by Edmund Hill. Hyde Park, NY: New City, 2002.

———. *On the Morals of the Manichaeans*. In NPNF[1] 4:69–89.

———. *The Trinity*. Translated by Edmund Hill. 11th ed. Hyde Park, NY: New City, 2015.

Ayres, Lewis, and Stephen E. Fowl. "(Mis)Reading the Face of God: The Interpretation of the Bible in the Church." *Theological Studies* 60 (1999) 513–28.

Balthasar, Hans Urs von. *The Dramatis Personae: The Persons in Christ*. Vol. 3 of *Theodrama: Theological Dramatic Theory*. Translated by Graham Harrison. San Francisco: Ignatius, 1992.

———. *Seeing the Form*. Vol. 1 of *The Glory of the Lord: A Theological Aesthetics*. Translated by Eramso Leiva-Merikakis. 2nd ed. San Francisco: Ignatius, 2009.

Basil of Caesarea. *The Hexaemeron*. In NPNF[2] 8:51–107.

Beale, G. K. *The Temple and the Church's Mission: A Biblical Theology of the Dwelling Place of God*. Downers Grove, IL: Apollos, 2004.

Benton, Michael J. *The History of Life: A Very Short Introduction*. Oxford: Oxford University Press, 2008.
Blanchette, Oliva. *Philosophy of Being: A Reconstructive Essay in Metaphysics*. Washington, DC: Catholic University of America Press, 2003.
Blenkinsopp, Joseph. "The Structure of P." *Catholic Biblical Quarterly* 3 (1976) 275–92.
Blowers, Paul M. *The Drama of the Divine Economy: Creator and Creation in Early Christian Theology and Piety*. Oxford: Oxford University Press, 2012.
Bockmuehl, Markus. "Creatio Ex Nihilo in Palestinian Judaism and Early Christianity." *Scottish Journal of Theology* 65.3 (2012) 253–70.
Bonaventure. *Breviloquium*. In vol. 2 of *The Works of St. Bonaventure*. Translated by José de Vincek. Paterson, NJ: St. Anthony Guild, 1963.
Bouyer, Louis. *Cosmos: The World and the Glory of God*. Translated by Pierre de Fontnouvelle. Petersham, MA: St. Bede, 1988.
Bulgakov, Sergius. *Bride of the Lamb*. Translated by Boris Jakim. Grand Rapids: Eerdmans, 2002.
———. *The Comforter*. Translated by Boris Jakim. Grand Rapids: Eerdmans, 2004.
———. *Lamb of God*. Translated by Boris Jakem. Grand Rapids: Eerdmans, 2008.
———. *Jacob's Ladder*. Translated by Thomas Allan Smith. Grand Rapids: Eerdmans, 2010.
Calvin, John. *Commentary on the Epistle to the Romans*. Translated by John Owen. Grand Rapids, MI: Christian Classics Ethereal Library, 1849. http://www.ccel.org/ccel/calvin/calcom38.xii.vi.html.
Chenu, M. D. *Nature, Man, and Society in the Twelfth Century: Essays on New Theological Perspectives in the Latin West*. Translated by Jerome Taylor and Lester K. Little. Toronto: University of Toronto Press, 1997.
Childs, Brevard S. *Biblical Theology of the Old and New Testaments: Theological Reflection On the Christian Bible*. Minneapolis: Fortress, 2011.
Cizewski, Wanda. "Reading the Word as Scripture: Hugh of St. Victor's *De tribus diebus*." *Florilegium* 9 (1987) 65–88.
Clark, Stephen R. L. "Progress and the Argument from Evil." *Religious Studies* 40 (2004) 181–92.
Clarke, W. Norris. "Action as the Self-Revelation of Being: A Central Theme in the Thought of St. Thomas." In *Explorations in Metaphysics: Being–God–Person*, 45–64. Notre Dame, IN: University of Notre Dame, 1994.
———. "Is a Natural Theology Still Viable Today?" In *Explorations in Metaphysics: Being–God–Person*, 150–82. Notre Dame, IN: University of Notre Dame, 1994.
———. "A New Look at the Immutability of God." In *Explorations in Metaphysics: Being–God–Person*, 183–210. Notre Dame, IN: University of Notre Dame, 1994.
———. "The Problem of the Reality and Multiplicity of Divine Ideas in Christian Neo-Platonism." In *The Creative Retrieval of Saint Thomas Aquinas: Essays in Thomistic Philosophy, New and Old*, 66–88. New York: Fordham University Press, 2009.
Cohen, Esther. *The Crossroads of Justice: Law and Culture in Late Medieval France*. Leiden: Brill, 1993.
Coolman, Boyd Taylor. "Pulchrum Esse: The Beauty of Scripture, the Beauty of the Soul, and the Art of Exegesis in Hugh of St. Victor." *Traditio* 58 (2003) 175–200.
———. *The Theology of Hugh of St. Victor: An Interpretation*. Cambridge: Cambridge University Press, 2010.

Cottingham, John. "'A Brute to the Brutes?' Descartes' Treatment of Animals." *Philosophy* 53 (1978) 551–59.
Creegan, Nicola Hoggard. *Animal Suffering and the Problem of Evil*. New York: Oxford University Press, 2013.
Cunningham, Conor. *Darwin's Pious Idea: Why the Ultra-Darwinists and Creationists Both Get It Wrong*. Grand Rapids: Eerdmans, 2010.
Curley, Michael J., trans. *Physiologus: A Medieval Book of Nature Lore*. Chicago: University of Chicago, 2009.
Daley, Brian J. "'In Many and Various Ways': Towards a Theology of Theological Exegesis." *Modern Theology* 28.4 (2012) 597–615.
Daniélou, Jean. *From Shadows to Reality: Studies in the Biblical Typology of the Fathers*. Translated by Don Wukstan Hibberd. London: Burns and Oates, 1960.
Danto, Arthur C. *Narration and Knowledge*. New York: Columbia University Press, 1985.
Darwin, Charles. "Letter No. 2814." Letter to Asa Gray, May 22, 1860. *Darwin Correspondence Project*, September 26, 2022. https://www.darwinproject.ac.uk/letter/dcp-lett-2814.xml.
Davies, Brian. *Thomas Aquinas on God and Evil*. New York: Oxford University Press, 2011.
Dawe, D. G. *The Form of a Servant: A Historical Analysis of the Kenotic Motif*. Philadelphia: Westminster, 1963.
Dawkins, Richard. *The Selfish Gene*. Oxford: Oxford University Press, 1989.
Dawson, John David. *Christian Figural Reading and the Fashioning of Identity*. Berkeley: University of California Press, 2001.
Deane-Drummond, Celia. *Christ and Evolution: Wisdom and Wonder*. London: SCM, 2009.
Dennett, Daniel. *Consciousness Explained*. New York: Back Bay, 1992.
Derrida, Jacques. *Writing and Difference*. Translated by Alan Bass. Chicago: University of Chicago, 1978.
Descartes, René. *Discourse On Method and the Meditations*. Translated by F. E. Sutcliffe. Middlessex: Penguin, 1968.
Doolan, Gregory T. *Aquinas on Divine Ideas as Exemplar Causes*. Washington, DC: Catholic University of America Press, 2008.
Dougherty, Trent. *The Problem of Animal Pain*. New York: Palgrave Macmillan, 2014.
Douglas, Mary. *Leviticus as Literature*. Oxford: Oxford University Press, 1999.
Duffy, Stephen. "Our Hearts of Darkness: Original Sin Revisited." *Theological Studies* 49 (1988) 597–622.
Dumsday, Travis. "Natural Evil, Evolution, and Scholastic Accounts of the Limits of Demonic Power." *Pro Ecclesia* 24.1 (2015) 71–84.
Dupré, Louis. *Passage to Modernity: An Essay in the Hermeneutics of Nature and Culture*. New Haven: Yale University Press, 1993.
Edwards, Denis. *Breath of Life: A Theology of the Creator Spirit*. Maryknoll, NY: Orbis, 2004.
Elnes, Eric. "Creation and Tabernacle, The Priestly Writer's 'Environmentalism.'" *Horizons in Biblical Theology* 16 (1994) 144–55.
Elwood, Robert, and Mirjam Appel. "Pain Experience in Hermit Crabs?" *Animal Behaviour* 77 (2009) 1243–46.

Ephrem the Syrian. "Commentary on Genesis." In *St. Ephrem the Syrian: Selected Prose Works*, edited by K. McVey, 67–213. Translated by E. G. Mathews and J. P. Amar. Washington, DC: Catholic University of America, 1994.

Farrer, Austin. *God is Not Dead*. New York: Morehouse-Barlow, 1966.

Feser, Edward. *Philosophy of Mind*. London: Oneworld, 2006.

Fish, Stanley Eugene. *Is There a Text in This Class? The Authority of Interpretive Communities*. Cambridge: Harvard University Press, 1980.

Fowl, Stephen E. *Engaging Scripture: A Model for Theological Interpretation*. Malden, MA: Blackwell, 1998.

Frei, Hans. *The Eclipse of Biblical Narrative: A Study in Eighteenth- and Nineteenth-Century Hermeneutics*. New Haven: Yale University Press, 1974.

———. *Types of Christian Theology*. New Haven: Yale University Press, 1992.

Fretheim, Terence. *God and the World in the Old Testament: A Relational Theology of Creation*. Nashville: Abingdon, 2005.

———. *The Pentateuch*. Nashville: Abingdon, 1996.

Gadamer, Hans-Georg. *Truth and Method*. 2nd ed. Translated by Joel Weisheimer and Donald G. Marshall. London: Continuum, 2004.

Gavrilyuk, Paul. "Creation in Early Christian Polemical Literature: Irenaeus Against the Gnostics and Athanasius Against the Arians." *Modern Theology* 29.2 (2013) 22–32.

———. "The Kenotic Theology of Sergius Bulgakov." *Scottish Journal of Theology* 58.3 (2005) 251–69.

Goodwin, Brian C., and Peter Saunders, eds. *Theoretical Biology: Epigenetic and Evolutionary Order From Complex Systems*. Baltimore: John Hopkins University Press, 1992.

Gregory of Nazianzus. *Second Theological Oration*. In *NPNF*[2] 7:288–301.

Griffin, Donald. *Animal Thinking*. Cambridge: Harvard University Press, 1984.

Griffiths, Paul J. *Decreation: The Last Things of All Creatures*. Waco: Baylor University Press, 2014.

Gross, Charlotte. "Twelfth-Century Concepts of Time: Three Reinterpretations of Augustine's Doctrine of Creation 'Simul.'" *Journal of the History of Philosophy* 23.3 (1985) 325–38.

Hanby, Michael. *No God, No Science: Theology, Cosmology, Biology*. Malden, MA: Wiley Blackwell, 2017.

Harkins, Franklin T. *Reading and the Work of Restoration: History and Scripture in the Theology of Hugh of St. Victor*. Toronto: Pontifical Institute of Medieval Studies, 2009.

Harrison, Peter. *The Bible, Protestantism, and the Rise of Natural Science*. Cambridge: Cambridge University Press, 2001.

———. "Descartes on Animals." *Philosophical Quarterly* 42 (1992) 219–27.

———. *The Fall of Man and the Foundations of Science*. Cambridge: Cambridge University Press, 2007.

———. "Theodicy and Animal Pain." *Philosophy* 64 (1989) 79–92.

———. "The Virtues of Animals in Seventeenth-Century Thought." *Journal of the History of Ideas* 59 (1998) 463–84.

Hart, David Bentley. *The Experience of God: Being, Consciousness, Bliss*. New Haven: Yale University Press, 2013.

Hasker, William. *Metaphysics: Constructing a Worldview.* Downers Grove, IL: InterVarsity, 1983.
Haught, John F. *God After Darwin: A Theology of Evolution.* 2nd ed. Boulder, CO: Westview, 2008.
Hick, John. *Evil and the God of Love.* Rev. ed. New York: Harper and Row, 1978.
Holder, Arthur G. "The Mosaic Tabernacle in Early Christian Exegesis." *Studia Patristica* 25 (1993) 101–6.
Holloway, S. W. "What Ship Goes There: The Flood Narratives in the Gilgamesh Epic and Genesis Considered in Light of Ancient Near Eastern Temple Ideology." *Zeitschrift für die alttestamentliche Wissenschaft* 103 (1993) 328–54.
Hugh of St. Victor. *The Didascalicon of Hugh of St. Victor: A Medieval Guide to the Arts.* Edited and translated by Jerome Taylor. New York: Columbia University Press 1961.
———. *Hugh of Saint Victor On the Sacrament of the Christian Faith (De sacramentis Christianae fidei).* Edited by John Saint-George. Translated by Roy Deferrari. Eugene, OR: Wipf & Stock, 2007.
———. "A Little Book About Constructing Noah's Ark (*De arca Noe mystica*)." In *The Medieval Craft of Memory: An Anthology of Texts and Pictures,* edited by Mary Carruthers and Jan M. Ziolkowski, 41–70. Philadelphia: University of Pennsylvania Press, 2002.
———. "Noah's Ark I (*De arca Noe morali*)." In *Hugh of St. Victor: Selected Spiritual Writings,* translated by the Community of St. Mary the Virgin, 43–153. London: Harper & Row, 1962.
———. "Notes of Genesis (*Adnotationes*)." In *Interpretation of Scripture: Practice: A Selection of Works of Hugh, Andrew, and Richard of St Victor, Peter Comestor, Robert of Melun, Maurice of Sully and Leonius of Paris,* edited by Franklin T. Harkins and Frans van Liere, 53–145. Translated by Jan van Zweiten. Hyde Park, NY: New City, 2012.
———. "On Sacred Scripture and Its Authors (*De scripturis et scriptoribus*)." In *Interpretation of Scripture: Theory: A Selection of Works of Hugh, Andrew, Richard and Godrey of St. Victor, and of Robert of Melun,* edited by Franklin T. Harkins and Frans van Liere, 203–52. Translated by Frans van Liere. Hyde Park, NY: New City, 2012.
———. "On the Three Days (*De tribus diebus*)." In *Trinity and Creation: A Selection of Works of Hugh, Richard, and Adam of St. Victor,* edited by Boyd Taylor Coolman and Dale M. Coulter, 49–102. Translated by Hugh Feiss. Hyde Park, NY: New City, 2011.
———. "Sentences of Divinity (*Sententiae de divinitate*)." In *Trinity and Creation: A Selection of Works of Hugh, Richard, and Adam of St. Victor,* edited by Boyd Taylor Coolman and Dale M. Coulter, 103–78. Translated by Christopher P. Evans. Hyde Park, NY: New City, 2011.
Irenaeus. *Against Heresies.* In *ANF* 1:307–567.
John Scotus Eriugena. *The Voice of the Eagle: The Heart of Celtic Christianity.* Translated by Christopher Bamford. Great Barrington, MA: Lindisfarne, 2000.
Johnson, Luke Timothy, and William S. Kurz. *The Future of Catholic Biblical Scholarship: A Constructive Conversation.* Grand Rapids: Eerdmans, 2002.
Jowett, Benjamin. "On the Interpretation of Scripture." In *Essays and Reviews,* 330–433. London: Parker and Son, 1860.

Justin Martyr. *Dialogue with Trypho.* In *ANF* 1:194–270.

Kalof, Linda. *Looking at Animals in Human History.* London: Reaktion, 2007.

Kauffman, Stuart. *At Home in the Universe: The Search for the Laws of Self-Organization and Complexity.* New York: Oxford University Press, 1995.

Kearney, P. J. "Creation and Liturgy: The Redaction of Ex. 25–40." *Zeitschrift für die alttestamentliche Wissenschaft* 89.3 (1977) 375–87.

Keck, David. *Angels and Angelology in the Middle Ages.* Oxford: Oxford University Press, 1998.

Keltz, B. Kyle. *Thomism and the Problem of Animal Suffering.* Eugene: Wipf and Stock, 2020.

Koons, Robert C., and George Bealer, eds. *The Waning of Materialism.* Oxford: Oxford University Press, 2010.

Kugel, James L. *Traditions of the Bible: A Guide to How the Bible as It Was at the Start of the Common Era.* Cambridge: Harvard University Press, 1998.

Legaspi, Michael C. *The Death of Scripture and the Rise of Biblical Studies.* New York: Oxford University Press, 2010.

Leiber, Justin. "Descartes: The Smear and Related Miscontruals." *Journal for the Theory of Social Behavior* 41 (2011) 365–75.

Leibniz, Gottfried Wilhelm. "Causa Dei (A Vindication of God's Justice Reconciled with His Other Perfections and All His Actions)." In *Monadology and Other Philosophical Essays*, 114–45. Translated by Paul Schrecker and Anne Martin Schrecker. New York: Macmillan, 1965.

———. *Theodicy: Essays on the Goodness of God, the Freedom of Man, and the Origin of Evil.* Translated by E. M. Huggard. New York: Cosimo, 2009.

Leithart, Peter. *Deep Exegesis: The Mystery of Reading Scripture.* Waco, TX: Baylor University Press, 2009.

Levenson, Jon. "The Temple and the World." *Journal of Religion* 64.3 (1984) 275–98.

Levering, Matthew. *Engaging the Doctrine of Creation: Cosmos, Creatures, and the Wise and Good Creator.* Grand Rapids: Baker Academic, 2017.

———. *Participatory Exegesis: A Theology of Biblical Interpretation.* Notre Dame, IN: Notre Dame University, 2008.

Lindbeck, George. "Scripture, Consensus, and Community." In *Biblical Interpretation in Crisis: The Ratzinger Conference on Bible and Church*, edited by Richard John Neuhaus, 74–101. Grand Rapids: Eerdmans, 1989.

Lloyd, Michael. "Are Animals Fallen?" In *Animals on the Agenda: Questions about Animals for Theology and Ethics*, edited by Andrew Linzey and Dorothy Yamamoto, 147–60. London: SCM, 1998.

Louth, Andrew. *Discerning the Mystery: Essay on the Nature of Theology.* Oxford: Oxford University Press, 1989.

Malebranche, Nicolas. *The Search After Truth.* Edited and Translated by Thomas M. Lennon and Paul J. Olscamp. New York: Cambridge University Press, 1997.

Margulis, Lynn. *Symbiotic Planet: A New Look at Evolution.* New York: Basic, 1998.

Marino, Lori. "Cetacean Cognition." In *The Oxford Handbook of Animal Studies*, edited by Linda Kalof, 227–39. Oxford: Oxford University Press, 2017.

Martelet, Gustave. *The Risen Christ and the Eucharistic World.* Translated by Renée Hague. London: Collins, 1976.

Martin, Francis. "Revelation as Disclosure: Creation." In *Wisdom and Holiness, Science and Scholarship: Essays in Honor of Matthew L. Lamb*, edited by Michael Dauphinais and Matthew Levering, 205–47. Naples, FL: Ave Maria, 2007.
Mascall, E. L. *Christian Theology and Natural Science: Some Questions on Their Relations*. New York: Ronald, 1956.
Maximus the Confessor. *On Difficulties in the Church Fathers: The Ambigua*. Translated by Nicholas Constas. Cambridge: Harvard University Press, 2014.
———. "On the Lord's Prayer." In vol. 2 of *Philokalia*, edited by G. E. H. Palmer et al., 285–305. Boston: Faber and Faber, 1981.
May, Gerhard. *Creatio Ex Nihilo: The Doctrine of 'Creation Out of Nothing' in Early Christian Thought*. Edinburgh: T&T Clark, 1994.
McFarland, Ian. *From Nothing: A Theology of Creation*. Louisville: Westminster John Knox, 2014.
———. *In Adam's Fall: A Meditation on the Christian Doctrine of Original Sin*. Oxford: Wiley-Blackwell, 2010.
McIntosh, Mark. "The Maker's Divine Meaning: Divine Ideas and Salvation." *Modern Theology* 28.3 (2012) 365–84.
McMullin Ernan. "Creation Ex Nihilo: Early History." In *Creation and the God of Abraham*, edited by David Burrell, 11–23. New York: Cambridge University Press, 2010.
Meer, Jitse M. van der, and Scott Mandelbrote, eds. *Nature and Scripture in Abrahamic Religions: Up to 1700*. Leiden: Brill, 2008.
Meiland, Jack W. *Scepticism and Historical Knowledge*. New York: Random, 1965.
Messer, Neil "Evolution and Theodicy: How (Not) to Do Science and Theology." *Zygon: Journal of Religion and Science* 53.3 (2018) 821–35.
Mews, Constant J. "The World as Test: The Bible and the Book of Nature in Twelfth-Century Theology." In *Scripture and Pluralism: Reading the Bible in the Religiously Plural Worlds of the Middle Ages and Renaissance*, edited by Thomas J. Heffernan and Thomas E. Burman, 95–112. Leiden: Brill, 2005.
Middleton, J. Richard. "From Primal Harmony to a Broken World: Distinguishing God's Intent for Life from the Encroachment of Death in Genesis 2–3." In *Earnest: Interdisciplinary Work Inspired by the Life and Teachings of B. T. Roberts*, edited by Andrew C. Koehl and David Basinger, 143–71. Eugene, OR: Pickwick, 2017.
———. *A New Heaven and a New Earth: Reclaiming Biblical Eschatology*. Grand Rapids: Baker Academic, 2014.
Milbank, John. *Theology and Social Theory: Beyond Secular Reason*. Oxford: Blackwell, 1990.
Milgrom, Jacob. "Israel's Sanctuary: The Priestly 'Picture of Dorian Gray.'" *Revue Biblique* 83.3 (1976) 390–99.
———. *Leviticus: A Book of Ritual and Ethics*. Minneapolis: Fortress, 2004.
Moltmann, Jürgen. *The Crucified God: The Cross of Christ as the Foundation and Criticism of Christian Theology*. Translated by R. A. Wilson and John Bowden. Minneapolis: Fortress, 1993.
———. *God in Creation: A New Theology of Creation and the Spirit of God*. Translated by Margaret Kohl. Minneapolis: Fortress, 1993.
Moritz, Joshua. "Evolutionary Evil and Dawkins' Black Box: Changing the Parameters of the Problem." In *The Evolution of Evil*, edited by Gaymon Bennet et al., 143–88. Gottingen: Vandenhoeck & Ruprecht, 2008.

Morris, Simon Conway. *Life's Solution: Inevitable Humans in a Lonely Universe.* Cambridge: Cambridge University Press, 2004.

Murray, Michael J. *Nature: Red in Tooth and Claw: Theism and The Problem of Animal Suffering.* Oxford: Oxford University Press, 2008.

Nagel, Thomas. *Mind and Cosmos: Why the Materialist Neo-Darwinian Concept of Nature Is Almost Certainly False.* Oxford: Oxford University Press, 2012.

Neusner, Jacob. *Praxis and Parable: The Divergent Discourse of Rabbinic Judaism: How Halakhic and Aggadic Documents Treat the Bestiary Common to Them Both.* Oxford: University of America Press, 2006.

Nieuwenhove, Rik van. "Retrieving a Sacramental Worldview in a Mechanistic World." In *To Discern Creation in a Scattering World,* edited by Frederiek Depoortere and Jacques Haers, 539–48. Leuven: Uitgeveru Peeters, 2013.

Origen. *On First Principles.* Translated by G. W. Butterworth. Notre Dame, IN: Christian Classics, 2013.

———. *Spirit and Fire: A Thematic Anthology of His Writings.* Edited by Hans Urs von Balthasar. Translated by Robert J. Daly. Washington, DC: Catholic University of America Press, 1984.

Papias. *Fragment 7.* In *ANF* 1:151–55.

Pedersen, Olaf. *The Book of Nature.* Vatican: Vatican Observatory; Notre Dame, IN: University of Notre Dame Press, 1992.

Peters, Ted. "Extinction, Natural Selection, and the Cosmic Cross." *Zygon: Journal of Religion and Science* 53.3 (2018) 690–710.

Polanyi, Michael. "The Stability of Beliefs." *British Journal for the Philosophy of Science* 3.11 (1952) 217–32.

Polkinghorne, John C. *The Faith of a Physicist: Reflections of a Bottom-Up Thinker.* Minneapolis: Augsburg Fortress, 1996.

Puntel, Lorenz B. *Being and God: A Systematic Approach in Confrontation with Martin Heidegger, Emmanuel Levinas, and Jean-Luc Marion.* Translated by Alan White. Evanston, IL: Northwestern University Press, 2011.

Rad, Gerhard von. *Genesis: A Commentary.* Translated by John H. Marks. London: Bloomsbury, 1976.

———. *Old Testament Theology: The Theology of Israel's Historical Traditions.* Translated by D. M. G. Stalker. New York: Harper & Row, 1962.

Radner, Ephraim. *Chasing the Shadow: The World and Its Times: An Introduction to Christian Natural Theology.* Eugene: Cascade, 2018.

———. *Leviticus.* Grand Rapids: Brazos, 2008.

———. *Time and the Word: Figural Reading of the Christian Scriptures.* Grand Rapids: Eerdmans, 2015.

———. *A Time to Keep: Theology, Mortality, and the Shape of a Human Life.* Waco, TX: Baylor University Press, 2016.

Rahner, Karl. *More Recent Writings.* Vol. 4 of *Theological Investigations.* Translated by Kevin Smyth. Baltimore: Helicon, 1966.

Ricoeur, Paul. *Interpretation Theory: Discourse and the Surplus of Meaning.* Fort Worth: Texas Christian University Press, 1976.

———. *The Symbolism of Evil.* Translated by Emerson Buchanan. New York: Harper & Row, 1967.

Ristau, Carolyn A., and Peter Marler, eds. *Cognitive Ethology: The Minds of Other Animals.* Hillsdale, NJ: Psychology, 1991.

Roberts, Alexander, and James Donaldson, eds. *The Ante-Nicene Fathers* [*ANF*]. 10 vols. 1886–1889. Reprint, Peabody, MA: Hendrickson, 1994.
Rollin, Bernard E. *The Unheeded Cry: Animal Consciousness, Animal Pain, and Science.* Ames: Iowa State University Press, 1998.
Rudolph, Conrad. *The Mystic Ark: Hugh of Saint Victor, Art, and Thought in the Twelfth Century.* New York: Cambridge University Press, 2014.
Russell, Robert John. *Cosmology: From Alpha to Omega.* Minneapolis: Fortress, 2008.
———. "Entropy and Evil." *Zygon: Journal of Religion and Science* 19 (1984) 449–68.
———. "The Groaning of Creation: Does God Suffer with All Life?" In *The Evolution of Evil*, edited by Gaymon Bennet et al., 120–40. Gottingen: Vandenhoeck & Ruprecht, 2008.
Scalise, Charles J. *Hermeneutics as Theological Prolegomena: A Canonical Approach.* Macon, GA: Mercer University Press, 1994.
Schaff, Philip, ed. *The Nicene and Post-Nicene Fathers*, Series 1 [*NPNF*^{1}]. 14 vols. 1886–1889. Reprint, Peabody, MA: Hendrickson, 1994.
Schaff, Philip, and Henry Wace, eds. *The Nicene and Post-Nicene Fathers*, Series 2 [*NPNF*^{2}]. 14 vols. 1890–1900. Reprint, Peabody, MA: Hendrickson, 1994.
Shanley, Brian J. "Aquinas on God's Causal Knowledge: A Reply to Stump and Kretzmann." *American Catholic Philosophical Quarterly* 72.3 (1998) 447–57.
Shepherd of Hermas. *Visions.* In *ANF* 2:9–55.
Sherrington, Charles. *Man on His Nature.* Cambridge: Cambridge University Press, 1940.
Sokolowski, Robert. *God of Faith and Reason: Foundations of Christian Theology.* Washington, DC: Catholic University of America Press, 1995.
Sorabji, Richard. *Animal Minds and Human Morals.* Ithaca: Cornell University Press, 1993.
Southgate, Christopher. "Divine Glory in a Darwinian World." *Zygon: Journal of Religion and Science* 49 (2014) 784–807.
———. "God's Creation Wild and Violent, and Our Care for Other Animals." *Perspectives on Science and Christian Faith* 67.4 (2015) 245–53.
———. *The Groaning of Creation: God, Evolution, and the Problem of Evil.* Louisville: Westminster John Knox, 2008.
Steiner, Gary. *Anthropocentrism and its Discontents: The Moral Status of Animals in the History of Western Philosophy.* Pittsburgh: University of Pittsburgh, 2005.
Tennant, F. R. *Sources of the Doctrine of the Fall and Original Sin.* New York: Schocken, 1903.
Theophilus of Antioch. *To Autolycus.* In *ANF* 2:89–121.
Thiel, John E. *Nonfoundationalism.* Minneapolis: Fortress, 1994.
Thomas, Keith. *Man and the Natural World: A History of Modern Sensibility.* New York: Pantheon, 1983.
Torrance, T. F. *Divine and Contingent Order.* Oxford: Oxford University Press, 1981.
Tracy, Thomas. "God and Creatures Acting: The Idea of Double Agency." In *Creation and the God of Abraham*, edited by David Burrell et al., 221–37. New York: Cambridge University Press, 2010.
Vanhoozer, Kevin J. *Is There a Meaning in This Text? The Bible, the Reader, and the Morality of Literary Knowledge.* Grand Rapids: Zondervan, 1998.
Vivian, Tim. "The Peaceable Kingdom: Animals as Parables in the Virtues of Saint Macarius." *Anglican Theological Review* 85.3 (2003) 477–91.

Waddell, Helen. *Beasts and Saints*. Grand Rapids: Eerdmans, 1996.
Walton, John. *The Lost World of Genesis One: Ancient Cosmology and the Origins Debate*. Downer's Grove, IL: InterVarsity, 2009.
Webster, John. "Theologies of Retrieval." In *Oxford Handbook of Systematic Theology*, edited by Kathryn Tanner et al., 583–99. Oxford: University of Oxford Press, 2009.
Weil, Simone. *Gateway to God*. Edited by David Raper. London: Collins Fontana, 1974.
Weiss, Amaroq E., et al. "Societal and Ecosystem Benefits of Restored Wolf Populations." In *Transactions of the 72nd North American Wildlife and Natural Resources Conference, Portland, OR, March 20–24*, 297–319. Washington, DC: Wildlife Management Institute, 2007.
Wenham, Gordon. *Genesis 1–15*. Waco, TX: Word, 1987.
Wennberg, Robert. *God, Humans, and Animals: An Invitation to Enlarge our Moral Universe*. Grand Rapids: Eerdmans, 2003.
Westermann, Claus. *Genesis 1–11: A Commentary*. Translated by J. J. Scullion. Minneapolis: Augsburg, 1984.
Williams, Norman P. *The Ideas of the Fall and of Original Sin*. New York: Longmans Green, 1927.
Williams, Rowan. *Resurrection: Interpreting the Easter Gospel*. 2nd ed. London: Darton Longman Todd, 2002.
Wilson, Jonathan. *God's Good World: Reclaiming the Doctrine of Creation*. Grand Rapids: Baker Academic, 2013.
Young, Frances M. *God's Presence: A Contemporary Recapitulation of Early Christianity*. New York: Cambridge University Press, 2013.
Zinn, Grover A. "De Gradibus Ascensionum: The Stages of Contemplative Ascent in Two Treatises on Noah's Ark by Hugh of St. Victor." *Studies of Medieval Culture* 5 (1975) 61–79.
———. "History and Contemplation: The Dimensions of the Restoration of Man in Two Treatises on the Ark of Noah by Hugh of St. Victor." PhD diss., Duke University, 1968.
———. "Hugh of St. Victor, Isaiah's Vision, and De Arca Noe." In *The Church and the Arts*, edited by Diana Wood, 99–116. Oxford: Blackwell, 1995.
———. "Mandala Symbolism and Use in the Mysticism of Hugh of St. Victor." *History of Religions* 12.4 (1973) 317–41.

www.ingramcontent.com/pod-product-compliance
Lightning Source LLC
Chambersburg PA
CBHW070326230426
43663CB00011B/2231